Combating International Crime

The realities of international law enforcement are widely misunderstood and generally mystifying to the uninitiated. Combating cross-border crime is a dynamic aspect of criminal justice that is becoming increasingly complex and directly relevant to national and local level policing. Unfortunately, most practitioners and policy-makers are unaware of the challenges involved in investigating and prosecuting criminals across frontiers. Professional experience of combating international crime is still restricted to relatively few.

This book maps the practicalities and challenges in making cross-border law enforcement work. It provides a professional assessment of the tactics currently deployed against trans-national crime and identifies those elements regarded as essential for successful international law enforcement co-operation. It explores the need for a comprehensive strategy against international crime and, using case studies by way of illustration and example, discusses the consequences and implications of an ineffective response.

Steven David Brown qualified as a barrister, before serving as a police officer with the Metropolitan Police in London. Having worked with the National Criminal Intelligence Service and Europol, he now acts as an independent consultant.

Combating International Crime

The Longer Arm of the Law

Edited by
Steven David Brown

Routledge
Taylor & Francis Group
LONDON AND NEW YORK

Published 2008
by Routledge
2 Park Square, Milton Park, Abingdon, Oxfordshire OX14 4RN

Simultaneously published in the USA and Canada
by Routledge
711 Third Avenue, New York, NY 10017, USA

First issued in paperback 2016

Routledge is an imprint of the Taylor and Francis Group, an informa business

Typeset in Sabon by RefineCatch Limited, Bungay, Suffolk

British Library Cataloguing in Publication Data
A catalogue record for this book is available from the British Library

Library of Congress Cataloging in Publication Data
Brown, Steven David
Combatting international crime : the longer arm of the law /
Steven David Brown.
p. cm.
Includes index.
1. Transnational crime. 2. Law enforcement–International cooperation. 3. Criminal justice, Administration of–International cooperation. I. Title.
HV6252.B76 2008
364–dc22

2007051790

ISBN 13: 978-1-138-97112-7 (pbk)
ISBN 13: 978-0-415-45828-3 (hbk)

For Phyllis, David and Éva

Contents

The authors

Neil Bailey

Neil retired in 2006 as a Director at the National Criminal Intelligence Service (NCIS) after a long and varied career in international law enforcement. At NCIS he was Director, International Division (in charge of the overseas liaison network) and latterly, Director Intelligence Services Division. Before joining NCIS, Neil rose to be Assistant Chief Investigation Officer with HM Customs and Excise. During his career with Customs, Neil served on the project team setting up Europol, was Assistant Co-ordinator of the National Drugs Intelligence Unit (at New Scotland Yard) and became Head of Customs International Branch. He now works as a consultant and advisor to international organisations and law enforcement agencies.

Steven David Brown

Having qualified as a barrister and completing pupillage, Steven joined the Metropolitan Police in London serving as an operational police officer before joining the National Criminal Intelligence Service as a staff officer and later moving on to Europol where his responsibilities centred on co-operation with non-EU states. He speaks Italian, German and Mandarin and for his Master's studies in organised crime, terrorism and security, Steven was awarded a distinction. He is an experienced project manager. He is trained in analysis and has authored a number of articles and reports related to intelligence-led policing, operational performance and strategic management. Latterly, his work on international law enforcement has taken him to Asia as well as to Central and Eastern Europe.

Stuart Cameron-Waller

Now working widely as a consultant in international law enforcement, Stuart held several senior management positions at Interpol including Head of Regional Co-ordination, Director of Regional Co-ordination and Development and Director for Specialised Crimes. He also project managed the development of Interpol's I-24/7 network, which today provides law enforcement agencies throughout the world with access to a global communication and information system. Stuart retired as a Detective Chief Superintendent with the Metropolitan Police.

Josip Cule

Josip has been Deputy Chief Public Prosecutor in Croatia since 2005. After passing the Bar Exam, he first became a Court Advisor in Split before being appointed judge for the criminal courts in 1991, in which capacity he worked on investigations, as a trial judge and on appeals. In 2006, Josip became President of the State Attorney Council. He has a special interest in transnational and cross-border co-operation and is the Croatian liaison judge for Eurojust. He has published and lectured on key issues, such as the suppression of corruption and the recovery of the proceeds of crime, and has also been a national delegate to UN and regional conferences (in particular with regard to the fight against corruption and the development of the judiciary).

Sandra L. Fowler

Sandra L. Fowler was a Federal Bureau of Investigation (FBI) Special Agent for 24 years. She served in five FBI field divisions (in a management capacity in two of these), did two management tours at FBI Headquarters in Washington, DC, and served six years overseas as the Legal Attaché in Brussels and as the FBI's first terrorism liaison to the Counter Terrorism Task Force at Europol. Following her return from her overseas assignments she was appointed to the position of Section Chief of the International Operations Section at FBI Headquarters. Sandra served in this capacity for almost two years. In addition to having responsibility for the growth and expansion of the Legat Program, Sandra also had oversight of its 300 employees stationed at FBI Headquarters and around the world.

Roger Gaspar

Roger Gaspar spent 36 years as a police officer and retired as Deputy Director General of the National Criminal Intelligence Service. He currently undertakes consultancy work and instructs on courses for senior (police) management and organised crime for international police leaders. He is an expert on anti-corruption (having led the Metropolitan Police Internal Investigations Branch) and on intelligence. He has been involved in many national and international policing projects including the Organised Crime Operations Group (as Chair), the Home Office Organised Crime Strategy Group, the Council of Europe's Group of Countries against Corruption (GRECO) and the EU Police Chiefs Task Force. In his spare time Roger is a keen yachtsman and has authored a forthcoming book on navigating the Thames Estuary.

Vladimir Gilca

As a colonel in the Moldovan National Police and the national representative at the Southeast European Cooperative Initiative (SECI) Regional Center for Combating Trans-Border Crime since 2004, Vladimir has extensive experience of cross-border law enforcement. He was Deputy Director of the Department for Combating Trans-Border Crime in Chisinau, has taught investigation techniques at the Moldovan National Police Academy, specialising in tax evasion and fiscal crime, and has been involved in the drafting of a number of national laws, in particular on combating corruption, the draft criminal code and the Government Decision on Wanted Persons. He has led and co-ordinated numerous international investigations and is currently researching his PhD thesis.

Mitja Močnik

Mitja has been the Director of the Southeast European Cooperative Initiative (SECI) Regional Center for Combating Trans-Border Crime since the beginning of 2006. He is a member of the Advisory Board for the International Centre for Migration Policy Development and the US Agency for International Development 'Programme to Support the Development of Trans-national Referral Mechanisms for Trafficked Persons in South East Europe'. He is an experienced member of the Slovenian diplomatic corps and has extensive experience in Eastern Europe and Central Asia (including in Budapest and Kiev) and with the Organization for Security and Co-operation in Europe. His public service has included senior postings with the Ministry of Interior.

In his early career, Mitja held a number of posts related to national security including as adviser on international security issues and anti-terrorism, for national security to the President of Parliament and as Secretary of the Parliamentary Committee for National Security. Mitja currently holds the rank of Minister Plenipotentiary at the Ministry of Foreign Affairs of Slovenia.

Kevin O'Connell

During a long career with the Metropolitan Police, Kevin acquired experience at every operational level including as Detective Superintendent in charge of international terrorism at Special Branch and as Commander in charge of royalty and diplomatic protection. He recently completed an appointment as Deputy Director at Europol where he was not only Chief Information Officer, successfully procuring and implementing the European-wide Europol Information System, but also had responsibility for information security and special projects. Kevin is an expert in the design, implementation and management of information processing and has now created E-I-Design, an expert forum exploring knowledge management and organisational solutions for public safety and security. Kevin speaks fluent French and basic Russian.

Michał Pesta

Michał joined the European Anti-Fraud Office (OLAF) in 2005 and works as an investigator on cases of fraud related to external EU aid in Africa, Asia and Middle East. He holds an MA in Political Sciences, an MA in International Relations and a post-graduate Diploma in Decision-Making in the European Union.

Prior to joining OLAF, Michał worked at the EastWest Institute, where he specialised in research focusing on the Commonwealth of Independent States countries (especially Ukraine, Moldova, the Caucasus, and Central Asia) as well as in broader aspects of the EU's policies towards these regions. In addition to his native Polish, Michał is fluent in English and French. He also speaks Dutch, Russian, Bulgarian, Ukrainian and modern Greek.

Kimberly Prost

Having graduated in 1981 from the University of Manitoba (with a Gold Medal for Highest Standing in Law), Kimberly became a Federal Prosecutor with the Canadian Department of Justice. Since then she has served as Counsel for the Crimes against Humanity/War Crimes Section, Senior Counsel for the Criminal Law Branch (where she handled extradition requests and provided advice on mutual legal assistance to law enforcement agencies) and Director of the International Assistance Group (Central Authority of Canada) from 1994 to 2000. In July 2000 she became Head of the Criminal Law Section and Deputy Director of the Legal and Constitutional Affairs Division of the Commonwealth Secretariat. In 2005 she joined the United Nations Office on Drugs and Crime as Head of the Legal Advisory Section before being appointed Judge *ad litem* to the International Criminal Tribunal for the former Yugoslavia in July 2006. She is currently a member of the Law Society of Upper Canada and has calls to the Bars of Manitoba and the Yukon territory.

Nick Ridley

Dr Nick Ridley is a worldwide authority on the financing of terrorism and financial analysis. He was a senior intelligence analyst with the Metropolitan Police and the National Criminal Intelligence Service before joining Europol at its inception. He retired from Europol and took a short-term post as associate professor at Università Cattolica in Milan teaching courses in terrorism and intelligence analysis. He lectures widely and has taught in Bulgaria and Turkey, providing training in anti-money-laundering awareness and anti-terrorism. He is currently a senior lecturer for the John Grieve Centre in Policing Studies at London Metropolitan University.

Phil Tucker

Phil Tucker is a serving Detective Superintendent and is currently Director of Intelligence for Essex Police in the UK. He has more than 27 years' police service, the vast majority of which has been spent as a detective at all ranks, including secondments to the National Drugs Intelligence Unit, Force, Regional and National Crime Squads, National Criminal Intelligence Service and Europol. He has substantial experience as a Senior Investigating Officer in both proactive organised crime and reactive homicide investigations and is a specialist in international investigations. As Head of the UK Liaison Bureau at Europol during the UK's presidency of the EU in 2005, Phil was responsible for introducing National Intelligence Model principles to Europe.

Johan Vlogaert

Johan was a lawyer in private practice, a judge (including in the Appeal Court) and an investigating judge in Belgium before becoming an expert on organised crime with the General Secretariat of the EU Council of Ministers. Then, following a brief return to the Appeal Court in 2001, he was recruited to the Europen Anti-Fraud Office (OLAF) where he led investigations into bribery and corruption involving EU aid in Africa, Latin-America, the Middle East and South-East Asia. He has also been responsible for building co-operation on an operational level, not only with new and candidate members of the EU, but also with a number of other international agencies. He is currently the head of OLAF's External Aid Investigations Unit.

Tim Wilson

Tim is a specialist in criminal justice, penal management and public infrastructure financing. Until 2005, as a senior member of the UK Civil Service, he was Head of the Forensic Science and Pathology Unit of the Home Office, a member of the National DNA Database Board and the Association of Chief Police Officers (ACPO) Forensic Portfolio Committee. He is currently Chairman of the Forensic Pathology Disciplinary Committee and, as a member of the Judd Place Partnership LLP, has also worked as a consultant to the Home Office, ACPO and the National Policing Improvement Agency (NPIA) on international forensic co-operation. He is a Visiting Fellow in the School of Geography, Politics and Sociology at Newcastle University and a lecturer in the MSc course on procurement management for sustainable development run jointly by Turin University and the International Labour Organization.

Foreword

Professional criminals are creatures of opportunity and exploit every possibility offered by the conveniences of modern living. The term 'globalisation' has become so commonplace that it risks becoming a cliché, but its reality represents ever greater challenges for the law enforcement community. Throughout the world, criminals and crime groups are increasingly familiar with the disparities and vulnerabilities in criminal justice systems which allow them to exploit gaps in the illicit marketplace. They have learned to spread the risk of detection and conviction across countries and even continents knowing full well that their competitive advantage improves with every border crossed.

Until recently, law enforcement generally paid insufficient attention to such multi-country challenges in any systematic way. There is always more than enough to do addressing national problems and locally recognised priorities. Unfortunately, this often means that the international aspects of an investigation are neglected or put into the 'too difficult' box and left on the shelf to gather dust. However, the threats from transnational crime can no longer be so easily ignored. Governments and national authorities are working to redress this past failure to engage properly against international criminality by backing a burgeoning array of international initiatives and frameworks.

The EU has formally declared its commitment to developing a region of freedom, security and justice. Citizens in every region of the world share these same aspirations and ambitions. In pursuit of these values, nation states have historically surrounded themselves with barriers to safeguard their sovereignty. These barriers may exacerbate national differences in language, culture, and laws, and the challenge for international law enforcement is to overcome these obstacles and negotiate a mutual understanding by which to achieve the universal purpose of law enforcement and criminal justice everywhere: bringing the crook to book.

But, the diversity of crimes, criminal justice systems, policing doctrines and operational structures means that it is impossible to find one solution to fit every set of circumstances. It also means that a solution found in one part of the world may not fit comfortably with that used in another. Where this is the case, it is essential that any conflict, misunderstanding or divergence is resolved by bridging the gaps.

Interpol has been guided by the principle of enhancing ways in which member countries' police services can co-operate across borders irrespective of their national policing or criminal justice systems. As the only international policing organisation with a global network and reach, Interpol actively researches and provides practical facilities for improving operational co-operation and information exchange. We aim to be at the forefront of promoting best practice and the dissemination of new technologies that can make a real difference in detecting, prosecuting and preventing crime. The strength of such initiatives is their focus on practicality and application in the operational setting, but the starting point for their development must always be the review of past and existing experience and practice as well as the relevant legal frameworks.

In the past there have been a number of notable and worthy academic studies looking at the phenomena of international or transnational crime. There have been fewer books focusing on international law enforcement, and fewer still offering an insight into how co-operation actually functions from the practitioner's point of view.

This is why, as Secretary General of Interpol, I am pleased to introduce a book which explores, explains and discusses the practical issues confronting investigators working across borders and the structures they use. The writers express personal perceptions based on their own professional experience, and while their views will obviously not be shared by all, they provide an invaluable framework and set of insights that complement academic perspectives that tend to look from the outside inwards. This book's contribution to the literature in the field is long overdue.

Ronald K. Noble
October 2007

Editor's note

This book is more than a series of essays. It seeks to provide the reader with a thematic development exploring the key issues in international law enforcement from the point of view of the practitioner. Although a number of the examples are drawn from the European experience, this is more a factor of historical developments on that continent. Indeed, the book has not been written with any particular national or regional audience in mind and for this reason the contributors have been at pains to explain those terms and concepts which, whilst they may be already familiar to some readers, might not be universally understood. The objective was not to write a manual, but to sketch out a map showing the main roads, routes and (information) highways for the investigator, lawyer, judge or strategic thinker who rarely travels this particular landscape and who needs to be able to recognise the landmarks.

The contributions reflect the personal views of their authors and were prepared in the summer of 2007. Their opinions and remarks are individual to them and may not necessarily reflect the views of the organisations for which they now work or have worked in the past; nor, indeed, will they always coincide with those of the other contributors. Readers should also be aware that there has been a certain amount of moderation in the editing so that, where one contribution has covered a particular subject in depth, another will have had any similar detail omitted.

Some common working definitions have been used: *International law enforcement* is taken to mean any activity involving the prevention, detection, investigation or prosecution of crime or criminality implicating more than one country. *International crime* is any activity which is conducted in more than one country and that offends against the criminal law of at least one of those countries.

This book is specific to combating international crime and for this reason does not explore the role or function of peacekeeping operations. Although those involved are sometimes described as 'international police officers', their activity is not 'international' in terms of the above definition, but 'local' even if conducted by an international workforce.

Steven David Brown
November 2007

Acknowledgements

The Editor would like to thank Miss Fiona Kinnear and Miss Kate Murphy of Routledge-Cavendish Publishers for their kind help and guidance in the production of this book; John Abbott's advice and ideas were, as ever, invaluable, as were the suggestions of Brian Taylor. The Editor would also like to thank Stanley Morris, Alan Wilson, James Heslop, Jim Busby and Mark Shaw, all of them experts in their respective fields, for their encouragement along the way and, especially, thanks to Ronald K. Noble, who, despite leading Interpol, the most important agency in global law enforcement, found time to contribute a foreword.

Part I

The context

The longer arm of the law

An introduction

Steven David Brown

Criminals have since time immemorial been cautioned and chastised to beware the 'long arm of the law'. This is a well-known English expression reflecting the popular view that the reach of law enforcement and justice exceeds its grasp, but more recently felons have come to learn that the reach of criminal justice all too often extends only as far as the nearest national border.

Our world has experienced enormous and unprecedented technological progress in recent years the rate of which shows little sign of slowing down. Unfortunately, along with the undoubted benefits, we are also confronted by a new complexity. Technology has influenced every aspect of our socio-economic existence and threatened the cultural balance established by centuries of development. In terms of the rule of law it has, as in so many other areas of life, presented both new challenges and new opportunities. It has created new crimes (such as phishing, internet child pornography, software piracy and credit-card cloning) and changed the way old crimes are committed (such as the advance fee frauds that now come courtesy of email), but at the same time law enforcement can also call upon new tools, techniques and methodologies that would have been inconceivable before now. Forensic science, for example, has with renewed vigour proved again and again the truth of Locard's principle of exchange:[1] it has allowed the origins of murder victims to be identified through trace contaminants in their bones, and brought murderers and rapists to justice by their DNA decades after their offences were committed. Communications technology has also come a long way since Crippen[2] received the unwelcome honour of being the first to be arrested as the result of a radio telegram in 1910. And then there is the development of professional skills to consider. For instance, the role of the card-index collator, once the mainstay of local police knowledge, has evolved out of all recognition into the hi-tech crime analyst

1 Where two objects come into contact with each other, they leave behind some trace of that contact.

2 Crippen murdered his wife then tried to flee the country with his mistress dressed as a young man. He was hanged.

(with organisations such as Europol and Interpol concentrating a hefty proportion of staff resources in this area). Unfortunately, improved communications, new technologies and international mobility have also provided criminals with an additional dimension and facility to their activity, helping them to mask their identities, avoid detection and escape justice as well as to hide their proceeds.

National law enforcement has been relatively slow to recognise the need to adjust to this phenomenon. National governments have been even slower. International police co-operation is expensive; it needs to accommodate differences in national policing, strategy and legislation, and depends on some level of surrender of control. In 1998 the G8 group of countries described the situation with some eloquence:

> Globalization has been accompanied by a dramatic increase in transnational crime. This takes many forms, including trafficking in drugs and weapons; smuggling of human beings; the abuse of new technologies to steal, defraud and evade the law; and the laundering of the proceeds of crime.
>
> Such crimes pose a threat not only to our own citizens and their communities, through lives blighted by drugs and societies living in fear of organised crime; but also a global threat which can undermine the democratic and economic basis of societies through the investment of illegal money by international cartels, corruption, a weakening of institutions and a loss of confidence in the rule of law.
>
> To fight this threat, international co-operation is indispensable . . . There must be no safe havens either for criminals or for their money.[3]

Political choices have to be made at the national level on how best to deal with international crime, but the menu of options is limited:

- reinforce national borders;
- reduce demand for contraband based crime;
- send personnel to foreign jurisdictions to liaise locally (or advise) on matters of national law enforcement interest;
- negotiate and support common international standards;
- provide aid to source and transit countries in order to enhance their law enforcement capacities (either directly or through an international proxy);
- influence governments in source and transit countries to commit their own resources to interdict crime locally;

3 G8 Communiqué 17 May 1998 Birmingham UK, www.g8.gov.uk/servlet/Front?pagename=OpenMarket/Xcelerate/ShowPage&c=Page&cid=1097587800968, accessed 10 May 2007.

- participate in international organisations which can then act as a central co-ordinating authority;
- build a non-centralised co-operative network with other countries to pool resources and manage information.

There is a further, controversial, option which has been judiciously avoided: the creation of a supranational investigative body with executive powers (i.e. a true international police force). Given the loss of political control (and accountability) represented by accepting a 'higher level' police authority, it is hardly surprising that a supranational police force has, to date, not found favour. Certain international groupings have attempted to approximate this concept: the International Criminal Tribunal for the former Yugoslavia (ICTY) and the International Criminal Court (ICC) have set up investigative departments with powers based on treaty and dedicated to offences with a specific significance; the European Union has the Office Lutte Anti-fraud (OLAF – the anti-fraud office)[4] for investigating irregularities involving the EU budget; and the UN has the Office of Internal Oversight Services (OIOS)[5] which travels the world investigating contraventions against its charter involving UN personnel. However, when it comes to the use of coercive powers and criminal prosecution, each of these agencies must have recourse to the local authorities.

IS CROSS-BORDER LAW ENFORCEMENT NEEDED?

The extent to which the international dimension affects the national crime picture has been disputed:

> The shallow nature of the arguments for further improvements in the quality of police co-operation . . . creating fantasies and fears about potential threats to internal security concerning a flood of illegal immigrants bringing with them drugs, arms dealing, organised crime and racketeers, may have a certain populist appeal, but it is not an adequate substitute for ethical arguments on which to base new obligations.[6]

4 OLAF has wide powers related to any issues related to threats to the financial and economic interests of the EU, www.ec.europa.eu/anti_fraud/index_en.html

5 UN OIOS conducts 'administrative investigations' based on the UN Constitution and with powers enforced through terms of employment.

6 M. Anderson 'The Agenda for Police Co-Operation', in M. Anderson and M. Den Boer (eds), *Policing Across National Boundaries* (London: Pinter, 1994), p. 9.

However, such arguments inadequately appreciate the interactivity of the global criminal economy:[7]

- heroin sold on the streets of western Europe is cultivated in Afghanistan;
- cocaine snorted in Milan is grown in Colombia;
- seven per cent of world trade is in counterfeit products, two-thirds of which are manufactured in China;[8]
- dirty money is laundered through the world's financial markets in New York, London, Frankfurt, Hong Kong and Tokyo;
- pills popped in the night clubs of Sydney were probably made in the Netherlands;
- a credit card scanned surreptitiously behind a bar in Cape Town can be cloned within 24 hours and used to purchase luxury items in Manhattan;
- the mobile phone slipped from the coat pocket on the Metro in Paris may be reprogrammed and sold on a market stall in East Africa;
- a luxury car may be stolen from the streets of Spain and sold in the Balkans;
- paedophiles travel to the developing world on sex tours or sit at home and log on to websites with servers located in distant lands.

Each of these offences would normally be viewed in terms of a national crime statistic, but they all have an international dimension, and, increasingly, the serious crime business model involves setting up in one jurisdiction, but operating in another. Without the close and constructive collaboration of national law enforcement bodies both investigations and prosecutions in such cases would be forlorn and impotent gestures.

There is an argument to say that international crime should not be viewed as a separate category. After all, the actual illegal acts committed by criminals across borders are generally the same as those committed nationally (except, of course, where importation is a key element of the offence). However, anecdotal evidence of an increase in cross-border criminal activity supports the view that the phenomenon of international crime deserves closer scrutiny.

International crime may be characterised differently not so much because of the type of act involved (acquisitive, violent, sexual, etc.), but because of the environment in which it is committed and the additional challenges entailed in its prevention, detection and prosecution. For example, it would have been

7 Roger Gaspar cites the work of Dr Ben Bowling in Chapter 1. In addition statistics show that in the first half of 2007, 20 per cent of crime in London was committed by foreign nationals: T. Harper and B. Leapman, 'Foreigners "commit fifth of crime in London" ', Sunday Telegraph, 23 September 2007.

8 D. M. Hopkins, L. T. Kontnik and M. T. Turnage, *Counterfeiting Exposed: Protecting Your Brand and Customers* (Hoboken: Wiley, 2003), pp. 3, 58, and T. Phillips, *Knockoff: The Deadly Trade in Counterfeit Goods* (London: Kogan Page, 2005), p. 4.

impossible for investigators dealing with the gangland execution of six Italians in August 2007 in Duisburg, Germany, to do so without close reference to the authorities in Calabria. And, at the same time, law enforcement in Italy needed to pay due regard to the local consequences of those distant killings. Calabrian crime groups (the 'Ndrangheta) are reported to have been buying into Germany for 20 years, to have property on five continents and investments in the Frankfurt stock exchange.[9] Clearly this phenomenon cannot be seriously viewed as a purely national threat.

International trade differs from national trade only because of the economic complexities involved in labour markets, raw material costs, international freight, the movement of funds between international financial markets and by its regulation. By analogy international crime has a similar relationship to national crime. The interactions exhibit the same complexity and, in the same way that international trade influences the costs on the high street, much internationally committed crime can be said to influence the quality of life in the local neighbourhood. For example, the virulent attentions of narco-conglomerates from Latin America threaten to overwhelm the legitimate community in tiny Guinea-Bissau in West Africa which finds itself on the front line of international drug trafficking, but without the wherewithal to fight back. Clearly Guinea-Bissau is not the destination for the drugs, just a bridgehead and vantage point for onward delivery.[10]

If the existence of international crime as a separate phenomenon can be accepted, then, of course, it follows that there is also a need for some degree of international response. Whether this can be accomplished solely at the national level has yet to be evidenced. So far, existing strategies have failed to stem the rise and impact of international crime. Countries with a federal structure have tussled with the challenge of crime operating across internal administrative borders and have found advantages in establishing some form of federal agency to confront it. However, on the international level, agencies have been defined chiefly as message-switching centres and depositories for information handling without the executive functions which give national law enforcement its bite. The G8 called international co-operation 'indispensable', but is co-operation by itself enough?

9 'More than 30 mafia suspects arrested over Germany killings' AFP 30 August 2007, www.afp.google.com/article/ALeqM5iFAT99yWz6TFEypv2Bn3F76C3x5w, accessed 3 September 2007. The 'Ndrangheta are Calabrian organised crime.

10 R. Callimachi, 'Africa a New Conduit for Europe's Drugs', Associated Press Report, 29 July 2007.

Chapter 1

Tackling international crime

Forward into the third era

Roger Gaspar

Bowling[1] argues that there is no part of policing that does not have an international dimension. He has observed that:

- local law enforcement has constructed co-operation and assistance arrangements with their counterparts in other countries;
- national policing structures regularly engage with neighbours on common problems;
- international[2] crimes have led to national law enforcement agencies working in other countries;
- transnational[3] crimes have demanded regional security arrangements; and,
- globally, Interpol provides worldwide operational assistance.

There may be some over simplification in this précis, but it is clear that globalisation has introduced international issues for law enforcement which were created within national boundaries and limited by sovereignty. It also follows that the need for internationalism within policing does not just lie with a response to organised crime.

To understand the scope of arrangements necessary to facilitate successful prevention and detection of crime with an international component, it will benefit us to broadly unpick the current nature of crime, reflect on our current investigative methodology and how it needs to be developed or mirrored, and to consider what international constructs are required.

1 B. Bowling, 'Sovereignty vs. Security: Transnational Policing in the Contemporary Caribbean' in Caribbean Journal of Criminology and Social Psychology, 10(1–2) (2005).
2 Between countries.
3 Activities which flow over national boundaries.

SOME TYPOLOGIES OF CRIME

To provide us with a broad picture of the nature of the problem created by the growth in internationalism, let us take a practical view of crime. There are, perhaps, four broad categories:

- spontaneous, unplanned crime committed by the opportunist;
- recidivist[4] crime committed by repeat offenders where the opportunity is sought rather than spontaneous; where plans and preferences are used;
- crimes that are organised and committed by determined individuals working alone, or with particular criminal associates, where an investment is made in research and planning or where victims are 'prepared' by grooming;
- organised crime where there is the notion of networks or infrastructure; connectivity between individuals in illicit markets or supply chains; an investment in control through corruption, violence or infiltration; substantial profits and elements of continuity.

The spontaneous crime may be committed by or on an international visitor. The recidivist may have chosen to cross borders to commit crime. The 'crimes that are organised' may involve international partnerships. Organised crime may transcend several borders and involve partnerships with people from several different countries.

Should we therefore add 'international' crime to these categories? I would argue no, for, as important as the international component is in the construction of a response to crime, it does not appear to be a separate typology.

A burglar, for example, who decides to travel from their home in Ghent, Belgium, to Paris, France, to commit burglary is using the same methodology as one who decides to travel from Ghent to Antwerp (which is also in Belgium) to commit the same offence. Both are seeking to increase their anonymity where they commit their crime. Where one sees it as sufficient to rely on poor exchanges of information between local policing commands within one country, the other seeks the greater protection of a national border that restricts the policing response, but not the offender's travel. The same principle applies whichever typology is used. All may have an international component but the methodology of the offender is consistent irrespective of the international component.

But whilst internationalism may not bring about a new typology, it certainly does present the most striking challenges in providing an effective response whether it be with our prevention strategies or our investigative response. Take the example of our burglar from Ghent. The traditional law enforcement

4 'person who habitually relapses into crime; one who apparently cannot be cured of criminal tendencies; persistent offender' Oxford English Dictionary.

response to burglary is a reactive investigation: a search for witnesses, a search for physical evidence, the use of crime-solving information and victim support. The Paris police can do this of course and will be experienced, competent and well resourced. However, assume there is a witness who provides a description. How is that converted into an identification? National systems exist for this but international ones do not. Of course Interpol exists with its notice system but this is not going to be the answer before the suspect is identified. Progressing through the investigation, what if DNA or fingerprints are found? Again Interpol could be used but, and this is no criticism of Interpol, their services are never going to be able to mirror the effectiveness of national systems when dealing with what is frankly an 'ordinary' crime.

Difficulties continue in this sample investigation. Some countries are making increasing use of criminal information to find patterns and similarities that assist the identification of suspects. But, again, these arrangements are drawn up on either a local or national basis.

So some fundamental problems exist in this routine investigation that are going to reduce efficiency. This is, though, but one example.

If we return to the four broad categories described above, how many distinct pathologies[5] can we find? Using this approach it is possible to see two primary pathologies. The first is a collective of the first three categories (the spontaneous, the recidivist and the 'crimes that are organised'). The impact of these crimes is very much local and the response starts locally. That response is largely reactive. The second is organised crime. Whilst there is always a local impact from organised crime and certain organised criminal activity will, when discovered, be investigated locally, action against the criminals' infrastructure, networks and markets is very much an activity for national law enforcement using a response that is primarily proactive.

The lines between these pathologies are not clear and solid; for example we do see a national response to some elements of the 'collective' of crimes. By and large, however, the crimes within the 'collective' are reported to or discovered by local police and we are locked into a reactive response which is both expected by the community and also the most appropriate for the majority of crimes in this category. However, the local reactive investigation of certain crimes in this pathology has not been considered sufficient and this has led either to the introduction of the local use of proactive techniques or to the construction of specialist investigatory arrangements. This latter activity may be either at a national level or a sub-national level and is, in the main, for low volume but more serious crime such as kidnapping, armed robbery, paedophilia and similar.

So, waiting to tackle the impact of internationalism within crime, we have

5 By 'pathologies' I mean distinct criminal methodologies that force investigators to respond with different techniques, structures or activities.

local policing structures and national structures, depending upon the nature of the problem. We will return to the pathologies and the consequences of international components in them shortly, but let us look at an investigatory doctrine.

AN INVESTIGATORY DOCTRINE

Whilst there are many ways in which law enforcement arrangements are constructed and managed and differences in their interaction with other national legal systems, there is only one basic model of investigation which any country can pursue. That model comprises three components, prevention, reactivity and proactivity, and can be summarised thus.

Prevention

Some crime is prevented (or immediately detected) by the presence of uniformed police patrols. This was the original concept of policing and remains present in all countries.

Reactivity

Where crime has been committed, a reactive response is provided by an investigator conducting an investigation. This is a scene-based process comprising a search for witnesses, a search for physical evidence, a search for crime-solving information and victim support. All reactive activity falls into these four processes and no others exist.

The search for witnesses looks first for eyewitnesses to the event but includes witnesses to prior and subsequent events, constructive, technical or expert witnesses. Depending upon the seriousness of the crime, a range of techniques are used such as the standard 'house to house' enquiry, reconstruction of the crime, the appeal for witnesses on anniversaries and the use of press conferences to maintain the case in the public eye. Interview skills have been advanced with the use of conversation management and cognitive interview. Supplementary aids to the process of moving from a description to possible identification of a suspect have also been developed, improving upon artists' impressions with photo-fit and e-fit equipment.

The search for physical evidence is to do with the finding of any latent material at the crime scene or on a suspect, or the tracing of any property or other tangible evidence that might trace or connect a suspect to the event. So this includes the search for DNA, fingerprints, blood or other secretions, handwriting, blood distribution or firearms residues and marks such as tool, tyre or foot. The tracing of tangible property includes the circulation of stolen property details, the maintenance of stolen property indices and specialist stolen arts and antiques registers.

The 'first' two processes are a direct hunt for evidence. The third process, *the search for crime-solving information*, is not directly evidential. It may become evidence but it is the use of information to add a third way of identifying a potential suspect. This can include, for example, the use of previous records to identify unusual methodologies or the use of an informant.

Victim support is first an acknowledgement that policing is a service to the public as much as a function to the state and, second, an essential process in obtaining and maintaining support for a prosecution or for countering repeat victimisation. This can range from the relatively simple provision of crime prevention advice to prevent a repetition of a crime, to prolonged support for a victim of a serious sexual offence or the family of a murder victim or the provision of a new identity or relocation where a serious risk to the life of a victim or witness exists.

The object of these four processes is to provide a service to the victim and for the identification and tracing of a suspect for interview. Of course, these processes can occur in any order and may be compressed in time or even simultaneous when a crime is discovered during its commission.

Depending upon the type of jurisdiction, law enforcement activity in these processes may be directed by judicial process, subject to special authorisation or merely established practice, but the point is that a reactive investigation will not alter from country to country. There may be differences in the resources applied to different parts of the process or in the support services available (such as specialist forensic scene examiners, forensic laboratories, databases or IT). There may also be differences in the resources applied to the process according to the seriousness of the crime but these three components are all that are possible in any reactive investigation.

Proactivity

It is also possible to be finite about the proactive opportunities that exist. There are only four. Within those, there are a range of techniques, but they all conform to one of these four activities: crime reduction; offender targeting; hotspot initiatives; and location targeting.

The crime reduction technique engages in partnership, for example, with government, the civil service, private businesses, industry, NGOs and the public. Police alone cannot prevent all crime: the numbers of police that would be required to impact crime on a large scale by random patrol would be huge. Of course the first and immediate activity in this technique is the use of directed uniform patrols in identified localities. This activity is driven by information analysis and effective fast-time briefing. But, by branching into partnership, other remedies become possible such as: civil partnerships to provide additional support for police (for example closed-circuit television); crime prevention initiatives; designing out crime prone areas; or adopting politically supported zero-tolerance areas. Any such plan must bear in mind and prepare to measure and tackle displacement.

Initiatives to help in specific crime types have their place here. The vetting of applicants for employment in security sensitive situations is one example. In a different vein, the analysis of organised car thieves' activities has led to partnerships with vehicle manufacturers to introduce specific measures to make both theft and the disguising of a stolen vehicle's identity more difficult. This is an early international example.

So, proactive crime prevention may be geographic specific or crime-type specific. Internationally, it is essential, whether it be initiatives to reduce the push/pull factors energising human trafficking and smuggling, tracking precursors or finding alternative solutions for poppy and coca farmers.

Offender targeting is the approach to tackle prolific offenders where there is significant information to indicate that an individual is regularly involved in crime but where evidence from any one reactive investigation is insufficient for the individual to be brought into judicial proceedings. It requires an intelligence package to provide the objective basis for suspicion and justification for action. This is derived from a number of analytical products and should lead to an operation which is essentially a plan to catch the offender during the course of his or her next crime. As a result covert information and evidential collection techniques will usually be employed to move from well-founded suspicion to evidence sufficient to arrest.

The risk to civil liberties is obvious. This approach must be accompanied by objective judgements about the quality of intelligence and evidence and a strictly ethical approach. Great care must be taken to ensure that the integrity of evidence collected is perfect and that innocent explanations for observed conduct are not overlooked. Judicial authorities may well be required in many countries to permit or authorise different activities in this approach.

This is a major technique in tackling organised crime and, consequently, may need to be run across borders and in a number of countries.

The hotspot initiative is the first of two geographic approaches and is used for persistent crime problems. Such an initiative involves the identification of and focusing of resources towards a crime prone area which suffers a higher than usual concentration of crimes of all types; thus it is about tackling a range of problems in a defined geographical area. It needs a process of analysis for identification of the target area and the components of criminal activity. Once identified the approach requires sustained and integrated tactics such as concentrated patrol or reactivity, a proactive operational response, crime prevention initiatives and the start of strategic partnerships to address these specific problems – usually with other public organisations and private businesses for the mutual benefit of all.

This process uniquely probably has little or no international relevance.

Location targeting is the second geographic approach and is used where a pattern has been identified which suggests that one individual or group of individuals is responsible for a continuing series of crimes of a particular type. There may be a description or forensic clues to the identity of the offender(s) available but they are insufficient for a prosecution or offender-targeting operation.

Typically this pattern will generally be linked by one or more of the following:

Time of day or day of week	Property involved
Place or type of venue	Forensic linking
Method	Victims

For this approach to work, a geographic area must be capable of being defined for the deployment of officers at a specified time with the object of arresting the offender either when he or she commits a further offence or some act which provides sufficient evidence that this is the person sought. There must be a feasible arrest plan and the risk to witnesses, victims, public and the police officers involved must be carefully assessed.

This is a technique used to great advantage against serial sexual offenders. In such cases the geographic 'area' may be quite large, perhaps even not finite, linked, for example, to major transport routes such as railways or arterial roads over a wide area. In an international context, there is little evidence of this technique being used yet. However, as collaborative information systems grow and fast-time identification of the methodology used by organised crime or in 'crimes that are organised' improves, it will be possible to share knowledge and information, for example, to target trafficking routes, particularly at geographical bottlenecks.

Again, as in the case of the reactive investigation, these four proactive opportunities are finite choices facing the investigator. There are no other alternatives. It may be that some countries do some or all of these techniques. It may be that a country does no proactivity other than crime reduction. But this is the art of the possible and the techniques that are globally available amount to:

- prevention by uniformed patrol or presence;
- reactive investigation comprising:
    - a search for witnesses;
    - a search for physical evidence;

  - a search for crime solving information; and
  - victim support;

- proactivity comprising:

  - crime reduction techniques;
  - offender targeting;
  - hotspot initiatives; and
  - location targeting.

This forms the basis of an investigatory doctrine. A country may not like a particular technique for cultural or other reasons. It may choose to invest more in one area than another. It may apply legal restraint to limit some processes or it may introduce legal gateways so that they are only used in serious cases. All this is understandable since an investigation inherently includes elements of intrusion into the private lives of citizens. This is one of the choices made by countries as a mark of their sovereignty. But if the international component in crime is becoming increasingly more common then there will be growing pressure for countries to provide international co-operation and make a success of investigations which cross borders. Countries will therefore come under increasing pressure to pursue all areas of this doctrine and for collaborative processes to be constructed.

To examine the extent to which international adoption of this doctrine would be beneficial or justified, we need to explore the national and international pressures on the business of crime prevention and investigation.

INCREASING COMPLEXITY AND GLOBALISATION: ARE WE MOVING TO A NEW ERA OF POLICING?

Most modern national policing arrangements are less than 200 years old. They started generally with an organised patrolling system of uniformed officers responsible for the prevention of crime. This was the first era but was soon superseded by the second as societies put pressure on their law enforcement structures for a response to committed crime. In the second era, reactive investigation sat alongside uniform preventative patrols as the national response. Some countries maintained a local domination of the management arrangements, some had national structures with devolved units, and others had (and still have) two structures either providing a separate national and local response or separate urban and rural responses.

The differences in management arrangements, structures and interfaces with the judicial system did not alter the development of the reactive investigation part of the doctrine. For example, excellence in forensic skills in particular developed from the use of fingerprints at the beginning of the twentieth century to DNA at the end of the century. However, with the exception of the introduction of some international support with the creation of Interpol in 1923, most of the development within the second era has been within national boundaries.

But the second era has probably passed. It has been a gradual process but, as in the first era the use of patrol alone was not sufficient, so in the second era the use of patrol and reactivity alone proved inadequate for the way in which crime problems developed.

The pressures that developed this inadequacy are these:

- the growth of wealth and the gap between rich and poor;
- the general increase in the population and the development of larger communities;
- more mobile national communities;
- greater international and intercontinental migration;
- the growth of communications;
- the globalisation of markets;
- the creation of cyberspace;[6]
- the sophistication of offenders;
- increased complexity in criminal businesses and enterprise.

An international component is present in all these factors.

The principle dynamics at work here have eroded the effectiveness of the patrol and reactive investigation. The growth in wealth has fuelled a rise in acquisitive crime making it more difficult for static law enforcement resources to maintain an equal level of service for all reactive investigations and the increase in public scrutiny and awareness has enabled some criminals to increase their sophistication making them more difficult targets to detect. At the same time, the development of larger communities has stretched patrolling resources, and national and international mobility has reduced the effectiveness of reactive investigation through greater anonymity, increased isolation between different communities and reduced community cohesion.

Increasing volumes of crime have led to a reduction in the time available for each enquiry; larger and more mobile communities have increased levels of anonymity within communities so the effectiveness of eyewitness accounts has diminished – effectively many people in large communities do not know their neighbours well and they may not feel confident about speaking out. At the same time, the same media which is used to great advantage in serious cases to find witnesses has meant that investigation techniques are known and discussed amongst criminals. The recidivist can now be routinely expected to take precautions to prevent leaving a forensic trail.

This practice of 'professionalism' within criminals started the move towards a new era and a broader spectrum of investigative activity. An example of

6 See Chapter 17 for the implications of cyberspace on e-crime.

armed robbery illustrates the dilemma. Offenders typically work in small teams of individuals who specialise in this type of offence. They plan carefully and know what they need to do to negate the reactive investigation. Typically a number of offenders, masked to prevent recognition or description and to eliminate the ability of witnesses to identify them, using 'clean' weapons and wearing overalls, follow a well-planned operation including for their escape and the effective disposal of anything likely to connect them to the scene. This type of methodology reduces the effectiveness of the reactive investigation model; it is still completed, of course, for evidential and information purposes but eyewitness accounts, CCTV and forensic material will not be as useful and, as a means of identifying the suspects, will probably be insufficient.

As a result, many countries have developed some capability in proactive techniques to investigate and detect resourceful and persistent offenders.

The 'collective'

The international impact on the 'collective' of crimes can appear anywhere in the process. Visitors to a country may engage in spontaneous opportunistic crime, they may be in the country for legitimate reasons but also plan to commit crime, or they may be there solely for a criminal purpose. However, we may expect the arrangements put in place for the prevention of crime to work equally well against the visitor as the resident. The issue is therefore more about the identification of offenders. For reactivity this is post-crime and involves the effectiveness of the reactive investigation model when conducted over one or more national borders; for proactivity, information is required prior to the event. If this is information that needs to be obtained from another country, we can have problems. What are the systems for requesting and obtaining the information? Does the information exist? Is there a common understanding about investigatory doctrine? Is there trust between the countries involved? Is it legal for such information to be shared? Should data be stored and shared centrally?

Countries can also have a problem with migrants who are criminals. Much of the information about recidivists is obtained as they grow up passing from petty crime to more serious matters or progressing through adolescence and inexperience as a criminal. Such information does not transfer with the migrant, even if systems and policies for the collection and retention of this information is the same from country to country. This leaves a gap in law enforcement knowledge. In the prevention of paedophile crimes, where some countries rely on such information for pre-employment vetting to prevent such offenders getting into occupations that bring them closer to children, the absence of such information can have profound consequences.

At the time of the creation of 'modern' policing, law enforcement was dealing with mainly indigenous populations where the community mindset was shared by the police, where cultural references were intuitively understood, and where linguistic inflexions and non-verbal communication were mutually comprehensible. Now, in many large conurbations throughout the world, purely local incidents have an international dimension and investigators need to take into account the diverse expectations, prejudices and pre-conceptions imported by the migrant communities. This is irrespective of whether the victim is a permanently settled but recent immigrant, second-generation descendant of immigrants or just on a business or recreational visit. This requires much better preparation of our domestic resources to understand the diverse nature of many modern societies.

The different expectations provide new challenges for the investigator. Forensic tests or other procedures expected and accepted by one group in the community may be an unacceptable intrusion to another. Support for the victim may be hampered by language difficulties or cultural perceptions; indeed cultural taboos may impede the collection of evidence[7] and the support for prosecutions. Investigators may be faced with a victim or witnesses who have returned to their native or former country or indeed, in the case of cyber-crime, with a victim or witnesses who have always been in another country. Typically, these difficulties can only be resolved on a police to police basis (where permitted by legislation) or through mutual legal assistance. The latter is frequently perceived as slow and inflexible and little suited to rapid post-crime investigation.

Organised crime

'Organised crime' is distinguished as a term in common daily use, behind which lies at least four decades of failed attempts to arrive at a single satisfactory definition. This is not the place to examine all its aspects nor to attempt to redefine it. Wright[8] maps these attempts but it remains problematic. As a result the UN[9] avoided the trap and limited their work to defining the nature of an Organised Crime Group. However, attempts at a definition are of little help in understanding the pathology which is more complex than the average two or three line definition.

Yet, generally, most people have a vision of what 'organised crime' means. It would include a mafia-type organisation or a network of individuals. If considered on a sole national basis, it would include activities such as protection rackets or sophisticated long-running criminal activities with some kind of infrastructure. Internationally, organised crime is typically seen as being behind the running of illicit commodity trading routes and markets.

Perhaps the only common feature of all these examples is that the reactive

7 Particularly in relation to serious sexual offences.

8 A. Wright, *Organised Crime* (Cullompton: Willan, 2006), pp. 1–26.

9 United Nations Convention against Transnational Organized Crime, Article 2 (a).

investigation model which, with high visibility patrolling, has been the principle law enforcement methodology in the second era, is unlikely to have any serious impact on the dismantling of such organisations or networks. Apply the reactive investigation part of the doctrine to the problems of tackling the illicit trafficking in human beings for slavery or sexual exploitation purposes or drug trafficking where there is cultivation in one country, production in a second and illicit markets in a third. The inadequacy is obvious.

The consequences

The consequences of these national and international developments are varied.

The principle international activity in the early days of 'modern' policing was the tracing of offenders who fled overseas. This is typified by the establishment of the International Criminal Police Organization (Interpol) in 1923. Interpol's notice system was an early development of the organisation, designed to provide a service to countries to locate, trace or bring about the arrest of offenders.

The twenty-first century view is that fleeing offenders can move even more quickly and more anonymously across borders which in many cases have been deliberately relaxed for the benefit of society and trade. But the investigator will also be faced with offenders who remain in another country while committing their crime, or in the case of organised crime, with international connectivity between offenders, each responsible for segments of an illicit commodity market. In organised crime, the new challenge for investigators is to balance the energy put into the dismantling of domestic networks with that contributing to the removal of connecting networks in other countries. Without that latter action, the supply to market will not be dismantled. For police services with a tradition of local service to the community, how is its responsibility to the servicing of perhaps extensive requests for assistance to the law enforcement of another country to be judged and balanced against local priorities?

A further complication arises with cybercrime. Here jurisdictional issues are at their most complicated. Offenders may not be actually present in the country from which an attack is launched and a complete picture of the criminal activity may only be possible with extensive international co-operation. Again, we have the new idea that law enforcement in one country may be expected to commit judicial and operational resources when the victim resides in another. Since national law enforcement organisations were conceived on the notion that they are there to prevent and investigate crimes committed within their geographic boundaries, this presents a new and difficult challenge and, for most, new and impossible demands on already overstretched resources.

So why should a country have to pay regard to this new level of internationalism in crime? The answer lies with globalisation. These events have the ability to negatively impact on local economies. In 2007, the kidnapping of a young child at a holiday resort in Portugal brought intense media scrutiny[10] and demonstrated that the performance of the local police was not just an issue for the victims, who in this case were not local nationals. Those watching from further away would be making judgements about the safety of the environment and the effectiveness of the police enquiry, and, using those judgements, decide where to holiday in the future. If their choice is to go elsewhere, this will impact heavily upon on the economy of the resort, making effective investigation of the individual crime an issue for the wider community.

And, of course, the judgements from those watching events from afar will be based upon their own expectations of law enforcement and media reports rather than realities on the ground. In terms of the wider impact of such events, it is not sufficient that the local police service did everything effectively and to the standard expected by their community. What also matters is how their performance is *perceived* by those who make judgments which impact on the economy.

Similar issues arise over trade. The general effectiveness of policing becomes a matter for a business looking to invest in another country. Will it have the same level of security as it enjoys at home? Are there protections against corruption, fraud or extortion?

> Crime and corruption flourish while development lags. This deepens social cleavages, scares away investors and encourages the flight of domestic capital and brain drain . . .
>
> Antonio Maria Costa, Executive Director UNODC[11]

The nature of the globalisation of markets has increased the risk of international crimes. As trade barriers have been removed so it has become easier for the criminal who deals in illicit commodities. This has broadened the nature of organised crime and places the investigator in the position of needing international co-operation in the generation of information, the design and execution of proactive operations and prosecutions.

All this points to a new and significantly different challenge to law enforcement and for that reason I believe we have or are moving into a third era of policing from both a national and international point of view. The national context is that a dependence upon patrol and reactivity is, for many, no longer adequate. There is no reason to expect this development not to spread globally. The international context is that collaboration between countries will be needed in all aspects of law enforcement work from prevention and reactivity to proactivity.

10 An essential part of a reactive crime investigation potentially contributing significantly to the discovery of witnesses.

11 UNODC, 'Crime and development in Central America – caught in the cross-fire' (Report, Vienna: UNODC, 2007).

MANAGEMENT, INFORMATION, CO-OPERATION AND COLLABORATION IN THE THIRD ERA

There are three significant elements which mark out a distinct shift from a second era to a third. First is the significant pressure on the reactive investigation model and the patrol alone to deliver effective prevention and investigation. Second, our arrangements for law enforcement have been created 'within borders' and form a key part of our national sovereignty. Those borders in places are at best porous, in other places deliberately absent, demanding a new view of relationships with neighbouring countries and others further away. Finally, societal changes and pressures on second era methodology means that investigation is not a solitary affair for the individual investigator. The proactive alternatives that are available require a managed approach to ensure the availability of resources, an objective process of both strategic and tactical choice and attention to due process. In short, a new level of organisation and infrastructure is required and a new focus around the use of information rather than on individual investigations.

Management

The distinguishing factor between the second and third era is the shift in management focus.

Patrolling officers, faced with limited resources and large urban, rural or border commitments, must be prepared with up-to-date knowledge of the problems and priorities and deployed by a managed process which produces the most effective use of those resources. Besides being the recipients of information to direct their activities, they will also be one of the prime sources of information to add to the corporate understanding of the problems to be tackled. This work must be steered by priorities set by managers.

Reactive investigation was an individually managed process in the second era and looked at one crime event in isolation. In the third era, there is a central management of crime conceived as a wider contextual problem supported by strategic (or threat) assessment and by the applied use of information through tactical assessments; this not only includes information derived from scene-based investigations but also information about crime from all sources, open and closed (including that from specific covert targeting and specialist operations).

Whilst proactive techniques initially originated from information gathered at reactive investigations, in the third era such myopia is perceived as insufficient. A smarter approach is required to the information-handling infrastructure, the related resource commitment and to the overall management of the process. Given the dynamics which forced the move from the second to the third era, national and international issues provide a single perspective which cannot be separated from each other.

In the second era, management commissioned reports that entailed a relatively simple assessment of rising or falling numbers of crime, noting whether there were any burgeoning areas and how successfully (or otherwise) law enforcement had been in preventing, reducing or detecting offences. These are still important issues in the third era but the management responsibility has become much broader. At a local level, there are choices to be made about allocating resources to patrol, to reactive investigation or to proactivity. There is management required as to the priorities to be set for both investigation activity and information collection as well as in the decision to adopt one or more of the proactive choices. To do this effectively managers will be in charge of the process of setting the priorities for information collection and enforcement and will themselves require information products that tell them what is going on and the opportunities and tactical choices. The construction of these products will require the support of analysts trained to assess all aspects of law enforcement work.

The acquisition and accumulation of knowledge is yet another new third-era function. It is aimed at contributing to the understanding of problems shared with neighbouring commands, the national picture and the international landscape. At a national level, there is a responsibility to understand the extent and nature of the problem and the dynamics at work, as well as to engage in partnership with neighbouring countries confronted by the same threats. Internationally, there is an as yet immature function to detect and describe emerging threats adequately in one country that will impact on another and to disseminate an early warning of them.

Assessing the threat

The first key to this broader approach is the strategic or threat assessment. The concept of this is new to many countries, but is gradually gaining acceptance as its value is realised. It is simply an evaluation of the current and emerging threats posed by crime within a particular context. It will normally contain an element of prediction in terms of how crime will develop and its value lies in allowing management decisions to be informed and based on evidence. When conducted at a local level they can be aggregated to contribute to a national view. National assessments can then be collated into regional threat assessments and so on. In the EU this has now resulted in the new European Organised Crime Threat Assessment produced by Europol.[12]

Typically such regional assessments look beyond crime methodologies and

12 www.europol.europa.eu/publications/European_Organized_Crime_Threat_Assessment_(OCTA)/OCTA2007.pdf, accessed 11 August 2007. See also T. Vander Beken, *European Organized Crime Scenarios for 2015* (Antwerpen: Maklu), 2006, for European Commission funded work on the use of risk-based methodology for analysing the threat of crime.

examine, in addition to crime diagnostics and impact assessment, the interdependence of security and development, the impact of crime in undermining development, 'points of vulnerability' and the resulting policy implications. The value in such research for the third era is not about considering whether to adopt a specific targeting operation (against a prominent crime figure or crime group). This is for the tactical assessment within discreet areas of operational focus. The regional strategic assessment drives progress on the proactive choice of crime reduction initiatives through international agreements and collaboration in the development of legislation and regional crime reduction strategies. It will influence both collaboration and national priorities.

Approaching the problem from the other direction, the UN Office on Drugs and Crime (UNODC), for instance, focuses upon problem or vulnerable areas to produce reports intended not just to inform those immediately involved but also those working at a global level. Perhaps the best-known example of this is the annual UN World Drug Report which looks at the trends in cultivation, production and distribution of illicit drugs on a global level.[13] This research can also be usefully compared with similar work done on the regional level by the European Monitoring Centre for Drugs and Drug Addiction (EMCDDA) and also published in an annual report.[14]

This embeds the third-era notion of strategic direction and the setting of priorities both for domestic agendas and regional partnerships. But it is from such collective knowledge that global initiatives can be formed. As an intergovernmental institution the UNODC seeks to address strategic issues through a search for consensus amongst its members and by negotiating a common agreeable framework in key crime areas. The principal results in this respect are the Convention on Transnational Organised Crime and its Protocols (on the trafficking of persons, the smuggling of migrants and the trafficking of firearms), the Convention against Corruption and the programmes of research, analysis and technical assistance.[15] The UN aspires to create minimum legislative standards throughout its membership, to spread knowledge and to build technical capacity. It concentrates on creating the right environment for enabling effective action.

The second key for managers is the tactical assessment. Produced by the analyst, this is the second vital information product but the one that drives the everyday business of setting and maintaining priorities for information collection, assessing the immediate crime demographics and presenting options for tactical deployments whether through patrol, additional reactivity or one of the four proactive choices.

13 www.unodc.org/unodc/en/world_drug_report.html, accessed 11 August 2007.

14 EMCDDA, www.ar2006.emcdda.europa.eu/en/page001-en.html, accessed 11 August 2007.

15 See p. 286 below.

Information

Knowing what resources are needed and where to deploy them requires accurate knowledge and understanding of what is going on. A crucial concern in the third era is, therefore, the fitness of our information collection and analysis processes for this purpose.

The mechanics of such processes will be discussed elsewhere in this volume, but proactive choices for local and international investigators dictate the need for a professional approach to the business of collecting, handling and analysing information as well as for an enhanced investment in infrastructure, training and resources. This must be comparable to that given to reactive investigation during the second era. These are expensive and difficult processes requiring the building of standards, objectivity and an infrastructure. Since operational partners may lie in different countries, international commonality in these areas becomes more of an imperative requirement than a desirable one.

Organised crime has a particular offender methodology at its core. Often organised criminal activity is not of the type normally brought to the attention of law enforcement by the public so that officers need systems not only to discover who is involved but also to understand what activities exist and how the criminal business operates. Whilst individual events may be successfully addressed through reactive investigation, the wider activities of organised crime groups are unlikely to be diminished by such methods with the crime bosses remaining isolated and immune and able to continue their business. They do not necessarily involve themselves in the physical 'criminal' act, but instead use others specifically brought into the organisation or network and contracted for the purpose. Often these groups have inter-territorial interests which weaken the nexus with the top figures even further and complicates the investigation with every extra jurisdiction involved. Indeed, a study by Mark Shaw of transnational organised crime groups, found that just under 50 per cent of such groups were categorised as spreading their business across five or more countries.[16]

Once again information is the core ingredient in understanding the linkages. However, information discovered during a single reactive investigation is unlikely to be sufficient to support proactive enquiries and new collateral sources are needed. These may include specific intelligence techniques employed by specialist officers trained in the use of covert techniques, the use of informants, data from open sources, but it will undoubtedly involve a collection process that stretches far beyond the immediate locality. Indeed, as crime reduction proactivity goes 'upstream' (perhaps to incorporate initiatives such as the eradication of poppy and coca plantations, the monitoring of the international movement of precursor chemicals or the control of illegal migrants) so must law

16 M. Shaw, 'Typologies of Transnational Organized Crime Groups', www.unodc.org/pdf/crime/training/typologies.pdf, accessed 1 August 2007.

enforcement work in partnership not only with its own foreign ministry, but also with international organisations, co-operative networks and foreign law enforcement.

As to infrastructure, we can take the way the second era developed as a guide. This produced specialists[17] where necessary and systems to support the reactive process. So, in the third era, specialists in the assessment and analysis of information are required, managers need to be trained in the wider processes and systems need to be developed for both national and international support of the business.

International standards for 'confidence'

The public are afraid of information systems. There are sufficient examples in world history of the misuse of data and of 'secret' organisations for this to be a valid and sensible concern. It is for this reason that, within each of our national structures of sovereignty, the activities of law enforcement are strictly regulated.

Yet, in the third era, law enforcement cannot be effective without a significant scaling up of its systems and effort in information handling. It is the only way in which a response can be provided to the changes in society facing us. This demands that the necessary sharing of information is done in a way that is acceptable to the public and law enforcement officers and in conformity to national laws. In other words public trust in law enforcement activities will feature even more highly in the third era.

Achieving trust is not easy but it comes about through real accountability and public confidence in law enforcement that is objective and professional in the conduct of its business. Tackling corruption is outside the scope of this chapter but is clearly important. No country is going to pass on highly sensitive information which might reveal the existence of a highly placed informant in the centre of an organised crime group to another country where corruption levels are high. Neither, though, is this type of exchange of information likely to take place with a country that has not applied professionalism to the discipline of handling information.

The public will see compliance with laws and principles designed to protect them against the abuse of information retention and use[18] as essential and will want the collection and dissemination of information to be regulated. This may require certain activities to be subject to independent authorisation but for confidence, the public will also require accountability in the same way that they seek it in the more visible aspects of law enforcement work. This may be

17 For example, specialist crime scene examiners and forensic science laboratories.

18 Known alternatively as Data Protection in the EU or the 4th Amendment and data privacy laws in the USA.

achieved through separate independent oversight or the right to make effective complaint. The courts will also need to exercise a 'fit for purpose' judgement.

For law enforcement officers there are new skills to learn. It will be necessary to make appropriate judgements about when to share information and when to restrict it. This requires an understanding of the tension that is inherent in the purpose of security controls and data protection and the benefits of information sharing. Also, so that unnecessary and purposeless collection and retention of information is not pursued (which would be against national data protection laws and would swamp our systems), we must learn objective review processes regarding priorities, information retention and use. And above all, if information is to be shared both nationally and internationally, we must accept that all data must be both assessed and graded at source so that third parties with whom it is shared can be clear about the quality of the source, the reliability of the information and the restrictions on sharing the data.

SUMMARY

The EU and Council of Europe have not been slow in the drafting of agreements to support and enhance effective crime investigation. It is possible to go immediately to over 1,000 pages of legal texts from the last 20 years;[19] from the creation of the European Police Office (Europol), through to the Schengen Information System for law enforcement co-operation to the draft Framework Decision on sharing criminal records,[20] and to find some progress made on information sharing to support both reactivity and proactivity. Even sub-groups of nations have gathered together to drive information sharing (in the Prüm Convention, etc.[21]). In all of these European-based efforts, major attention has been paid to the rules regarding the handling of data and perhaps less to investigative doctrine. And this is just within the EU.

Bowling[22] has discussed the international impact on law enforcement at local, national, international, transnational and global levels. At a local level, collaboration with other law enforcement agencies principally concerns action with victims, witnesses and the tracing and arrest of fugitives. Interpol provides a global service to assist this process through its communication and notice systems but it is not helpful, for example, to relax border controls for the

19 G. Vermeulen, *Essential Texts on International and European Criminal Law* (4th edn, Antwerpen: Maklu, 2005).

20 Draft Council Framework Decision on the organisation and content of the exchange of information extracted from criminal records between Member States, www.eur-lex.europa.eu/LexUriServ/site/en/com/2005/com2005_0690en01.doc, accessed 3 August 2007.

21 The Prüm Convention is also considered in other chapters and in particular at pp. 31 and 177 below.

22 Op. cit., Bowling, fn 1.

ordinary citizen whilst maintaining slow, cumbersome and restrictive extradition processes designed for a time when internationalism in crime was not a significant feature.

At the national level, law enforcement is engaged with colleagues in other countries through joint work on proactive operations (such as controlled deliveries), but also through an expanding network of liaison officers and information sharing with regional organisations.

Transnationally, strategic partnerships have also been formed for crime reduction. Notwithstanding the substantial work of the EU, OECD, OSCE, the Council of Europe, etc. in international capacity building, the UNODC has taken the lead globally in developing legislation and minimum standards, in conducting research into major problems and in providing technical assistance. Interpol, whilst also providing strategic solutions, provides the only worldwide assistance on tactical issues as well as contributing significantly to international and transnational partnerships through its information systems and sub-regional bureaux.[23]

However, essentially this is all piecemeal. There is no global doctrine on methodology and, consequently, developments in different parts of the world look and are different. National sovereignty sits firmly in the way of criminal justice even where countries have embarked on reducing barriers and borders. An investment in third-era thinking and infrastructure is required to overcome this insularity whilst a shared understanding of methodology and a commitment to building 'confidence' in the greater use of information and proactivity are essential.

The requirement for a step change in the handling of information and integration between local policing and national and international effort is obvious, but such initiatives that exist at present are based more on facilitating progress though differences in legal systems rather than moving together on investigative doctrine and information sharing.

And then there is the issue of subsidiarity to consider (the principle that you should only do things centrally where there is a clear benefit to doing it there). The advocates of subsidiarity argue that groups are most motivated when allowed to set their own rules and methods of working. So any rule imposed from outside has to have clear benefits to outweigh the reduction in motivation it will cause.

There is no doubt that both the principles of sovereignty and subsidiarity are issues for thought consequent on the demand for greater information sharing. If access to information on an international basis is important should national systems be open to search by another country or should data be exported to some international 'warehouse'? Both systems have fundamental problems: if a country does not have the systems in place, it can do neither option. If it has

23 Stuart Cameron Waller explores Interpol more fully in Chapter 3.

data but no infrastructure, systems or doctrine, it will not understand which data are important, nor how to make them available with the necessary safeguards. If it has these principles established within its borders, the issue then becomes one of trust in the law enforcement of others. Certainly it would be preposterous to propose global-data warehousing. Data, systems and trust on that scale just do not exist (then again, the business need is not established at that level). But for regional or bilateral problems, data sharing is certainly necessary and it is no resolution for this to be barred because of the difficulties of establishing trust and mutual co-operation. These problems are not solved by allowing a criminal fugitive refuge because s/he cannot be identified, traced or returned. Bear in mind that despite having clearly defined criminal procedures for the return of fugitives, we still have very poorly defined systems for the identification of offenders who travel in pursuit of their crime.

One remedy lies in developing existing reactive and national methodologies into a third era of law enforcement where the use of information is the key and where law enforcement is a management-driven process informed by objective assessments and supported by a new level of investment. Above all, this investment must result not only in an effective information infrastructure but also in the adoption of international standards that promote the development of understanding and trust. This can have positive benefits beyond those of criminal justice. Neither sovereignty nor our people are served by allowing crime groups to continue to operate an alternative criminal economy.

Chapter 2

Ready, willing and enable

A theory of enablers for international co-operation

Steven David Brown

Although this book is mainly concerned with the actual practice of combating international crime, this chapter will discuss in a little more detail some of the contextual factors that can affect its overall success. Notwithstanding its importance as a law enforcement strategy,[1] international co-operation cannot be conjured out of thin air. Proper foundations need to be laid and appropriate structures need first to be developed at the national level before they can be launched into the international sphere. One can, perhaps, identify four main factors that influence the environment for co-operation and without which progress in this area is unlikely. These 'enablers' are: Politics; Law; Culture; and Capacity.

POLITICS

The political dimension of law enforcement co-operation has been described by some observers as the macro level 'at which political agreement and consensus has to be sought as a precondition for action'.[2] So, at least from this perspective, political will is a prerequisite without which co-operation cannot exist. In practical terms, the importance of political support for international law enforcement is that it enables:

- the negotiation of international agreements;
- the creation of national laws that give those agreements effect;
- the setting of priorities that include international co-operation;
- the allocation of funding and other resources.

There are a number of business drivers that can influence political will.

1 See the comments of the G8 in this regard reproduced above at p. 4
2 J. Benyon, L. Turnbull, A. Willis and R. Woodward, 'Understanding Police Co-Operation in Europe: setting a framework for analysis', in M. Anderson and M. Den Boer (eds), *Policing Across National Boundaries* (London: Pinter, 1994), p. 50.

Globalisation has become a convenient phenomenon by which to explain failures in many areas of modern governance, but, of course, it does have a genuine and decisive impact on political thought and subsequent policy. As has been commented elsewhere:

> The actions of states must be understood as the culmination of both external pressures and domestic political struggles in which national and transnational organisations and movements shape the actions and opinions of diverse societies.[3]

Governments are under constant pressure to perform on a number of different levels at the same time. Their ultimate objective is to remain in power with a mandate for implementing their policies and, in giving the impression that they are the best choice for the job, they have to balance competing interests and demands without alienating their powerbase. In a liberal democracy this usually means cultivating support by attempting to satisfy electoral expectations (perhaps by giving a boost to popular initiatives, but precluding any unpopular, if otherwise desirable, action). In other types of regimes such responses are likely to be geared more directly to the appeasement or pleasing of partners in the power network. In neither case will governments normally act on an issue unless there is a pressing need – there are simply too many other calls on both resources and energies. Action in criminal justice will, therefore, by and large have to wait until prompted by a rising set of circumstances that has become too apparent to be ignored or which has been vocalised by increasingly intolerant client groups. Once the tipping point has been reached those groups will demand to know what their politicians are doing about crime, the media will advance difficult questions about law and order performance (at least where the media are free to do so) and popular attitudes will grow uneasy. Feeding this unease, governments will also face pressure from opposition parties exploiting any perceived failures and publicly castigating the government for inaction.

Domestic crime sits more naturally at the forefront of the national political agenda. Citizens quite rightly expect value from their taxes and efforts against national criminality will have a much more immediate and obvious effect on local perceptions than 'upstream' strategies which are not only expensive, but also appear somewhat remote. After all, criminal activity prevented before it enters national boundaries is difficult to quantify and, in effect, constitutes crime that statistically never happens. However, where national crime problems can be demonstrated as having their origins in or strong connections to the international dimension, government support for international law enforcement must surely follow. This poses a challenge for those involved in combating

3 P. Andreas and E. Nadelmann, *Policing the Globe: Criminalization and Crime Control in International Relations* (Oxford: Oxford University Press, 2006), p. 18.

international crime to demonstrate clearly such connections and to market the threats in terms of local impact.

Where a heightened international threat is proven it is not uncommon for national crime issues to drive an international anti-crime agenda. Governments are well known to leverage unilateral strategies aimed at reducing their own crime levels perhaps by underwriting offers of aid (a strategy which generates good will) or threatening economic sanctions (which does not). Such leverage may be direct or indirect, persuasive or prescriptive, or tie the provision of different types of aid (economic, welfare or developmental) to targeted improvements in other sectors (such as the judiciary or human rights). Western governments have, for instance, sought to use a variety of measures to reduce or limit the cultivation of drugs by using carrot and stick strategies from licensing opium production or paying subsidies for alternative crops to bombing suspect fields with defoliant chemicals.

An offer for financial aid or other support from the developed world is rarely without strings, but the promise of help can be especially useful where the beneficiary is a transit or source country for a form of criminality which, whilst affecting the West, has little or no domestic impact. In such cases there may be no incentive for a government to act except in response to pressure from the destination countries. However, such leverage has to be applied judiciously as it is quite possible for this action to actually undermine the local economy (which, it has been suggested, could potentially be the case even in an economy as large as China's[4]) or threaten political alliances on which the partner government depends for power.

Organisations, such as the UN, the OECD and the OSCE, as well as individual donor countries, all use 'soft power' to try to introduce best practice and raise standards. The EU, in particular, is forthright in monitoring standards in countries applying for EU membership and measuring them against those of existing EU states. However, concepts of best practice and standards are often nationally or regionally specific and may not travel so well. Groups of governments may also seek to influence developments less directly. For instance, the seven countries[5] that signed the Prüm Convention on co-operation and sharing of police information, have manoeuvred to introduce the treaty into the EU acquis (the EU's body of law), and thereby impose it on the other 20 countries, even though legal documents containing similar powers, and formally negotiated under the EU banner, already exist or are under negotiation.

A more obvious and direct illustration of the influence of foreign governments on national criminal justice can be seen in so-called 'technical assistance'

4 The example concerns a sudden and complete suppression of the manufacture of counterfeit goods: D. M. Hopkins, L. T. Kontnik and M. T. Turnage, *Counterfeiting Exposed: Protecting Your Brand and Customers* (Hoboken: John Wiley and Sons, 2003), pp. 172–3.

5 Austria, Belgium, France, Germany, Luxembourg, the Netherlands, Spain.

projects that provide infrastructure, equipment, training and know-how for the benefit of law enforcement and criminal justice generally. However an unfriendly regime cannot, of course, expect aid or equipment that might help to entrench its position, and the level of support for other states will always be subject to a prioritisation linked to the donor's national interest.

Unfortunately, international co-operation, in criminal matters as much as in any other, is vulnerable to unrelated political events in the wider context. A good example of this was seen in the furore that accompanied the US Congressional vote in support of a Bill condemning as genocide an incident where Ottoman Turks were alleged to have massacred Armenians in 1915. This led to the withdrawal by Turkey of its Ambassador to the US and to the Turkish president to declare that the US had, 'once again sacrificed important matters to petty domestic politics despite all calls to common sense.'[6] And yet, the situation with Turkey and northern Cyprus has attracted very little comment even though that territory has been a haven for fugitive criminals. The political reality is that Turkey is a valued partner in countering the drug trade, illegal migration and the trafficking in human beings, as well as a major contributor to regional stability, and serious consideration must be given to maintaining good working relations.

LAW

The enabling effect of the law is totally dependent on the political will of the legislature. When engaging at the international level, there are two chief factors to consider in this respect: the negotiating of international agreements and their national implementation. Framing international laws that can accommodate the different types of legal jurisdiction and practice is no easy task.

In general, there are two types of international agreement: multilateral and bilateral. Examples of multilateral treaties would be, for instance, the UN Convention against Transnational Organized Crime (Palermo, 2000), the Council of Europe Convention on Mutual Legal Assistance (Strasbourg, 1959) or the Convention for Police Co-Operation in South-Eastern Europe (Vienna, 2006). In such documents, countries agree to comply with certain standards or to introduce certain concepts into national law that have been described in the treaty. The complexity in drafting such legislation should not be underestimated, but neither should the difficulties caused by an imbalance in the measure and application of powers from one country to another.

National and international agreements will also govern the way in which information can be requested from or provided to other countries. In particular,

6 M. Tran and Agencies 'Turkey Condemns US over Armenian Genocide Resolution', www.guardian.co.uk/turkey/story/0,,2188509,00.html?gusrc=rss&feed=networkfront, accessed 11 October 2007.

although police officers can often exchange data on a police to police basis,[7] coercive measures within a foreign jurisdiction (that is to say involving an unwilling individual) require an official letter of request to a judicial authority. Such letters may cover anything from a request to take a witness statement, to the seizure of assets or to the arrest and extradition of a suspect. They are an essential mechanism for bringing a suspect to justice, but the power to send and receive them is mired in a patchwork of complex treaties and, if the stipulated format or legal conditions are not properly fulfilled, the request, if not the entire prosecution, will fail.[8]

Treaties form the legal basis for international organisations and have been growing in significance as legal structures for law enforcement co-operation. Such treaties (sometimes called conventions) must formally recognise the body as an independent entity and define the rights and obligations of the signatory states as well as the scope and activities of the organisation itself. Whether countries play host to a network of foreign liaison officers or create their own abroad, international agreements and national laws are also necessary to authorise the presence of such officers and to establish the limits to their powers. Sometimes, but by no means always, liaison officers are attached to an embassy as an accredited diplomat. Sometimes officers will visit on an ad hoc basis (perhaps where an officer is covering a region rather than a single country).[9] There have been cases, however, where an officer, not understanding the restrictions on exercising powers in another jurisdiction, has taken it upon him or herself to travel abroad and make local enquiries without the necessary clearances. Apart from causing some diplomatic distress, the officer involved is acting illegally and actually becomes liable to prosecution.

There is another category of international legislation exemplified by the EU Council Decisions emanating from Brussels. These documents derive their power from earlier treaties and describe a set of principles which each country has to interpret and introduce in ways best suited to the national legal framework. This means that the actual wording agreed at the diplomatic level can have a slightly different effect in each of the countries.

The situation with EU legislation can be rather confusing, but it is an interesting testing ground for the future development of international criminal justice. For the time being, and until the constitutional treaty is ratified, EU Member States individually retain most of the decision-making power over criminal justice. Unlike in economic sectors such as agriculture, the central EU Bureaucracy, the European Commission, has as yet no formal power in this area (except in the area of immigration) but is able to suggest policy and offer draft legislation for the consideration of national ministers who make up the various

7 The information exchange networks are considered in Chapter 12 pp. 173–8.

8 This is explored more fully by Judge Prost in Chapter 10 p. 141.

9 Chapters 7–9 look more closely at different types of liaison officers and how they work.

EU Councils. In addition, the only elected institution, the EU Parliament, unlike parliaments on the national level, does not have a veto on the laws but merely the power to 'consider' them. Instead, decisions are based on a consensus arrived at in meetings of justice and home affairs ministers from national governments often without national parliaments having the opportunity to make their feelings felt.[10] However, unless national willingness is present to give proper effect to such treaties, ratification can be inordinately delayed[11] and may never be implemented.

One example is the attempt within the EU to create legislation authorising the use of liaison officers from one EU Member State to undertake enquiries on behalf of another.[12] This is an interesting legal proposition because, at least on one level, it suggests a central doctrine should influence the bilateral relationships of individual Member States with third parties. Whilst it would be of undoubted benefit to those smaller countries who cannot afford to maintain their own liaison network, those others that have invested widely in such networks would be subsidising those that are unable or unwilling to finance one of their own. The proposal also raises questions of liability and accountability where an officer has been accredited on the basis of a bilateral treaty, but is then asked to perform duties on behalf of a party outside of this bilateral relationship. However, in an example of the imbalance between diplomatic language and that of legal certainty, the wording of the EU Council Decision has been criticised as 'insufficiently legally binding'.[13]

Although there is a long history of countries collaborating with each other in the conduct of investigations, the EU has also attempted to formalise the use of multinational teams on common investigations in law. In the past the guest law enforcement officer has acted merely as an observer offering advice, but the EU's Joint Investigation Teams concept[14] takes this a step further by allowing guest officers to exercise the same powers as officers of the host country. However, the speed of implementation of this initiative has been too slow for

10 A. Coughlan, 'Why the EU cannot go on like this', www.euobserver.com, 14 May 2007, accessed 14 May 2007.

11 Consider for instance, the European Convention on Mutual Assistance in Criminal Matters (2000) which needed eight Member States to ratify in order to come into force, but is still pending at the time of writing.

12 EU Council Decision 2003/170/JHA of 23 February 2003 'on the common use of liaison officers posted abroad by the law enforcement agencies of the Member States', Official Journal L67/27, 12 March 2003.

13 M. Roure, 'Policing Europe – Europol Liaison Officers', www.europarl.europa.eu/news/expert/briefing_page/6149–087–03–13–20060313BRI06148–28–03–2006–2006/default_p001c014_en.htm, accessed 25 August 2007.

14 See, for instance, 'Initiative of the Kingdom of Belgium, the French Republic, the Kingdom of Spain and the United Kingdom for the adoption by the Council of a draft Framework Decision on joint investigation teams', (2001) Council of European Union, 11990/01, www.statewatch.org/docbin/freedomobsodcs/11990en1, accessed 5 May 2007.

some. Even before this protocol/convention has received sufficient support to enter into force, some Member States have formed their own co-operative clique under the Prüm Convention. In addition to providing facilities for officers in one country to search databases in another, this treaty, subject to national rules, expresses the intention to allow officers to act in foreign jurisdictions during mutual operations, armed and in uniform. The real mettle for such a collaboration will be tested when things go wrong and by the fairness and objectivity with which any grievances are addressed.

At the moment, the nearest example to a supranational criminal law is perhaps to be found in the statutes of the International Criminal Court (ICC), but the court is severely limited in its jurisdiction and scope and is not really related to the kind of law enforcement considered in this book. The ICC will normally deal with cases committed solely within one country (albeit where the perpetrators may be invaders or the rule of law may have collapsed) and its jurisdiction is limited to genocide, crimes against humanity (that is, widespread or systematic attack against a civilian population) and war crimes.[15] Those who have the difficult job of investigating crimes under the ICC statute exercise their powers on the basis of a comprehensive set of regulations but their practical effect is limited wherever domestic authorities are reluctant to comply (or where the suspects are from a non-signatory country).

The examples above demonstrate the need for a sufficient network of laws to enable countries to provide assistance to one another, to exchange information and to accommodate liaison officers. They also show how groups of countries can work together to create mutual doctrines or policies concerning criminal justice, but face practical and sometimes fatal limitations where national implementation is necessary. Generally they demonstrate yet again how a favourable political will is imperative.

CULTURE

Whilst politics and the law help to set the framework within which co-operation can take place, it is the prevailing culture that actually sponsors co-operation in practice. The culture factor comes into play in two respects: first, opportunities for sharing can be created, but officers must be both aware and willing to take advantage of them; second, in building co-operation, one partner has to be sensitive to the limitations on and the cultural preferences of the other. National cultures can be vastly different and such differences must be fully

15 The court was conceived in 1998 on the basis of a treaty now signed by more than 100 countries (with the notable exception of the USA) and came into force on 1 July 2002, www.icc-cpi.int, accessed 15 August 2007.

understood if any co-operative relationship is to be truly fruitful. Indeed, in some respects, culture is more significant as a factor than the other enablers in that it not only influences politicians and the drafting of the laws, but also disposes officers and prosecutors towards pursuing international lines of enquiry rather settling for a quick result in the national courts.

Mistrust, historical associations and stereotypes play as much a role in law enforcement as they do in other fields and idiosyncratic judgements about another's culture may also operate directly against the desire to co-operate. As an enabler for international co-operation, 'culture' not only influences the mind-set of the investigator, but also his or her preconceptions of how a requested country will deal with an enquiry. For instance, an officer will be less inclined to share sensitive information with a country where he or she suspects a lack of integrity, fears that the information may be sold on or is concerned that poor local handling of the case might otherwise jeopardise the outcome; and where previous attempts at co-operation have gone awry or have taken inordinately long periods of time, this experience may prejudice an officer against further co-operation or carry such an expectation of failure that he or she is dissuaded from making the effort.[16] Unfortunately, the formal routes for co-operation have a reputation for being overly bureaucratic, inefficient and slow.

The consequences of losing control over information are often identified as a major obstacle to sharing it. This is not only due to the fear that confidential information might be passed on to the criminals, but also to the worry that the kudos for 'their' case might be stolen by other officers or agencies (sometimes national departments may be more reluctant to share data between themselves than they are with other countries). On the other hand, the consequences of withholding data can outweigh the potential repercussions. All such issues come into play when managing international co-operation because even though information is shared in a relationship of trust, once data have been provided to another, their control is forfeit.

Some cultures view formal organisational structures with suspicion or contempt and officers will find co-operation facilitated through personal relationships rather than by any legal agreement because reciprocity and personal respect are considered more important than procedures prescribed by law. When someone from such a culture engages at the international level, they will quite naturally want to conduct business in a similar manner. Liaison officers help to build such relationships but, in the developed world, reliance on technical infrastructure for communication has generally all but supplanted face to face relationships and the existence of a law creates an expectation of

16 Consider, for instance, the impact of revelations in the wake of the arrests for the murder of Anna Politkovskaya in Russia where serving and past FSB officers have been linked to Chechen organised crime and how that may deter the future exchange of information: S. Gutterman, '10 Held in Russian Journalist's Killing', Guardian Unlimited, www.guardian.co.uk/worldlatest/story/0,,-6878634,00.html, accessed 27 August 2007.

compliance. Somewhere in the middle, these differing preferences are to be reconciled.

Those sharing data also have to take into account the diversity of organisational and management culture in co-operation partners. For instance, in many parts of the world the highest roles in law enforcement are reserved as political appointments subject to replacement at any time and with any change in government. In others the police chief may be elected by popular vote. This may result in the most senior figures in law enforcement management being politicians without previous experience either in law or in law enforcement and therefore lacking the common vocabulary of the investigator or an understanding of the challenges involved. It may also mean that the degree of political patronage is significantly more intrusive than might be encountered elsewhere.

Variations in accountability may breed significant differences in the way international law enforcement partnerships function. Where the form of government is authoritarian, the values and ideals of 'policing by consent', even if professed, are likely to be absent and law enforcement may act as it likes with impunity. In more liberal societies, on the other hand, members of the public may have a role in overseeing police performance with officers expected to subscribe to the notion of public service. Understanding the differences in approach will not only help build international relationships but will also assist in managing risk.

CAPACITY

All the political will, legal framework and enthusiasm in the world will come to nothing if the physical ability or actual capacity to implement the desired co-operation is lacking. Inadequate resources, training or funding in law enforcement generally will, of course, always result in the need for prioritisation, but where should international issues sit in the preferences? Reciprocity is a solid push factor in this regard, but will only operate where all parties concerned believe they stand to gain in the long run and are aware of the potential benefits of a continuing relationship.

Investment in organisations like Interpol and the extensive facilities and opportunities they offer will also be less effective if officers in the front line actually tasked with an international request lack the technical means to receive the details, to conduct the necessary enquiries or, having done so, to transmit the result.[17] In many countries it is still the case that correspondence between different agencies, or even different departments in the same agency, is

17 Interpol has recognised this and sought to extend its communications network beyond the NCBs. See pp. 45 *et seq*.

communicated in hard copy and countersigned by the head of department. In societies where automation and information technology are well established, officers will be used to employing technical solutions, but when dealing with agencies that are less well-equipped, their requests need to take into account the fact that colleagues may be working without computers, with neither fax machine nor photocopier, in offices where the mains electricity supply is unstable and where telecommunications infrastructure is non-existent.

In some quarters, technology has acquired the status of universal panacea for the ills of criminal justice and can indeed confer very many benefits but, since the chain of communication is only as strong as its weakest link, the lack of resources at any point in the chain can impact on the chances of success even in a country which boasts the latest hi-tech resources. For example, technical surveillance to the effect that a target is travelling across a country carrying a large consignment of contraband is of no value if that country's law enforcement has no facilities for identifying the target or of placing it under surveillance.

An equally enthusiastic trend in crime fighting has been the increased reliance on forensic science as an investigative tool but, again, it needs to be stressed that not all co-operation partners have access to properly equipped laboratories with well-trained staff, not all local investigators understand the importance of crime scene preservation and/or have the wherewithal to collect the samples. And even where they do, poor handling procedures can lead to contamination or contrary analysis or to a failure in evidential integrity. It does not matter how good your domestic procedures are if, before you even receive it, the evidence has been rendered useless.

International capacity-building measures are a useful way of redressing such imbalances, but there is a danger that they may themselves become a short-term unsustainable fix that fail as soon as support is withdrawn. Gifts of equipment have only limited benefit if, as soon as the equipment breaks down, there is no local funding available for its replacement or repair. Indeed, the lack of continuing support can even exacerbate the original difficulties it was intended to solve if the beneficiary country has become reliant on the donations and assistance. For instance, a beneficiary may, at the behest of the international community, fully adopt new techniques and methodologies into its procedures and national legislation but, once the external support ends, it can suddenly find itself in an operational vacuum unable to afford the new ways of working to which it is now committed. This can happen in something as simple as the need to upgrade software with the payment of expensive licences, or where a single essential piece of specialised and costly equipment becomes obsolete or needs replacing. In such circumstances perhaps a more imaginative solution to the same problem based on local resource limitations might provide greater longevity.

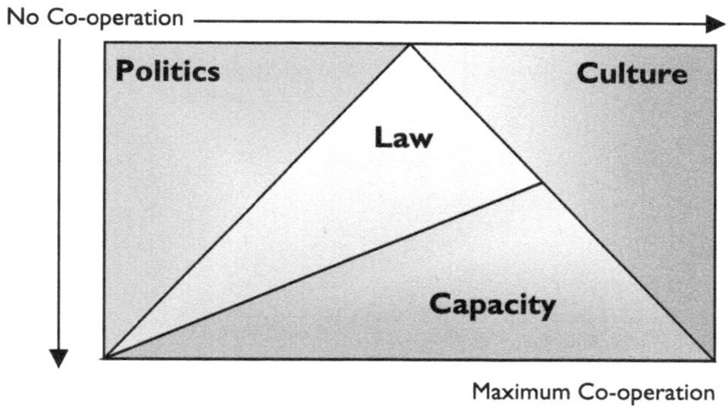

Figure 2.1 Four enablers diagram

ENABLED OR FINAGLED?

The way in which the four enabling criteria need to correspond and interact in support of successful international co-operation can be represented diagrammatically (see Figure 2.1). The positioning of each enabler in the diagram reflects the relative associations and interdependence of the four components whilst a top-left to bottom-right movement across the diagram (in the direction of the arrows) depicts the way in which new avenues of co-operation require each enabler to impact on and facilitate the others.

The existence of the right political will, the appropriate legal framework and a culture favourably disposed to international law enforcement supported by a sufficient capacity, are each required for the propagation of successful co-operation, but these enablers also have to achieve a balance. Where political influence is too strong, decisions and choices will be made according to expediency in support of the government's interest. If the law is too prescriptive and the field is over-regulated, the opportunities for international co-operation will become paralysed in trying to comply with conflicting legal approaches. On the other hand, if the legal basis is inadequate, the necessary co-operation and support for partners may be illegal. Where the culture supports co-operation only weakly, investigators will be disinclined to engage with the laws and opportunities available, nothing will be shared and the investment in setting up the systems will be wasted; and where international law enforcement is inadequately resourced, investigators will struggle to meet the expectations of co-operation partners or to accomplish their duties. This is not to say that such activity would be impossible, just that it would struggle and struggling to compete against the threat of international criminality leaves us all at a disadvantage.

Part II

Co-operation

Chapter 3

Interpol

A global service provider

Stuart Cameron-Waller

Interpol is perhaps the most well known amongst international police organisations. Founded in 1923 and now with a membership of 186 countries it is the only structure that enables law enforcement agencies from across the whole world to collaborate bilaterally or multilaterally using a single platform.[1] Through its General Secretariat in Lyon, France, and with its network of national, the National Central Bureaux (NCBs),[2] and sub-regional offices, any request for information or assistance is directed to wherever it is required anywhere in the world.

THE CONTEXT

In today's so-called global village, any viable strategy for combating cross-border crime or indeed any crime with an international element (for example where evidence or assistance may need to be gathered or provided in more than one country) must include arrangements for communication, information sharing and other forms of international police co-operation. When a criminal investigation is being conducted, assistance from abroad may range from relatively simple and straightforward information such as whether a vehicle or passport is stolen, through to the provision of sensitive information on the movement of target criminals, drugs, firearms or other commodities – sadly such 'commodities' can even include human beings. The range of circumstances where foreign or international police assistance may be needed is so wide

1 The actual membership of Interpol comprised 186 countries in 2007. It should be noted, however, that Interpol also has standard operating procedures which enable law enforcement officials of member countries to be put in touch with their counterparts in the few remaining non-member countries to pursue operational activities. Interpol can thus claim to have a truly global reach.

2 The decision to establish NCBs in each member country was taken by way of a resolution of the General Assembly of Interpol's precursor organisation, the International Criminal Police Commission, in 1927.

as to defy listing. The good news is that there are mechanisms in place that can help.

Despite efforts to include international collaboration on the syllabus of police training courses, the means by which foreign assistance may be obtained (and, indeed, provided proactively) remains a mystery to many investigators. Navigating alone through a maze of foreign languages, different policing systems and varying legal infrastructures is not recommended for the novice. The consequences can be dire, not just in terms of not getting the job done but also because it entails a risk of provoking a diplomatic row if the 'proper channels' are not used. In these circumstances a single point of contact in each country for international enquiries has obvious benefits.

For many years Interpol provided this facility for its member countries simply because it was the only international law enforcement link that existed. That picture is now very different. Many countries have placed law enforcement liaison officers directly in key foreign countries so that they may work directly with foreign counterparts on specific cases. Regional task forces, police committees and secretariats have been created to promote and deliver more intense local co-operation. New permanent institutions, notably Europol and the SECI Center, have been set up with representatives of the member countries and directly employed officials working alongside each other in an international environment. As regional and other liaison networks and collaboration systems developed (particularly in the 1980s and 1990s), there was a trend towards establishing distinct points of contact for each system without any obvious co-ordination at the national level. The potential for disaster here hardly needs spelling out. Increasingly, however, this situation is slowly being rectified by countries creating single management structures[3] responsible for the overall co-ordination of international crime enquiries. Where these have been established they have usually amalgamated Interpol's NCBs with the other offices set up as the point of contact for regional activities or organisations.

So how can Interpol help in an investigation being conducted in one of its member countries? It is probably useful first to underline the distinction between services provided directly by the NCBs and those provided by Interpol's General Secretariat whilst at the same time remembering that close collaboration between the two is central to any successes Interpol may have.

NATIONAL CENTRAL BUREAUX

As mentioned above, each member country has an NCB. The NCBs, which are part of the national administration and not subject to any external executive

3 As, for example, was done in the UK within the National Criminal Intelligence Service (NCIS), and later within the Serious and Organised Crime Agency (SOCA).

authority, are staffed by officials who are the point of reference for any requests for information or other assistance emanating from or directed to that country. Whether an incoming request is simply for a piece of readily available information or requires an in-depth enquiry or some other operational activity, these officials will know which (geographical or functional) service has jurisdiction, whether the request is of a nature that may be legally acceded to and how to get it dealt with as efficiently as possible. They also have the added advantage of language skills. Interpol uses four official languages (Arabic, English, French and Spanish) and, in theory at least, each NCB should be able to handle enquiries in any of those languages. Whilst this does not rule out the need for translation somewhere along the line, it does mean that individual NCBs should be able to communicate directly with each other to resolve any difficulties or misunderstandings. Communicating via the NCBs, law enforcement officials are able to send any police enquiry or request for assistance just as if they were sending it to a police station in a neighbouring village or city. Where there are likely to be procedural formalities, such as the need for a prosecutor's letter of request for formal evidence, the NCB can first advise on the correct procedures to be followed and then be used, if required, to fast-track the request while the original document is transmitted through diplomatic or other channels.

THE GENERAL SECRETARIAT

Interpol provides a range of communication, data and police services through its General Secretariat and Sub-Regional Bureaux.[4] The General Secretariat and Sub-Regional Bureaux are staffed by a combination of permanent officials recruited directly by the General Secretariat and representatives of the member countries (generally, but not exclusively, law enforcement officers) seconded to Interpol for a period which is usually from three to seven years.

CORE FUNCTIONS

The backbone of Interpol's service provision is its secure global communication and information network, called I-24/7. This is a secure network using internet protocols which enables its users to communicate with their international counterparts and the General Secretariat by encrypted e-mail. It also gives its users online access to Interpol's main data bases including nominal (persons known or wanted internationally for criminal activity), lost and stolen travel documents, stolen vehicles, fingerprints, DNA profiles and stolen works of art. I-24/7 is also the medium through which a range of web-based services,

4 The role of the SRBs is discussed below in the context of Interpol's regional approach.

including online searches of and applications for Interpol notices and the distribution of crime-specific intelligence bulletins, are available. Interpol notices, in particular the Red Notice, have long been one of the organisation's most important tools. The Red Notice is a circulation which alerts Interpol member countries that an individual is the subject of a criminal arrest warrant (for prosecution or to serve a sentence) and that the individual's extradition will be sought when he or she is detained. The notice, in addition to details of the case in respect of which it has been issued, contains the identifying details of the individual concerned including fingerprints and photograph where these are available. The Interpol United Nations Special Notice has recently been introduced and is issued for groups and individuals who are the targets of UN sanctions against Al Qaeda and the Taliban. Another recent innovation is the Orange Notice which is designed to warn police, public entities and other international organisations about potential threats from disguised weapons, parcel bombs and other dangerous materials.

Primary access to I-24/7 is via the NCBs. Once its member countries[5] had been connected via their NCBs, Interpol also made I-24/7 available to law enforcement services beyond the NCBs (to the extent that individual member countries wished this to happen). Those responsible for border security, for example, are thus able to know instantly by consulting the Interpol records online whether people leaving or entering their country are wanted, using lost or stolen travel documents or driving a stolen vehicle. I-24/7 is also being used in some cases to enable countries to access each other's databases via a business to business (B2B) connection thus potentially vastly increasing the amount of information available to them.

The network and the databases are of prime importance in that they provide an instant, easily accessible yet secure global police communication and information service. In addition Interpol carries out or facilitates a range of activities described as 'operational police support services' including crime analysis and intelligence activities whereby, through reporting systems (generally via I-24/7), working meetings and conferences, specialists in their fields share information which is pooled, analysed and fed back in intelligence packages either as alerts or as the basis for co-ordinated operational activity. The services have been upgraded to the extent that, whereas until relatively recently Interpol simply provided one of the options for case officers to secure foreign assistance, today it would be almost negligent not to consider Interpol, or at least consider consulting Interpol's databases, in a whole range of international criminal enquiries.

5 In March 2007, of 186 member countries only Somalia was not yet connected to I-24/7.

INTERPOL'S REGIONAL APPROACH

Interpol has embraced a regional approach to co-operation where distinct groups of countries have regional desks[6] at the General Secretariat, as well as regional offices (the Sub-Regional Bureaux) in Central and Western, Eastern and Southern Africa, Central and South America and South-East Asia.[7] The officials who work in these offices are able to facilitate the efficient handling of international enquiries and requests for assistance by intervening as necessary to find solutions to any difficulties or potential difficulties that may arise.

The regional offices also play a key role in supporting regional committees of chief police officers that have been established in the regions they serve. The first example of this was in Southern Africa where, at a meeting convened by Interpol in Harare, Zimbabwe, in 1995, the chief police officers of the region established the Southern African Regional Police Chiefs Co-Operation Organisation (SARPCCO). It was also agreed that a SARPCCO secretariat would be housed at the Interpol Sub-Regional Bureau for Southern Africa and would help to co-ordinate the activities of the SARPCCO sub-committees on operations, legal matters and training. SARPCCO has since established an impressive record both in terms of its support mechanism (roll-out of training, co-operation agreements, etc.) and in terms of a succession of joint operations against crime problems. A key feature of the arrangements put in place is that the government ministers responsible for policing matters in the region meet immediately after and at the same venue as the SARPCCO meeting. This means that they are briefed on and then have the opportunity to offer immediate and unambiguous political support for any measures proposed at the SARPCCO meeting. The SARPCCO model was later promoted by Interpol in Central, Eastern and Western Africa and these regions subsequently established their own regional committees of police chiefs, each serviced by an Interpol Sub-Regional Bureau which acts as its secretariat. A similar arrangement exists in Central America where the Interpol Sub-Regional Bureau in San Salvador interacts directly with the Association of Chiefs of Police of Central America and the Caribbean.[8] Although this Sub-Regional Bureau does not formally act as this committee's secretariat, its importance in the overall scheme of regional security is evidenced

6 At the General Secretariat there are desks for Africa, the Americas, Asia, Europe and the Middle East.

7 These offices are situated in Abidjan (Côte d'Ivoire), Nairobi (Kenya), Harare (Zimbabwe), San Salvador (El Salvador), Buenos Aires (Argentina) and Bangkok (Thailand). There is also an Interpol liaison office at the UN Headquarters in New York. Central and Western Africa are both served by the office in Abidjan but on 26 March 2007 an agreement was signed between Interpol and the Republic of Cameroon to open an SRB for Central Africa in Yaoundé, Cameroon.

8 Belize, Costa Rica, Dominican Republic, El Salvador, Guatemala, Honduras, Nicaragua, and Panama. Mexico is not a member of this association but participates in the meetings.

by mention of the role of this office in the Granada[9] (20 June 2002) and Mérida[10] (27/28 June 2002) Declarations by the Heads of State of Central America at their 21st Ordinary Meeting of Heads of State and Government of the System of Central American Integration (SICA) and 5th Summit of the Tuxtla Mechanism for Dialogue and Concertation respectively.

Interpol has also concluded formal co-operation agreements with over 30 regional organisations (including several of those mentioned in Appendix 1) and recently reiterated its general support for regional policing initiatives while tasking the Secretary General to consider how Interpol could best support the Central Asian Regional Information and Coordination Center (CARICC),[11] Gulfpol,[12] ASEANAPOL, the Pacific Transnational Crime Coordination Center (PTCCC)[13] and Frontex (as well as other regional law enforcement initiatives) with a view to enhancing police co-operation at the operational level.[14]

TRAINING AND BEST PRACTICE

Another service offered by Interpol consists of training and the development and promotion of best practice. Examples of the work done here include the Global Standards to Combat Corruption in Police Forces and Services (which were developed and promulgated by the Interpol Group of Experts on Corruption[15]) and the creation of the Interpol Bioterrorism Prevention Resource Centre. Both of these initiatives have produced tools of direct value which are immediately available to law enforcement and which may be accessed via the Interpol website.[16] These examples demonstrate Interpol's capacity to employ the expertise of experts who are not available to the organisation on a permanent basis but who are often willing to give their time to promote excellence by, for example, participating in working groups or workshops.

9 www.minec.gob.sv/policom/media/downloads/Union%20Aduanera/Declaracion%20de%20Granada%20fin.doc, accessed 15 September 2007.

10 Fifth Declaration of Tuxtla.

11 In February 2006, Azerbaijan, Kazakhstan, Kyrgyzstan, Russia, Tajikistan, Turkmenistan, Uzbekistan decided to set up the Central Asian Regional Information and Coordination Center (CARICC), in Almaty, Kazakhstan, to fight illicit drug trafficking.

12 In March 2006 it was announced that countries of the Gulf Co-operation Council (Bahrain, Kuwait, Oman, Qatar, Saudi Arabia and United Arab Emirates) are planning to set up a joint police organisation to combat cross-border criminal activities in the region.

13 In June 2004, the Pacific Transnational Crime Coordination Center (PTCCC) was established in Suva, Fiji, with a mission to co-ordinate the flow of information between Transnational Crime Units (TCUs) in Fiji, Tonga, Samoa, Vanuatu and Papua New Guinea and foreign law enforcement agencies.

14 By way of a resolution of the 75th session of its General Assembly in Rio de Janeiro, Brazil, from 19 to 22 September 2006 (AG-2006-RES-07).

15 Adopted by Interpol's General Assembly session in 2002.

16 www.interpol.int.

MODERNISATION AND POSITIONING OF INTERPOL

Getting into a situation where Interpol can offer this range of services has been quite a journey. Early in the 1990s the General Secretariat was still in the process of conducting a back-record conversion of data held on paper files to its first computerised information database. Under the stewardship of former Secretary General, Raymond E. Kendall, this was the first of a series of urgently needed initiatives designed to modernise the organisation and bring its services in line with the contemporary needs of its members. During the next few years, Interpol rolled out what was then regarded as a state-of-the-art communication network and introduced its first automated remote data search facility for NCBs. It also introduced crime analysis to its daily work, set up the network of regional offices, worked with the member countries to set up the African regional committees described above and, rather belatedly, established service standards for the NCBs.

Since 2000, under the current Secretary General, Ronald K. Noble, Interpol has confronted many new challenges. The introduction of I-24/7 was a response to one of the first of these: the need to replace a system that had become quickly outdated by the dramatic advances in communication and information technology. In addition to the logistical and technical challenge of rolling out I-24/7 to over 180 countries, Interpol also had to overcome the reluctance of some countries to trust their information to an internet-based system. Those security concerns were addressed in the system design to the satisfaction of its members and it is now standard practice to connect the NCB of new member countries as soon as they join.

Subject to concluding formal agreements or special arrangements specifying conditions for access and use, Interpol is also able[17] to grant third organisations access to its telecommunications and databases.

Also in the spirit of offering a 24/7 service, the General Secretariat moved from a (European) night-time reserve and call-out system dealing only with matters of urgency to establish a 24-hour Command and Co-ordination Centre. The Centre monitors the flow of messages and serves as the first point of contact in a crisis, disaster, or other emerging situation where the resources of the General Secretariat might need to be deployed.

POST-9/11

It is perhaps not surprising that the events of 9/11 changed the way Interpol does its business. Interpol had even before 9/11 already identified public safety

17 Rules governing access by an intergovernmental organisation to the Interpol telecommunications network and databases, www.interpol.int/Public/ICPO/LegalMaterials/constitution/accessdatabase/Default.asp, accessed 15 August 2007

and terrorism as a priority crime area but its efforts post-9/11 have seen a far more aggressive approach to sharing and analysing terrorism-related information so as to help member countries identify active terrorist groups and their membership. This approach, which led to the founding of the Interpol Fusion Task Force, has seen a fourfold increase in the number of profiles in Interpol's terrorist registry since 1999 and the creation of a contact network of nearly 200 officers in more than 100 member countries. Interpol claims this is 'an unparalleled resource – a solid, practical international contribution to national anti-terrorist measures.'[18]

Another emerging issue of concern during this period was the relative freedom with which terrorists and other criminals were using false travel documents. Interpol's response was to introduce a global database of stolen and lost travel documents (SLTD) accessible via I-24/7. Securing the commitment of countries to input their data into the SLTD required a new approach as the original data is often held by non-law enforcement entities such as foreign ministries and passport agencies, but by March 2007 over 13 million entries from some 120 countries had been added to this database. Switzerland and France, together with the Caribbean (in the context of the 2007 Cricket World Cup), have led the way in making this database available to key border control points. In Switzerland, for example, over 400,000 searches are made each month and generate some 100 hits (that is to say 100 persons are found to be using travel documents that have been reported stolen or lost).[19]

PROTECTING OUR CHILDREN

There is no more poignant example of how advances in technology can be used for evil as well as good than the abuse of the internet for making available and distributing child pornography. Interpol recognised very early that many countries were working independently to identify, and often rescue, the victims of such sexual exploitation whose images had been distributed via the internet. Where best practice prevails, investigations are not just directed at seizing the images. They go further and attempt to identify and locate the children concerned. A specific problem that arose was that, with the global distribution of and access to such images, different countries could well be working on the same picture without realising that there were parallel investigations in train elsewhere. The creation of Interpol's Child Abuse Image Database (ICAID) now means that investigators working in this field may send seized images (for example those found on a computer during a police operation) and have them compared with the half million or more pictures held on the database. By doing

18 www.interpol.int/Public/FusionTaskForce/default.asp, accessed 15 August 2007.
19 www.interpol.int/Public/ICPO/speeches/SG75thGA20060919.asp, accessed 15 August 2007.

so they can ascertain whether the seized images have been seen before and whether any of the children featured have been identified and/or located. Interpol also adds value by analysing the detail of the image and advising whether there is a specific line of enquiry that might usefully be followed either in the country from which the enquiry has been received or elsewhere. This gets results. Interpol can point to many cases where it has successfully co-ordinated enquiries of this nature.

THE EXECUTIVE COMMITTEE

Subject to the obvious requirement to work within its budget,[20] it is relatively easy for Interpol to take on new responsibilities or provide new services to law enforcement. Interpol's constitution permits it to ensure and promote the widest possible mutual assistance between all criminal police authorities within the limits of the laws existing in the different countries and in the spirit of the 'Universal Declaration of Human Rights'.[21] Whenever a new anti-crime initiative is proposed or developed, there is considerable discretion to introduce new activities to the work programme. Any new activity giving rise to major policy issues would usually be brought in due course by the Secretary General to the attention of Interpol's Executive Committee and, as necessary, to the General Assembly, for advice or approval.[22] The Executive Committee, therefore, has a key role. Formally it is required to supervise the execution of the decisions of the General Assembly, prepare the agenda for sessions of the General Assembly, submit to the General Assembly any programme of work or project which it considers useful and supervise the administration and work of the Secretary General.[23] In practice the calibre of the individuals elected to serve on the Executive Committee can impact directly on the good health of the organisation by influencing the relevance and importance of ongoing and new initiatives. The committee members are frequently, but not always, very senior officials in their own administrations and should have a clear understanding of what is required of Interpol. They have the responsibility of driving new ideas forward at the policy-making level and to help ensure that the organisation is not only doing what is needed but, just as importantly, also not doing what is not needed.

20 Interpol's annual budget is funded largely by statutory contributions from its member countries. The total called up from member countries for the financial year 2007 was set at €41,398,000, and its budget at approximately €45,000,000.

21 Article 2 of the Interpol Constitution.

22 Interpol's Executive Committee, which meets three times per year, comprises 13 members elected on a regional basis (Africa, the Americas, Asia and Europe) by the General Assembly. The members participate in the Executive Committee in their own right and not as representatives of their countries.

23 Article 22 of the Interpol Constitution, www.interpol.int/Public/icpo/governance/ec/default.asp, accessed 15 August 2007

INTERPOL MAKING A DIFFERENCE

Interpol has the advantage of global reach, a sound technological infrastructure, a professional staff recruited locally or drawn from its member countries and access to experts to help deal with specific crime problems. Does it work and does it make a difference?

When it comes to bilateral co-operation (requests sent from NCB to NCB) much inevitably depends on the capacity of the law enforcement services within the countries concerned. The communication system (I-24/7) ensures that the messages are sent and received in an instant, but what happens next? Interpol, as long ago as 1994, established service standards for NCBs so that, for example, time limits were set for responding to messages (namely requests from other NCBs) according to their nature and classification. There is, therefore, a baseline for performance, but all depends on:

- how adequately individual NCBs are staffed (in terms of numbers and language ability);
- what computerised information systems are available to provide the answers to simple requests;
- the links the NCB has with other national services when it is obliged to pass the request on for action to be taken; and,
- the capacity of the national law enforcement infrastructure itself to handle such enquiries efficiently.

Even if all these are positive, there must also be a willingness to treat an international enquiry with the same (or even higher) priority than it would be given had the incident under investigation been committed in that country.

In the absence of any empirical research, it is difficult to generalise about how efficiently the NCB system works. There will always be good examples and poor examples and there will always be room for improvement. The service standards were revised as recently as October 2004 and their implementation has been helped by initiatives such as the establishment of the regional desks and Sub-Regional Bureaux (whose principal role is to support the operation of the NCBs) as well as the creation of an Exchange of Good Practice programme for NCBs. These initiatives demonstrate the 'corporate' focus on performance, but the capacity and response of individual member countries are the determining factors.

Compared with the services provided by the NCBs, over which the Interpol General Secretariat exercises no executive authority, it should at first sight be easier for the General Secretariat to establish and maintain a high quality service delivery from the centre. There are, however, a number of challenges. The first, as with any organisation, is the budget. As mentioned earlier, the total of annual statutory contributions to be called up for 2007 is approximately €42 million. For an organisation which serves 186 countries from its

General Secretariat in France and a number of regional centres throughout the world, the size of this budget might reasonably be regarded as somewhat limited. Notwithstanding the impact on investment and new initiatives of such a restricted budget, one important consequence is that Interpol is largely dependant upon the generosity of individual member countries to second the police officials who make up approximately one third of the staff (and the majority of the experts) who work at the General Secretariat and Sub-Regional Bureaux. In recent years the recruitment of seconded staff has presented some problems and it is hardly surprising that many countries hesitate to bear the costs of sending highly qualified and experienced officials to work for a third organisation. Unfortunately, the limitations on Interpol's budget do not allow it to meet the salary costs of all its staff and, therefore, it does not have total control over the recruitment pool.

SOURCING INFORMATION

A second perpetual challenge for Interpol as an information and intelligence provider is the need to source accurate, timely and relevant information. To a limited extent this is being addressed by automating the processes (for example through 'B2B' links where they are accepted), but there are still many situations where Interpol depends upon human intervention at the investigator, prosecutor, NCB or other national level to feed information that might be of interest to the centre. It is only by receiving relevant information that Interpol is able to 'join the dots' and present the big picture. For many years there has been a regular supply of information relating to drugs seizures as a result of which there has been a steady feedback by way of intelligence bulletins and other analytical packages. There is evidence that this approach has driven operational deployment at national level and led to significant seizures and many arrests. Project Fusion has, more recently, demonstrated that this can work just as effectively when sensitive terrorism-related information is involved and there are other crime areas that may be cited as good examples. Trust and confidence in both the organisation and individuals are essential for this to work effectively, but there is also a great dependency on the enthusiasm, drive and commitment of the staff both of the General Secretariat and of national law enforcement agencies to develop and make available a useful product. It is very easy to close a case file without thinking through how the information contained in it might usefully be exploited for the greater good. The NCBs inevitably carry a heavy burden here as the Interpol community depends upon them to drive action within and for their own countries. There is always the risk that the staff of an NCB might not believe that their information or enquiry is sufficiently important to warrant making contact with other countries affected. Nothing could be further from the truth. The quality of the NCB staff, their energy, enthusiasm and alertness to what is relevant all have a significant effect on

Interpol's overall performance. A proactive approach by NCBs to seeking and sharing information (including from and with their own national agencies) is key to success in tackling international crime.

Although there are many fields of crime where the sharing of information has proved effective, these arrangements are always quite fragile. Trust and confidence in the process is important. In this regard there is an obvious need for the information or intelligence generated to be handled securely and for any conditions imposed by the original information providers to be respected. Any failure in this department is bound to impact on the quality of future collaboration. Even where the highest level of trust has been achieved, staff rotation can have a severe impact on those relationships (especially at the centre where expert staff are on limited secondments).

EXAMPLES OF SUCCESS

Interpol makes use of its website to publicise cases where successful operations may, at least in part, be attributed to judicious use of Interpol services. A few examples help to illustrate the scope of these services:

- An Italian with a long criminal history who escaped from prison in 1981 was arrested in Brazil in 2007 following collaboration between Brazilian, French and Italian authorities. His 'wanted' status was determined by reference to Interpol's nominal database. It is reported that, when his apartment was searched, a false French travel document registered in Interpol's SLTD was found.
- In New York a fugitive from Ecuador, subject to a Red Notice in relation to the death of a politician and two other men, was arrested in 2007 having been identified following a routine traffic stop for not wearing a seat belt.
- During a two-day police operation conducted in Tanzania in 2006, of 1,382 motor vehicles inspected, more than 70 resulted in positive hits when checked against the Interpol stolen motor vehicles (SMV) database.

These are routine cases which demonstrate how Interpol makes a contribution to the daily work of law enforcement agencies throughout the world and demonstrate how single checks against 'hit or miss' databases can be of use.

When the information is collated, analysed and fed into an intelligence package they can also drive operational activity. Classic examples of this are the alerts produced based on information supplied relating to drugs seizures. Whenever a drugs seizure of a quantity over an agreed threshold is made, Interpol member countries are encouraged to report full details to the General Secretariat. These details include not only the names of persons arrested and the type and quantity of drug seized, but also such information as the route via which the drug had been trafficked, the transport used and methods of concealment. When a trend is noted (for example regular seizures on the same route, same type of transport used, same method of concealment or storage used) alerts are posted and border control officials notified so that the profile might be used to decide how to deploy staff or what interventions are to be made. There are many examples where this has led directly to further seizures and more information leading investigators closer to the main organisations behind the trafficking.

As long ago as 1999 the US Postal Investigation Service dismantled a website that was supplying child pornography over the internet. The data seized revealed that over 389,000 individuals from over 60 countries throughout the world had subscribed to this service. Interpol's General Secretariat analysed this information and produced individual intelligence packages which were distributed to law enforcement agencies for action. Different countries responded at different speeds and the follow-up enquiries, known as Operation Landslide, went on for several years with thousands of searches made and huge quantities of child pornography seized. A large number of individuals, many of whom worked with children or held public office, have been brought to justice.

Interpol was probably the only organisation capable of effectively co-ordinating an operation of this scale. Its key role in dealing with the sexual exploitation of children, and in particular, on-line pornography has been recognised by the G8 group of leading industrialised nations which has pledged funds to enable Interpol to expand use of and improve access to ICAID through the Interpol Child Sexual Exploitation Image Database (ICSE) project.

JOINED-UP REGIONAL POLICING?

There is something approaching global coverage by the various regional law enforcement entities which now exist although it should also be noted that there are several countries – some of which are key contributors to the whole process of international law enforcement collaboration – that do not participate directly in the activities of any regional group.

In an ideal world, all the initiatives for regional and global co-operation would be 'joined up', with common standards, operational procedures and parallel missions. When work in one region spills over to one or more other regions, the relevant law enforcement agencies (with their information and other resources) would be brought together seamlessly into ongoing or planned operations. In reality, insofar as direct co-operation between regional entities and third parties is concerned, it is not always so clear cut. Indeed, some regional arrangements actually bar the release of their shared 'regional' information to third parties either absolutely or, as is the case with Europol, unless a formal co-operation agreement has been concluded. One of the chief reasons given for this relates to concerns over the confidentiality of the information shared and whether any conditions stipulated by the data provider would be respected by a recipient organisation.

At first sight the most efficient way of sharing police information internationally might seem to be the use of a B2B linkage of national databases. This would enable users to search their own and other national databases throughout the world. The reality is that, despite the range of information and intelligence systems available in some parts and the progress made by some countries in networking their data systems, we are a still long way from having a global information exchange facility. Irrespective of any issues of compatibility, many countries in the world today do not even have national or local databases of key and critical law enforcement information.

In this light, one might ask what chance there is of having a comprehensive international information or intelligence sharing system. There is, however, an increasingly mature approach to information sharing and the value of criminal intelligence at the national level.[24] It is perhaps a statement of the obvious that where the sharing of information can be shown to be useful and where the recipient(s) may be relied upon to respect the level of confidentiality attached to it, the chances of effective international information exchange are significantly increased. Sadly, experience shows that the reverse is also true, but this is sometimes forgotten in the enthusiasm and rhetoric when new initiatives are being planned.

It is clear that there is no 'one size fits all' solution to regional policing infrastructures. To some extent other regions have set out to imitate the Interpol or Europol models on a local basis with individual solutions being tailored in response to specific needs and aspirations but to fit within local means. Whereas some regional groups are able to fund new projects and initiatives as soon as they become political imperatives, others struggle to find funding for what might be regarded as basic needs. Although most regional initiatives have been set up independently of Interpol, increasingly they are aligning themselves so that their global and regional efforts may be complementary, the number of re-invented wheels minimised and the prospects of integrating all regional groups into a global network become more realistic.

DOING WHAT IS NEEDED?

As stated above, the Executive Committee of Interpol is expected to ensure that Interpol is doing what is needed. How does Interpol as an organisation – how does any organisation – decide what it needs to provide across a globally diverse constituency?

24 See, for example, the UK's National Intelligence Model which the UK government has placed at the centre of the Police Reform Agenda, www.police.uk/nim2/.

At Interpol there is, to some extent, a reliance on seconded and other officials being posted to the General Secretariat with a broad range of experience and a keen understanding of their particular subject areas. These officials, often working closely with expert groups convened for the purpose, are able to identify where improvements in investigative techniques and tools can be made, and promote solutions that, if accepted, could contribute to the greater good. Another mechanism, implemented to ensure that I-24/7 continues to meet the needs of member countries, has been to establish a Users' Advisory Group. Both these approaches, the expert/officials and Users' Advisory groups, have the advantage of getting direct feedback from those who make operational use of the services provided.

In addition to different meetings and working groups on specific fields of crime there are also meetings of contact officers, regional committees, regional conferences, Executive Committee meetings and the annual General Assembly. These act as channels for communication with the different client groups and offer opportunities for bringing new ideas and initiatives forward for consideration. Although the number of meetings organised by Interpol peaked at over 140 in 2001, the following year saw a fall of some 23 per cent in a concerted effort to reduce costs.[25] The number of meetings held by Interpol is, however, just a drop in the ocean of international crime-related meetings held and attended by law enforcement representatives from across the world. Hosting these meetings and conferences has become big business and increasingly they are organised by external organisations and linked with exhibitions so as to make them self-funding or, in the best-case scenario, even a source of income.

THE FUTURE

It is not hard to understand that where groups of countries with shared interests and values decide to intensify their collective efforts against serious and organised international crime, an international organisation can be the outcome. Nevertheless no single regional entity can deal with international crime without seeking help from others outside the region. The spread of regional anti-crime initiatives is well-advanced and, particularly as they are usually driven by politics, no reversal of this trend is likely in the near future. Provided they are adequately resourced (both in terms of physical means and the skills and ability of their personnel) they have the potential to overcome some of the barriers to collaboration that might exist on a wider scale. On the other hand there will always be tools and other facilities made more effective by global approach.

25 www.interpol.int/Public/ICPO/GeneralAssembly/AGN72/Reports/agn72r01.pdf, accessed 15 August 2007.

The key here is co-ordination: first, to ensure that the spread of regional entities develops into a real network rather than just a collection of independent and unconnected parts and, second, to find the balance between those activities that genuinely call for a centrally driven global response and those that can be handled more effectively at local or regional level. One thing is certain: police and other officials will go where they can to get what they need. They will be influenced by results both in terms of what they can get and how quickly they can get it. There will always be some degree of competition and this can only serve to encourage improvement. In the long term resources will be invested where it is judged they give the greatest return. There is no simple one-time solution here.

Opinion is probably divided as to whether new regional organisations constitute a threat to Interpol, whether they actually offer new opportunities or merely cause duplication of effort. The situation in western Europe serves to illustrate the lack of true co-ordination in international strategy. When Europol was conceived, some suggested that the EU wanted a Europol because Interpol was not providing what it needed. Europol, however, was initially given very specific terms of reference that essentially required it to focus on the top level of international criminality in the EU whereas Interpol had a much more general mandate. The distinction between these roles, particularly with regard to the development and handling of criminal intelligence, has perhaps become a little blurred in practice as Interpol's service delivery has become more comprehensive and Europol has been expected to adapt in response subsequent demands for specific services. Their roles may nevertheless be regarded as complementary and Interpol continues to provide unique and valued services to all regions including the EU. Now the introduction of the Prüm Convention is seen by some commentators as a sign that still more radical measures are necessary to tackle serious and organised international crime in the EU than have hitherto been available. There has often been speculation about whether there will ever be a European FBI[26] with enforcement powers based on an EU-wide legislative framework that would permit it to work effectively. Whether a consensus on that approach will ever be achieved remains to be seen. However, Interpol is and will remain a major and important service provider for its member states in the EU as well as for those in the rest of the world.

26 W. Bruggeman, 'Europol – A European FBI in the making?' (2000), www.cicerofoundation.org/lectures/p4bruggeman, accessed 2 May 2007.

Chapter 4

The EU solution

Europol and Eurojust

Steven David Brown

The European Community has been a bold adventure in economic and political unity that has dominated western Europe for 50 years. Slowly, but surely it has progressed with a long-term strategy of increasing political integration, even though it has yet to acquire legal personality. In terms of international co-operation, the EU has had to resolve significant cultural and historical differences to invent for itself workable and acceptable mechanisms to achieve success. This is true not least in the field of criminal justice.

However there is a danger in trying to export law enforcement models created under the EU banner to other parts of the world[1]. EU models function under a very particular framework of nations that, because of close economic ties and growing harmonisation, carry with them a much stronger motivation for participation than will be the case elsewhere and for countries wanting to join the economic bloc, membership of Europol and Eurojust (as well as the Schengen Information System) is compulsory. Even so, active support for these mechanisms by the individual Member States has been variable.

EUROPOL

The European Police Office (Europol) was born out of a proposal made in 1991 by the then Chancellor of Germany, Helmut Kohl, who called for a European Police Force based along the lines of the Bundeskriminalamt (the German Federal Criminal Police or BKA). However, whilst the link to the BKA remains strong (the first two Directors of the organisation have been serving BKA officers) and the BKA is among the most active of its partners, Europol is not a police force. Europol officials do not actually have any police powers and are not authorised to conduct investigations. After all, there are no EU criminal offences for them to investigate and no EU criminal court in which they could be prosecuted.

1 It took over 30 years of economic co-operation before the possibility of a common police office was mooted.

Indeed, unless they remain employed as officers of a law enforcement agency at home, something which is not open to officers from every Member State, Europol officials have no affiliation to any police force or other agency.

Europol is described as:

> . . . the European Union law enforcement organisation that handles criminal intelligence. Its mission is to assist the law enforcement authorities of Member States in their fight against serious forms of organised crime.[2]

It derives its organisational identity from an international treaty called the Europol Convention.[3] The Convention, although a significant diplomatic achievement at the time, has come under considerable criticism since it came into force on 1 October 1998 for its rigidity and lack of clear definition, but amending it has proved to be such a difficult proposition that steps are now being taken to change the legal basis in order to make the organisation more flexible and responsive to change.

Structure

Having said that, there are in essence two Europols, each supporting the common mission but each with different functions and lines of management reporting. These can become, and often are, easily confused when discussing organisational activities.

One Europol consists of a series of independent, but related offices staffed by law enforcement officers from each of the 27 EU Member States (plus a few other guest countries). These officers work under national laws and are managed from their home countries and, although they are called 'Europol Liaison Officers', it would perhaps be more appropriate to term them, 'Liaison Officers to Europol'. They constitute approximately 20–25 per cent of those who work in the Europol building in The Hague, but are responsible for the great majority of the operational activity and tactical information exchanged under the Europol banner.

The 'other' Europol consists of a secretariat and support function which is managed, staffed and regulated according to Europol rules and legislation. A quick comparison with the Interpol structure will show that this part of Europol undertakes activities very similar to those of the Interpol General Secretariat in Lyon.

The 'secretariat' part of the organisation has units that work on narcotics, human trafficking and immigration crime, hi-tech crime, terrorism and finan-

2 www.europol.europa.eu/index.asp?page=ataglance&language=, accessed 4 May 2007.
3 www.europol.europa.eu/index.asp?page=legalconv, accessed 4 May 2007.

cial crime. Europol has also been designated as the central European office for dealing with euro counterfeiting and works closely with the European Central Bank in this regard. However, the biggest unit at Europol deals with analysis.

All Europol officials must be EU citizens and be able to speak at least two of the official EU languages. Those officials working directly on law enforcement activity, rather than on administrative functions, are recruited from national 'competent authorities' and, as with Interpol, are on fixed-term contracts of limited duration. However, unlike at Interpol, very few of these officials are on secondment or attachment and are usually directly employed by the organisation – with consequences for the comparative size of the core budget. The term 'competent authority' is used a good deal in EU documents related to justice and law enforcement, but it does not always mean the same thing. In the Europol Convention it is defined as:

> . . . all public bodies existing in the Member States which are responsible under national law for preventing and combating criminal offences.[4]

In some Member States this has been interpreted as only relating to national crime police which then connects with other law enforcement bodies nationally. However, even though Europol is called a 'police' office, it actually has staff from all different sorts of law enforcement including customs, border guard and security services. This greatly broadens the base of the available expertise and enriches the organisational culture.

What it does

Europol's remit can be summed up as:

- information exchange;
- analysis;
- training; and
- dissemination of best practice.

Since Europol was formed, the EU has gone on to create the EU Police College (CEPOL)[5] which would appear to have assumed a role that duplicates (at least in part) these latter two functions.

4 Convention Based on Article K.3 of the Treaty on European Union, on the Establishment of a European Police Office (1995) Article 2(4), www.europa.eu/scadplus/leg/en/lvb/l14005b, accessed 4 May 2007.

5 www.cepol.net/KIM/, accessed 4 May 2007. Europol signed a strategic co-operation agreement with CEPOL in 2007.

The Europol Convention restricts the activity of Europol to those offences in which:

> . . . there are factual indications that an organised criminal structure is involved and two or more Member States are affected by the forms of crime in question in such a way as to require a common approach by the Member States owing to the scale, significance and consequences of the offences concerned.[6]

The Convention further stipulates that Europol can only deal with the specific crime areas of terrorism, drug trafficking and 'other serious forms of international crime' which are listed in an annex. This list is quite comprehensive, but nominating such a list is not without problems when trying to find an international equivalent.[7] For example, the English version (although not all the other-language versions) refers to 'organised robbery', and not to 'theft' or 'burglary'. A supplementary attempt was made to amend this through a declaration that the word 'robbery' should be read as 'theft' without amending the Convention, but, since all language versions of the document are considered equally valid and since this was clearly a mistake in translation, the oversight does not appear to have had much impact. However, such errors can become an issue for national parliaments who will normally scrutinise and approve the text by reference to their own language versions. Although the idea of a Europol was floated in 1991 and originally set up as the European Drugs Office, it was not until 2001 that the organisation was able to deal with all the crime areas in the list

A permanent solution to these difficulties may be in the offing. After new developments agreed in early 2007, Europol's remit will be extended so that it will also be able to deal with any serious crime which is not organised as well as international public order events (although it has already undertaken work with regard to certain international football tournaments and the Olympic Games).

Europol is a popular and convenient umbrella for conducting meetings or conferences on crime matters and allows experts to network and to exchange knowledge about their subjects. Europol also hosts and conducts training seminars and has been especially active in analysis training and in the safe dismantling of synthetic drug factories (which can be a risky business)

Information

The creation of a Europol Information System (EIS) as a central depository for Member States' information relevant to Europol's activities was seen as a key aspect of the Europol Convention and of the thinking behind EU police co-operation. The EIS has only comparatively recently become operational. It is

6 Op. cit., Europol Convention Article 2(1), fn 3.

7 Cf. the non-list based system used for extradition agreements, Chapter 10, p. 135.

managed and maintained by Europol, but is accessible by the Member States, if only through restricted outlets.

As mentioned above, the vast majority of operational information is shared between the different liaison bureaux at Europol through the use of a secure messaging system. In 2006, 210,272 messages were exchanged via this system in relation to 7,246 cases.[8] The contents of such a message can only be viewed by the sender and the intended recipient, but the system also records certain management information related to the classification and timing of each message. New messages with a new subject are allocated a unique sequential number and any subsequent message retains this number. Each message is automatically timed and dated and, if a request has not been answered, the system keeps it open in both the sender's and the recipient's mailbox so that it can be followed up. Although this system is used mostly for sending information to and from other countries, liaison officers can also forward the information or request to the EIS, to one of Europol's specialist units or for inclusion in a specific analytical project called an 'Analytical Work File' or AWF.

Analysts at Europol work on a limited number of AWFs each of which has clearly defined written terms of reference. They are, in effect, information silos the content of which is strictly limited to those terms of reference and which can only be accessed by the designated analysts. Each AWF has a project group consisting of EU Member States that opted into the file and the results of any analysis are distributed between them. However, personal data submitted by one country remains under the control of that country and permission is required before they can be disseminated.

Europol was recently assigned the role of producing the European Organised Crime Threat Assessment (OCTA) and the EU Terrorism Trends and Situation Report (TE-SAT),[9] both the first editions of which were published in 2007 (previously Europol had been publishing a collection of EU information in a European Crime Situation Report). As a central body with significant analytical resources, Europol is very well placed to collate and analyse the EU perspective in these areas, but the result depends greatly on the quality of the contributions and the data submitted.

Data protection has a high profile in the EU, but the stringent limitations and controls on the use of personal data by Europol have been recognised as being 'too rigid' and 'outdated'.[10] It remains to be seen whether such difficulties can be resolved in the next incarnation of the organisation.

8 Almost 30 per cent of these cases related to drugs, *Europol Annual Report 2006* (The Hague: Europol, 2007), p. 20.

9 Although the Situation Centre (SITCEN) in Brussels would seem to be equally well placed in terms of counter terrorism.

10 'Friends of the Presidency's report to the future of Europol', (2006) Council of the European Union, 9184/1/06, www.statewatch.org/news/2006/may/eu-fop-future-of-europol-06, accessed 4 May 2007, p. 24.

Building bridges

In addition to Member States' liaison bureaux there are also a number of other countries represented by virtue of bilateral agreements between Europol (the secretariat) and the country concerned. EU Member States are, as a result, able to use Europol to forward messages to such countries even when there are no direct bilateral country to country mechanisms or agreements in place (of course, the content of such messages should conform not only to the Europol mandate, but also to any restrictions in the relevant Europol agreement).

Europol is not allowed to liaise or co-operate with just any country that takes its fancy. The European Council has an approved list of countries with which agreements may be negotiated and to get a potential partner onto that list requires a business case and the sanction of the Europol Management Board before it is even considered by the ministers. Once a country is on the list, but before negotiations on the text can be started, Europol has to conduct a 'data protection audit' in the country concerned and then seek further approval from both the Management Board and the Council of Ministers. In addition, the Joint Supervisory Board (see below) must also be allowed to give its opinion on the data protection situation in the potential partner. Only then can the actual text of the co-operation agreement be negotiated, but even this is not the end of the procedure. Once the text has been agreed between the parties, the same approval hierarchy has again first to be satisfied before the agreement may be signed. Thus the whole process requires a considerable investment in time and patience.

Europol has developed a practice of recognising two degrees of co-operation: strategic and operational. A strategic co-operation agreement means that only technical information can be exchanged, but an operational agreement also allows for the exchange of personal data. At the time of writing,[11] Europol has operational agreements with Norway, Iceland, Switzerland, Canada, the USA, Australia and Croatia (as well as with Interpol and Eurojust). Where countries have been judged not to offer an 'adequate' level of data protection, they will normally be offered a strategic agreement instead. Europol has signed strategic agreements with Colombia, Russia, Turkey, the Former Yugoslav Republic of Macedonia, Bosnia and Herzegovina, Albania and Moldova.[12] Unfortunately, strategic agreements are of somewhat limited value in terms of operational co-operation because, although the partner may provide any kind of information it likes to Europol, Europol may not supply any personal data in return.

As already stated, Europol has an operational agreement with Eurojust, but the real value of the relationship is in the co-operation between the Eurojust national members and the national liaison bureaux at Europol. In many cases

11 May 2007.

12 Europol also has strategic agreements with the Commission, ECB and CEPOL among others.

this is extremely close with activities being cross-referenced to ensure appropriate co-ordination.

Questions are often asked about the relationship between Interpol and Europol. Europol has observer status on Interpol's European Regional Committee and both organisations have now exchanged liaison officers.[13] In reality, much of what Europol does is also done by Interpol: the communication of information; maintenance of specialised databases; analysis; training; expert groups, etc. There was a time when information exchanged through Interpol was sourced predominantly from western European countries. In the early 1990s (as the concept of Europol was being mooted), 80 per cent of Interpol message traffic originated in Council of Europe countries (40 per cent from the then 12 members of the EU[14]), but the incorporation of countries from the Commonwealth of Independent States (CIS) into the Interpol network has reportedly changed this dynamic. However, it is still the case that all members of Europol are members of Interpol and are paying for participation in both networks as well as for the Schengen Information System.[15]

Governance

At least for the moment, the Commissioners in Brussels do not have management responsibility for Europol. It is overseen (and paid for) directly by the Member States. The first line in the governance of Europol is an international committee called the Management Board. This body, which monitors the financing and strategic direction of the organisation, consists of one representative from each of the Member States (normally from the Ministry of Interior or Ministry of Justice) and is chaired by a representative from the same country holding the current EU Presidency. Someone from the Justice and Home Affairs Directorate of the European Commission also attends as observer. Management Board members are supposed to reflect the highest levels of their competent authorities or government, but this is often not the case and decisions are regularly referred back for ratification. Currently any important proposal has to achieve a consensus, but, given the 27 different perspectives of the countries concerned, this is easier said than done. A further bone of contention lies in the different national perceptions of the role and function of the Management Board. Some consider it should merely monitor performance and set the strategic direction (leaving the Director to run the business); others

13 The Interpol office at Europol was opened in August 2007. Europol also maintains a liaison office in Washington.

14 J. Benyon, L. Turnbull, A. Willis and R. Woodward, 'Understanding Police Cooperation in Europe: Setting a framework for analysis' in M. Anderson and M. Den Boer (eds), *Policing across National Boundaries* (London: Pinter Publishers, 1994), p. 57.

15 In some cases the countries are also paying for other co-operation groups too, such as the Baltic Sea Task Force and the SECI Crime Center.

believe that their function should be much more 'hands on' and expect to be consulted on day-to-day management issues as well.[16] Given the consensus model of decision-making, this unfortunate divergence in national perspective can lead to an oscillation in management emphasis from one six month presidency to the next. A major innovation in this approach is the proposal that the European Commission should have 10 per cent of the voting rights on the Europol Management Board (and 18 per cent on budget issues) whilst each Member State will only have 3 per cent.[17] Given that the Management Board will renounce the consensus model for decision-making in favour of one based on a two-thirds majority, this will provide the Commission with a significant say in these third-pillar activities.

Above the Management Board sits the EU Council of Justice and Home Affairs Ministers which has to agree and sign off on the recommendations of the Management Board on behalf of the Member States. However, before any decisions get to the Council, they have to pass through a working group called the Article 36 Committee (named after the relevant Article in the Treaty of European Union) and the Committee of Permanent Representatives (COREPER) which filters, reviews, advises on and prepares the documentation for the Council. All this means that making any decision is a long-term undertaking. The planned changes to the Europol legal basis hope to rectify these problems by making Europol decision-making subject to qualified majority voting without the need to ratify any changes in national parliaments.[18]

A further level of co-ordination is provided by the Heads of Europol National Unit (HENUs). This is a committee consisting of those national officials from the Member States who have direct management control of the liaison officers and Europol National Units at home. They are normally subordinate to those in the Management Board and may not come from the same organisation or even the same ministry, so the level of co-ordination between them varies from state to state, but the HENUs have a direct line of sight into the operational activity undertaken by the ELOs and are a valuable asset for future planning.

There is also a group called the European Police Chiefs' Task Force which was formed in 1999. It is not an EU institution, but it does have a role in influencing Europol activity. It began as an informal forum of chief officers from the national police services of EU Member States. It has become more formal as time has passed (with members being allocated policy portfolios and

16 Op. cit., 'Friends of the Presidency's report to the future of Europol' (2006) fn 10, p. 30.

17 The proposal allows the Commission three votes on normal decisions and six votes on budget decisions whereas Member States only have one vote. Art. 36(1) Proposal for a Council Decision establishing the European Police Office COM(2006) 817 final, 2006/0310, Brussels: European Commission, 20 December 2006.

18 This is an EU voting mechanism where the votes of the bigger Member States carry more weight than those of the smaller countries.

individual responsibilities) and now has a small secretariat collocated with Europol in The Hague. Although there is no formal procedure by which the Police Chiefs' Task Force can officially task Europol, Europol does attend the task force meetings and accepts their requests for assistance or suggestions for initiatives (in many respects the task force is a potential tasking and co-ordination forum in terms of a European intelligence model). However, there is no guarantee, again, that those on the Police Chiefs' Task Force come from the same agency as the Head of the Europol National Unit or, indeed, as that of the Management Board member.

There is an additional independent layer of external monitoring related to the protection of personal data. The Joint Supervisory Body consists of data-protection experts from each of the EU Member States and is empowered to inspect Europol's use of personal data (but not that of the liaison officers who are subject to national supervision) and to make recommendations for improvement. The Joint Supervisory Body is also able to review complaints submitted by EU citizens about the way Europol has handled their own personal data and offers opinions about any activity that involves data protection (for instance, as mentioned above, where new agreements with countries outside of the EU are proposed).

Who pays for it?

Europol currently receives its money directly from the Member States in the form of a levy. Budget plans have first to be approved by the Management Board and then agreed by the Council of Ministers. This means that budget planning starts about two years before the year in which it applies. Although (at the moment) every member country has equal status and casts an equal vote, the national levy reflects the fact that not all members have the same size of economy and contributions are formulated according to a complex calculation based on Gross National Income. In 2007, the Europol budget was approximately €65 million (€55 million of which was paid through Member States' contributions). However, the 12 countries which have joined the EU since 1 May 2004 are responsible for paying only 8.7 per cent of the total.[19]

The result

Europol was created as a political initiative in the spirit of a political union which has never quite managed to subordinate national ownership of justice and home affairs matters. However, this does not abrogate the very real need for an effective and a co-ordinated capability for dealing with transnational crime.

19 The 2007 levies were based on the 2005 Gross National Income statistics, www.europol.europa.eu/publications/Other/Budget/Budget2007, accessed 7 May 2007.

The scale and proportion of the threats in the EU, together with the dismantling of internal border controls, reinforce the particular necessity for such a body in Europe. Europol has not achieved its potential in this area. Despite the hard work and strong motivation of those involved, it has been hampered by a poor structure and a legal basis which have allowed it to be subjected to strong political influences, but without the substantive national political support to give weight and priority to its efforts. In the coming years the new legal framework, plus moves to address the wider EU decision-making stalemate should take effect, but it is too early to tell what that effect will be. In the meantime, Europol will persevere and the liaison officers will continue to transfer messages and oil the wheels of international law enforcement operations.

EUROJUST

The EU's Judicial Co-operation Unit (Eurojust) was established as recently as 2002 and has been described as sitting at 'the crossroads between two conflicting models: one seeking to increase harmonisation of criminal law and procedures and centralised EU structures and the other based on mutual recognition of Member States' laws and procedures and enhanced co-operation between them'.[20]

Eurojust, which has, like Europol, adopted English as its working language, is based in The Hague, the same Dutch city as Europol, but is currently housed alongside the International Criminal Court offices at some distance from the Europol building. Early in 2007, plans were unveiled which will mean that Eurojust will eventually be relocated to a site near to the new Europol headquarters, but not yet.

Eurojust has been assigned the task of enhancing 'the effectiveness of the competent authorities within (EU) Member States when they are dealing with the investigation and prosecution of serious cross-border and organised crime'.[21] This mission is to be achieved through:

- stimulating and improving the co-ordination of competent authorities in the Member States;
- improving co-operation between them; and
- providing other support in order 'to render their investigations and prosecution more effective'.[22]

20 The evidence of Hans Nilsson to House of Lords: House of Lords EU Committee, 'Judicial Cooperation in the EU: the role of Eurojust', 23rd Report of Session 2003–04 (London: The Stationery Office Limited, 2004), p. 8.

21 www.eurojust.europa.eu/index.htm, accessed 5 May 2007.

22 Eurojust Decision, Article 3, www.eurojust.europa.eu/official_documents/eju_dec.htm.

Thus, Eurojust has been assigned a function broadly similar to that of Europol (which is also required to improve the 'effectiveness and co-operation' of those same 'competent authorities'[23]). The activities of Eurojust are, however, focused on investigations (although Europol currently has no power to investigate as such its officials may participate in Joint Investigation Teams) and prosecutions in relation to those crime areas for which Europol is competent (that is to say those sanctioned by the Europol Convention), but explicitly in relation to:

- computer crime;
- fraud and corruption and any criminal offence 'affecting the European Community's financial interests';
- laundering the proceeds of crime;
- environmental crime;
- participation in a criminal organisation (where it is an offence to do so); and
- any other offences committed with any of the above.[24]

The reference to Europol's crime areas but the use of different language creates an unnecessary ambiguity because, whilst the Europol Convention only covers crimes which are both serious and organised, Eurojust is permitted to deal with crimes that are either serious or organised, or both.[25] In addition, whilst a Europol case must relate to a type of criminal offence that 'affects' two or more Member States, two Member States must actually be involved for Eurojust to be able to take action.

Structure

Eurojust has adopted a collegiate structure that is considerably different to that of Interpol, Europol or the SECI Center. Each of the 27 EU Member States is required to second one national 'member' (usually supported by an assistant member) to participate in the College who may be a judge, a prosecutor or a police officer 'of equivalent competence'. Such a structure places the members at the heart of the business, giving them a direct role in the decision-making

23 Europol Convention, Article 2, www.europol.europa.eu/index.asp?page=legalconv, accessed 23 April 2003. 'Competent authorities' are defined as 'all public bodies existing in the Member States which are responsible under national law for preventing and combating criminal offences'. The Eurojust Decision (see fn 22) does not define the term separately.

24 Most of these additional crime areas are also covered by the list in the annex to the Europol Convention (although not the protection of the EU finances which is allocated to OLAF, nor the reference to participation in a criminal organisation), but are mentioned separately in the Eurojust Decision. This may have been because the Europol Annex was not in force at the time of the drafting and negotiation of the Decision.

25 Proposed changes to Europol's legal basis are expected to bring this remit into line with Eurojust.

process to which they can apply their personal knowledge and experience. The members are, in effect, their own Management Board. The College meets twice a week and decisions require a quorum of 17 members (which is unfortunately not always achievable due to other commitments of the members). In operational matters, the voting of the College is decided by a two-thirds majority.

This combination of roles means that each national member wears two hats: that of national representative (similar to Europol Liaison Officers) and that of member of the College. Whilst participating as part of the College, national members are divided into teams each of which focuses on one of the agency's portfolios of activity (at the time of writing these were: Brussels; Casework Strategy; Cybercrime; Data Protection and E-POC project; Drug Trafficking; European Arrest Warrant and European Evidence Warrant; European Judicial Network and Liaison Magistrates; Environmental Crime; Europol; Football Crime; Fraud; Money Laundering and Asset Recovery; Office Lutte Anti-fraud (OLAF); People Trafficking; Performance Management; Presidency; Terrorism; Third States; Vision; Western Balkans). Each team prepares relevant policy and strategy considerations before presenting their findings to the College in plenary for the decisions to be taken.

The powers, job description and terms and conditions of members are determined nationally (including their salaries and duration of appointment) and their work as national representatives is governed by national laws. A member's workload, therefore, relies both on the extent of the national representation undertaken (including the transferring and progressing of requests for assistance or information) and on the team work for the College. As national representatives, members retain a national status and may act within their home jurisdictions directly under their residual powers as judges or prosecutors. However, this has resulted in an inequality of influence in respect of some members, not only because, as in the case of the UK, prosecutors have greater limits to their authority, but also because those countries with a federal and state structure compartmentalise the judicial process (for instance, in Germany, the Eurojust member, as a Federal Judge, has a different range of powers to that assigned to judges in the Länder[26]). In October 2007, the EU Commissioner for Freedom, Security and Justice, Franco Frattini, announced the Commission's intention to propose new EU legislation in 2008 to increase the powers of Eurojust as an agency and to harmonise the powers of the different Eurojust members.[27]

26 Op. cit., House of Lords fn 20, p. 19.

27 R. Goldirova, 'Brussels Set to Strengthen EU Crime Body', EU Observer, Brussels, 24 October 2007.

What it does

Apart from co-ordinating investigations and prosecutions, Eurojust members provide an advisory service constituting a centre of excellence for information on national criminal law and procedure (the recent advent of the European Arrest Warrant and European Evidence Warrant offers an additional breadth to the advice on offer).

Where the work of Eurojust discloses suspicious cross-border activity, Eurojust members, acting singly or as a College, may request competent authorities to undertake an investigation (six such cases were recommended in 2006).[28] This is a recommendation only, but if a request made by Eurojust acting as a College is denied, the relevant competent authority (i.e. law enforcement agency) must explain their reasons for the refusal and face the prospect that the details may be published in an annual report – the only actual sanction available is this naming and shaming. An additional function relates to conflicts of jurisdiction where there is a disagreement over the best place to prosecute an international case. Under such circumstances Eurojust can adjudicate and make a recommendation that one country would be a more appropriate jurisdiction than another. There is an inherent danger in such a power that there may be a temptation to transfer proceedings in order to obtain an unjust advantage for the prosecution, such as by choosing a venue where the rules of procedure are more amenable or harsher sentences are possible. Eurojust has issued guidelines to offset this risk.[29]

One of the main challenges for Eurojust has been to address the differences in approach between civil law and common law systems. Whilst both systems aim at achieving justice, the most obvious distinction is how, in the civil law system, a state-appointed independent authority (the judge or magistrate) personally questions witnesses and elicits evidence, whereas in the common law system, lawyers representing the parties involved present the evidence in court and question witnesses as adversaries presenting opposing scenarios. On the basis of this 'ritual combat' a jury of 12 members of the public decides on the facts (guilt or innocence) whilst a judge decides on the law. A further distinction found in common law systems is the reliance on previous court decisions (precedent) in deciding how the law should be interpreted, whereas in civil law countries, a judge tends to apply the law primarily by reference to the relevant legal 'code'. These differences have become blurred as time has passed and it should be acknowledged that, for instance, German and Austrian courts pay considerable attention to case law and that, in the USA, where the law is to a great extent codified, the use of juries is far more extensive than elsewhere (for instance with the used of a Grand Jury to consider whether there is sufficient evidence to indict a suspect).

28 Europol has a similar power inserted into the Europol Convention Art. 3b by a Council Act of 28 November 2002, Official Journal C312/1, 16 December 2002, p. 2.

29 Op. cit., House of Lords, fn 20, p. 22.

Communications

Like Europol, Eurojust also has points of contact within each EU Member State that act as a clearing house for information and, in early 2007, it was piloting a secure email connection system as part of the E-POC (European Pool against Organized Crime) project which will allow enhanced case management. The system uses a central database held at Eurojust connected to subsidiary local investigation databases located in the national authority.[30] The E-POC architecture will provide for both information exchange and for an analytical capability to search for links between cases.

As part of the information exchange framework, Eurojust has formulated and adopted its own data protection rules that are managed internally by a Data Protection Officer but, in accordance with best practice, monitored externally by the members of a 'Joint Supervisory Body'. As with Europol this body consists of experts designated by the Member States, but, unlike Europol, they are required to be 'judicial' figures. The need for these experts to be judges was challenged in some quarters on the grounds that sufficient expert knowledge would not be available within the judiciary. However, in order to satisfy such concerns, some Member States have simply designated members of their national data protection authorities as 'judges'.[31]

Co-operation

Since Eurojust is an EU agency within the 'third pillar' of the European Communities it is accountable to the EU Council of Ministers rather than the Commission.[32] Its authority and legal personality derive from an EU Council Decision[33] that locates Eurojust clearly within a wider landscape of EU law enforcement co-operation and which demands 'close co-operation' with Europol and OLAF and 'privileged relations' with the European Judicial Network.

Despite the priority given to communication and the sharing of data, there has been a familiar reluctance in some countries to co-operate with Eurojust.[34] Even so, Eurojust's workload has been increasing year on year. In 2006, Eurojust National Members dealt with 771 registered cases (which represented an increase of 31 per cent over 2005). The main crime areas involved were swindling and fraud (23 per cent); drug trafficking (22 per cent); and, crime against

30 www.giustizia.it/newsonline/data/multimedia/1243.pdf, accessed 25 May 2007.

31 Op. cit., House of Lords, fn 20, p. 24.

32 The Commission has to be 'fully associated' with the work of Eurojust Governance and there are regular co-ordination meetings.

33 The Eurojust Decision, www.eurojust.europa.eu/official_documents/Eurojust_Decision, accessed 23 April 2007.

34 'Findings of Eurojust in the Area of International Cooperation – Difficulties and Successes' (2007) Strasbourg: Council of Europe, www.coe.int/t/dg1/legalco-operation/ccpe/meetings/bureau/CCPE-Bu(2007)02%20Eurojust%20activities_en.asp, accessed 15 May 2007.

property or public goods including fraud (17 per cent).[35] Eurojust also held 91 co-ordination meetings (55 of which were multilateral).[36]

OLAF

The involvement of Eurojust in offences related to the EU's financial interests has created a potential for considerable overlap with the role of OLAF.[37] This is especially the case since OLAF has its own sizeable liaison magistrates unit. In fact, co-operation between OLAF and Eurojust has been described as 'hampered by suspicion and antagonism,'[38] even though a memorandum of understanding between them stresses the importance of co-operation. A tangible example of joint working can be seen in the first joint seminar (on fraud and corruption) held in March 2007.

In this regard, the proposal for a European Prosecutor is also relevant.[39] The text of the European Constitution (currently on ice, but rapidly thawing into the new Treaty) suggested that such a Prosecutor should be 'from Eurojust'. The exact meaning of this is unclear but what is clear is the intention that such a Prosecutor will initially focus on EU fraud (with the possibility that the Prosecutor will take on more general additional powers at a later stage).[40] This eventuality would have clear implications for the work and positioning of OLAF and it has even been suggested that OLAF could become the investigative wing of Eurojust.[41]

European Judicial Network (EJN)

Co-operation between Eurojust and the EJN is assisted by the collocation of the EJN Secretariat with that of Eurojust in The Hague.[42] Eurojust and the EJN have found a practical division of labour by which the national liaison magistrates of the EJN concentrate on bilateral cases whilst Eurojust focuses on

35 Eurojust Annual Report 2006, www.eurojust.europa.eu/press_annual.htm, accessed 23 April 2007, p. 29.

36 Ibid., p. 27.

37 Interestingly, OLAF also has powers in respect of Eurojust because Eurojust receives its budget from the Commission.

38 Op. cit., House of Lords, fn 20, p. 28.

39 S. Brown 'A Police Perspective on the Future of European Judicial Co-operation' in M. Leaf (ed) *Cross-Border Crime: Defence rights in a new era of international judicial co-operation* (London: Justice, 2006), p. 136. See also 'IGC 2007: Draft Treaty amending the Treaty on European Union and the Treaty establishing the European Community', Article 69i Conference of the Representatives of the Governments of the Member States, CIG 1/07, 23 July 2007.

40 Op. cit., House of Lords, fn 20, pp. 33 *et seq*.; European Public Prosecutor, www.europa.eu/scadplus/leg/en/lvb/l33159.htm, accessed 28 May 2007.

41 Op. cit., House of Lords, fn 20, p. 33.

42 Op. cit., Eurojust Decision, fn 33, Art 26.

multilateral activity. Members of both organisations are at liberty to attend the other's meetings (with the EJN holding meetings three times a year).

Europol

As already stated, Eurojust has signed a co-operation agreement with its sister organisation Europol, but negotiating that agreement was not without difficulty.[43] Partly this was due to the need to reconcile the mutual data protection frameworks, but there was also a political issue in terms of seniority. It has been commented that members of the Europol Management Board were wary of any form of words which could imply 'supremacy' for Eurojust.[44] However, the fact remains that, within the continental law enforcement tradition, prosecutors and judges do provide a supervisory function for their police services and the option for Eurojust to supervise Europol has elsewhere been welcomed as a possibility for the future.[45]

Because it has legal personality, Eurojust is also able to conclude co-operation agreements with countries outside of the EU or other institutions. Currently Eurojust hosts liaison magistrates from Norway and the USA and has a co-operation agreement with Iceland.

Administration

The work of the College of Eurojust is supported by an administration managed by an Administrative Director (with responsibility for human resources, information technology, finance and security) and by a Press Officer, College Secretary and a Data Protection Officer working directly to the College.

Unlike the direct levy arrangements for funding Europol, Eurojust receives its finance in the form of a 'subsidy' from the general European Communities budget. The College reviews the draft budget prepared by the administration which is then submitted to Commission for approval. The budget for 2007 is €18.9 million including the salaries of 147 staff (the national members and their deputies, however, are paid directly by their national authorities).[46]

Great expectations

The real strength of Eurojust is the fact that it brings together under one umbrella a coalescence of the specialist experience, knowledge and understanding essential to formal co-operation in transnational criminal procedure and

43 Op. cit., House of Lords, fn 20, p. 29.
44 Ibid.
45 Op. cit., S. Brown, fn 39, p. 136.
46 Official Journal L126/735, 16 May 2007.

that this expertise is made available and accessible to ordinary prosecutors and investigators throughout the EU. The raison d'étre for such a central facility has been clearly stated by the UK's House of Lords:

> It is unrealistic to expect individual national prosecutors to be familiar with the evidential and other requirements of a large number of different jurisdictions and to be able to co-ordinate unaided a complex investigation involving several different Member States.[47]

The potential of Eurojust is that it may make such unrealistic expectations redundant.

A COMPARISON

The creation of two separate entities for criminal justice co-operation reflects the tensions one finds at national level between the Ministries of Justice (who tend to govern the prosecutors) and the Ministries of Interior (with responsibility for policing). The division may have a discernible logic given the continental civil law distinction between the intelligence (or pre-investigation) phase, which deals with 'soft' data and is normally managed by the police, and the investigation proper (related to hard facts) which is normally supervised by prosecutors. However, it is hard to see a justification for perpetuating these national divisions with a separation at a supranational level – particularly when objectives and areas of competence are drawn in such similar terms. Would it not have been far better to integrate the two functions and create a coherent EU-level response rather than have to duplicate administrative and support measures (especially those related to information management and exchange)?

Undoubtedly, an increasing amount of information flows through these channels of liaison and criminals have been brought to justice because of the efforts of them both, but there has been no research into whether the use of these options has achieved results or performance unachievable by alternative bilateral methods of co-operation. Such research would help to satisfy doubts as to the effectiveness of these organisations and provide evidence to justify increased national commitment.

The Eurojust structure has much to commend it in that it puts the weight of activity and performance at the core of the organisation by directly engaging the national authorities. However, it does not benefit from the level of access to the potential network of police and customs information available and implicit in the Europol Convention. The proposed changes to the legal basis of Europol do not reproduce the advantages of the Eurojust structure and actually appear

47 Op. cit., House of Lords, fn 20, p. 39.

to reduce the levels of national oversight that presently exist. On the other hand, should the intention be to build a central police agency with operational powers, then it could be argued that isolation from national influence is a desirable attribute, but that argument must first be justified in terms of a rational and effective law enforcement strategy and reconcile likely concerns over accountability and competence.

There is, unfortunately, a sense that Europol was not equally welcomed by all Member States and, as a result, its formation in the early 1990s was bound to reflect the best possible compromise. At the time, however, Europol was breaking new ground from which experience Eurojust can be seen to have benefited. Given that experience, a subsequent initiative to bring both agency structures together in substance and with national representatives placed at the operational and strategic focus, would have perhaps promised a more integrated approach to international crime in Europe.

Chapter 5

OLAF

Fighting fraud in the EU and beyond

Johan Vlogaert and Michał Pesta

The European Anti-Fraud Office, OLAF,[1] was created on 1 June 1999 with the aim of helping European institutions[2] fight fraud and financial irregularities, including where the EU has provided development assistance or aid to non-EU countries. Its mission is to protect the financial and other interests of the Community against fraud and irregular conduct liable to result in administrative or criminal proceedings.[3]

It has a hybrid status: formally part of the European Commission (EC), but also enjoying a budgetary and administrative autonomy designed to make it operationally independent. To this end, the Office exercises the powers of administrative investigation (conferred on the Commission through Community legislation[4]) in complete independence.

POWERS

OLAF's core business is the conducting of administrative investigations, defined as:

> all inspections, checks and other measures undertaken by employees of [OLAF] in the performance of their duties . . . and to establishing, where necessary, the irregular nature of the activities under investigation. These

1 OLAF: l'Office européen de lutte anti-fraude.

2 Main European institutions comprise: the European Parliament (EP), the Council of the European Union, and the European Commission. For more info on EU Institutions and other EU bodies see www.europa.eu/institutions/index_en.

3 Its remit covers all Community revenue and expenditure and extends to all measures affecting or liable to affect the Community's assets and certain other, non-financial interests. OLAF Manual (Brussels: European Commission, 2005), p. 13.

4 Regulation (EC) No 1073/1999, www.eurlex.europa.eu/pri/en/oj/dat/1999/l_136/l_13619990531en00010007.pdf, accessed 6 August 2007.

> investigations shall not affect the powers of the Member States to bring criminal proceedings.[5]

OLAF may also assist EU Member States in their investigations by providing information gathered at Community level or through co-ordinating operational activity in transnational cases and this includes tactical intelligence for specific operations as well as strategic analysis and risk assessment.[6]

Where EU 'structural funds'[7] are involved, agencies in the Member States retain responsibility for managing and monitoring expenditure, but OLAF may nevertheless intervene when the allegations of irregularities or fraud are serious.

A further area of OLAF activity involves work traditionally undertaken by customs officials. This can include:

- evasion of all types of customs fraud related to industrial products, textile products and fish, including their smuggling, the false declaration of goods or value, false declarations of origin, and the evasion of anti-dumping duties;
- attempts to obtain illegal supplies of precursor chemicals;[8]
- cigarettes and alcohol: smuggling, diversion and counterfeiting of these products;
- VAT and mineral oils: international VAT carousel fraud and other intra-Community VAT fraud. Some units also provide assistance in combating the smuggling, misdescription and diversion of mineral oils.

In these areas, OLAF works in partnership with the Member States and the countries concerned.

In fact, OLAF assigns a high priority to partnership working and maintains direct contact with national judicial, law enforcement and administrative authorities. It has formal 'co-operation agreements' not only with other international investigation services, such as the Integrity Department of the World Bank, but also with those authorities in non-EU countries that have responsibility for dealing with financial crime and donor funds.

THE STAFF

OLAF is divided into four Directorates: Directorates A and B perform operational and investigative activities; Directorate C is responsible for intelligence

5 Ibid.

6 Op. cit., OLAF Manual, fn 3, p. 16.

7 I.e. Community funding aimed at assisting in the development of social and economic capacity in Europe.

8 Chemicals used in the manufacture and processing of illicit drugs

and for following up OLAF investigations (disciplinary, financial, judicial and administrative); and Directorate D covers policy work, preparation of anti-fraud legislation and the provision of logistical support.

OLAF staff members are Commission employees subject to the staff regulations and other general rules applicable to Commission staff. However, contrary to other EC departments[9] where a majority of permanent EC civil servants are employed, most OLAF officials are on fixed-term contracts, either as temporary agents or contract staff, or are seconded national experts. This is because the skills and qualifications required are highly specialised and not generally available in the Commission. Many OLAF employees are in fact former prosecutors, judges, police investigators, tax inspectors, auditors or representatives of anti-fraud organisations from the Member States. Nevertheless, there is now a trend to retain investigative experience in-house so that the number of the permanent OLAF staff is steadily growing. In mid-2007, there were approximately 420 persons employed at OLAF, of whom nearly 120 were investigators working on cases related to diverse fields of EU expenditure.

INVESTIGATIONS

OLAF conducts both internal and external investigations. Internal investigations are those administrative investigations related to financial irregularity within the Community bodies, but also cover matters of serious staff misconduct which may result in disciplinary or criminal proceedings. External investigations, on the other hand, are similar to internal investigations, but relate to activity outside the Community bodies.

In this respect, a distinction should also be made between administrative investigations and audits. Audits are checks on whether relevant procedures have been properly applied and have the objective of detecting any administrative failures or irregularities; in contrast, administrative investigations consist of more detailed inquiries aimed at detecting irregular behaviour liable to give rise to administrative or criminal proceedings and/or to the recovery of any taxes evaded or misspent funding.

Although OLAF is empowered to investigate, it cannot conduct investigations on its own initiative but only in response to an allegation received. Such information can be received in various ways: it can, for example, arrive in the form of a letter or e-mail from a concerned citizen, from a whistleblower working in one of the EU institutions or agencies,[10] disclosed in the media, or simply detected by OLAF in the course of its duties. Cases may also be referred, for

9 Called Directorates-General.

10 There is also a special telephone number in every EU Member State, called the 'OLAF Freephone', which allows members of the public to report fraud directly to the Commission departments.

instance, when the EC, as a contracting authority, encounters problems with paperwork such as interim or final reports that are supposed to establish the fact that the financed activity has actually taken place. There have, indeed, been cases where NGOs have failed to submit any data or reports and have simply vanished into thin air. Where external aid is involved, serious irregularities are often discovered in the first instance by other Commission bodies, by the local EU Delegation, or sometimes thanks to a standard audit.

Once information has been received it is first registered before being forwarded to the investigation unit with responsibility for the relevant area[11] where the head of unit will appoint one or two members of staff to assess the allegation.[12] During this assessment phase, which usually lasts two months, these staff check whether EU finances are concerned (that is to say whether OLAF has competence to deal with the matter), contact the source of the information to verify the facts and obtain any clarification needed and will gather any relevant documentation. Where necessary they will also contact the OLAF Intelligence Unit to request supplementary information and analysis.

The evaluator(s) will then draft an initial assessment. This is an internal OLAF document that describes the allegation, assesses its importance and financial impact, gauges the reliability of the source, and proposes whether or not an investigation should be opened. Where investigation is proposed, the evaluator will in addition state the legal basis for the investigation, prepare an investigation plan and suggest possible officers for the investigation team. The evaluation report is then considered by the OLAF Executive Board who will make a recommendation to the Director on what further action should be taken. However, the actual decision whether to investigate or not rests solely with the Director.

NO OLAF INVESTIGATION

Where it is concluded that there are no grounds or need for further OLAF action, an allegation will be classified as a 'non-case'. This occurs, for instance, where EU interests do not appear to be at risk or where only one Member State is concerned and is already dealing with the matter satisfactorily. Where appropriate, OLAF may also pass information to a Member State where possible offences have been uncovered but are unrelated to EU interests.

Even though a full investigation is not undertaken by OLAF it may maintain a watching brief when EC funds are involved but where another body or authority would be in a better position to deal with the matter (this is formally called a 'monitoring case').

11 The Directorates for Investigations and Operations carry out investigations and conduct other operational tasks and are arranged into teams or units each responsible for specific areas of activity.

12 Except where the information is unequivocally and clearly outside OLAF's area of competence.

There are two further possibilities for OLAF involvement. This happens, for instance, when another national or EU body is working on a case which would ordinarily be undertaken by OLAF, but where involvement is limited to facilitating contacts and encouraging inter-agency working by, among other things, supporting the gathering and exchange of information. These are called co-ordination cases. To this end, OLAF has developed the Anti-Fraud Information System, a secure network for exchanging information with the Member States.[13] The second type of involvement occurs where an irregularity is the subject of a criminal investigation by a national agency and OLAF is asked (or offers) to provide assistance. These latter are called 'criminal assistance' cases.

Allegations received by OLAF in 2006 were categorised as:[14]

Internal Investigations	37
External Investigations	112
Criminal Assistance	20
Co-ordination	26
Monitoring	59
Non-cases	210

AN ACTUAL CASE

The Lesotho Highlands Water Project is a multi-purpose project comprising dams, water transfer tunnels and an underground hydroelectric power plant. The project was developed in several phases to supply water to South Africa and indirectly to produce electricity for Lesotho. The EU has been involved in this project since the 1980s. The European Development Fund provided financing of €61 million and the European Investment Bank €122 million. Other donors included the World Bank and the Government of Lesotho. It appears that one Lesotho official was in a position to influence the awarding of contracts. Following legal proceedings in Lesotho, several bank accounts were identified in Switzerland containing more than €3 million considered to be from bribes. The official was found guilty and sentenced to 15 years' imprisonment. In 2003, following a meeting and exchange of information with the prosecutor in charge of the case in Lesotho, OLAF opened its own external investigation into the allegations and at the same time provided assistance to the prosecuting authorities of Lesotho. These and other ongoing enquiries have assisted the Lesotho authorities to continue to examine further suspect transactions and contributed towards a guilty plea by a multinational company to corruption charges in

13 Co-ordination is also facilitated by the Advisory Committee for the Coordination of Fraud Prevention (COCOLAF), www.ec.europa.eu/dgs/olaf/mission/mission/cocolaf/en.

14 OLAF Seventh Activity Report, www.ec.europa.eu/anti_fraud/reports/olaf/2006/report_en.

Lesotho. Two other companies have been convicted in Lesotho and OLAF is continuing its enquiries into the activities of other companies.

INVESTIGATIVE OPTIONS

An OLAF investigation may deploy any or all of the following techniques.

Intelligence analysis

Checks can be performed against various databases (with the assistance of OLAF analysts). OLAF has access to all Commission data with regard to financing and contracts and is currently using and – with the help of the EC's Joint Research Centre (JRC) in Ispra, Italy – further developing a search tool for Commission-based sources and databases. This has already been used successfully on several occasions, for instance, in uncovering cases of multiple financing of the same project by different donors.

Further audits

Where an investigation has been prompted by an audit, further analysis and collaboration with the auditor is normal. Additional or forensic audits can be also requested and financed from OLAF's budget. Where tenders have been forged using false bids, auditors will often be tasked to look into all similar contracts (often numbering several hundred) to check for other frauds. OLAF investigators can even accompany the auditors while they conduct their audits.

On-the-spot checks

In association with the authorities in the Member States, OLAF investigators may perform checks on the premises of any beneficiary or economic operator (contractor) receiving EU funds.[15] During these checks investigators can seize documents and computer hard disks, analyse paper or electronic data and inspect any other information related to EU funding.

Interviews and inspection visits

These can include interviews with witnesses and visits to any companies concerned in order to validate invoices or inspect other related financial documentation.

15 Regulation 2185/96.

Co-operation with national investigators

Whenever possible OLAF seeks to collaborate with law enforcement in Members States and non-EU countries. This is crucial in countries where cultural, linguistic and infrastructure barriers might otherwise seriously hamper the investigative process. Familiarity with and understanding of local realities as well as a knowledge of local criminal law has proven to be indispensable. Where parallel investigations are ongoing in several countries at once, co-ordination through OLAF is also possible, with OLAF disseminating relevant information to the local law enforcement agency/prosecuting body in charge of the investigation.

Contact other donor agencies

Where multiple financing is suspected, OLAF may also contact other donor agencies, foundations or governments and propose that they cross-check information related to the beneficiary in question.

Satellite imaging

Again thanks to co-operation with the JRC, investigators may, when circumstances so require, request satellite imaging in support of an case.

It must be stressed that OLAF's powers of coercion, especially in non-EU countries, are fairly limited and cannot be compared to those enjoyed by mainstream law enforcement. However, the fact that any lack of co-operation with OLAF investigations may potentially lead to the halting of EC funding and to the recovery of funds already donated, normally prompts rather a high level of access and co-operation. Furthermore, OLAF is not bound by the unwieldy mutual legal assistance arrangements which often delay investigations, but can speak directly to government representatives and private partners. This facilitates and expedites OLAF's operations considerably.

EXTERNAL AID

In providing almost €10 billion of funding each year, the EC is one of the most important international players in the field of development and humanitarian aid. While at the beginning of 2000 only very few cases of irregularity in external aid were reported to OLAF, by mid-2007 there was a caseload of some 58 ongoing investigations and 46 initial assessments of information.[16]

16 In 2006 there were 11 cases involving Africa, four cases in Asia, two in Central Asia, two in the Middle East, one in Oceania and three in South America: op. cit., OLAF Seventh Activity Report, fn 14.

Cases involving countries outside the EU are allocated to teams specialising in the geographical area concerned. The investigators working in this field require an extensive knowledge of all the relevant financial mechanisms and often have a good command of several languages. In such cases the EC's (and naturally OLAF's) rights to carry out checks are regulated by the financial agreements signed with the government of the country concerned and are usually also written into the contract with the beneficiary. These contracts provide OLAF with the right to conduct administrative investigations and to access all files connected with the EU funding. Moreover, the beneficiary must consent to retain documentation for a certain period of time (for example up to five years from the end-date of the activity) to assist in any subsequent enquiries. Investigators working on external aid cases spend approximately 60 days per year travelling and conducting on-the-spot checks.

Multiple financing of the same project activity – a common fraud typology encountered by OLAF investigators – is often exacerbated by the shortcomings in, and sometimes total absence of, co-ordination among the different global and international donor organisations in their grant award procedures, their auditing, monitoring and evaluation as well as in their early warning systems. The abundance of different projects, programmes and beneficiaries combined with the large number of different legal environments and financial systems makes the overseeing of the use of such funds very challenging. Unfortunately, there are no standardised, universal or commonly approved ways of reporting or any established verification systems that prevent donor organisations from over-funding the same activity. OLAF is actively engaged in seeking long-term solutions that will improve the exchange of information, enhance co-ordination and adopt joint approaches for tackling such problems.

RESULTS

OLAF has no powers to impose sanctions, but can only liaise and make recommendations to those agencies that have the necessary powers to do so. These recommendations may be of a financial nature (for example to recover funds), administrative (for example to improve contractual provisions or legislation, to alter the distribution of funds or to improve overall control and effectiveness), disciplinary (for example for disciplinary procedures against a staff member), or judicial (for example to launch criminal proceedings against individuals or companies).

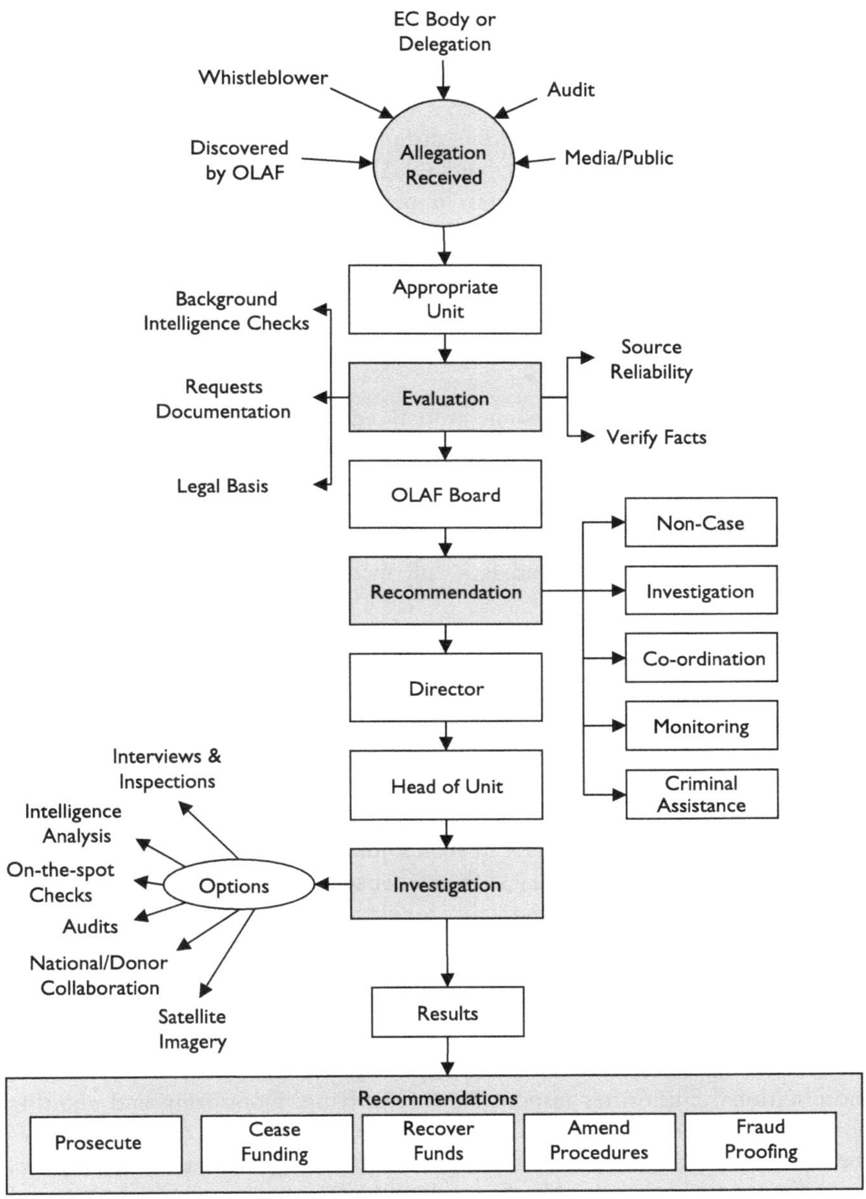

Figure 5.1 Schematic depicting the OLAF investigative process

PRACTICAL DIFFICULTIES

On-the-spot checks in non-EU countries

One of the key problems that emerge when investigating fraud in non-EU countries (especially countries in more distant regions such as Africa) is the fact that the European Commission, and OLAF in particular, is not very well known. This can cause difficulties in performing on-the-spot checks even though such checks are permitted by the contract. Experience has shown in the past that these checks are in most cases only effective if performed in close co-operation with the authorities of the beneficiary country.

Co-operation networks

Because it is free from cumbersome mutual legal assistance formalities, OLAF has been free to build its own networks within the law-enforcement community in general. OLAF works closely on a daily basis with prosecutors' offices, investigating judges, police and customs bodies both in the Member States and in non-EU countries and has formal co-operation agreements with Interpol, Europol and Eurojust and is a full member of the European Judicial Network.

What is less widely known is that, for several years now, there has been close co-operation between the investigative services of the UN (the Office of Internal Oversight Services), the World Bank (Department of Institutional Integrity), the European Investment Bank, the regional development banks and OLAF. This group of so-called 'international investigators', for whom OLAF provides the secretariat, meets on a regular basis to improve both the sharing of information and with regard to the creation of Joint (Administrative) Investigation Teams (OLAF recently took part in such a joint team with investigators from the UNDP in an African country with positive results). The group also holds an annual conference and there is a facility for exchanging staff between OLAF, the UN and the World Bank.

Looking at the challenges ahead, OLAF has, in close co-operation with EuropeAid[17] and the European Investment Bank, started to build its own network of partners in Africa and, for the first time, in 2007, organised a meeting with the co-operation of the Inspectorate General of Finance of Morocco with those national authorities responsible for verifying, monitoring and auditing donor funding in 27 southern Mediterranean and sub-Saharan countries. This is the start of a developing partnership network involving national administrative, law enforcement and judicial bodies and OLAF. The Forum of African General Inspections of State (FIGE), which currently represents 10 African nations,

17 The EU institution that implements the EC's external aid. See www.ec.europa.eu/europeaid/who/index_en.

signed a co-operation agreement with EuropeAid and OLAF in September 2007 and it is also worth mentioning that several prosecuting authorities in Latin America have already signed or asked to sign similar agreements (and that agreements with many other countries are also in the pipeline)

CONCLUSION

In dealing with investigations, particularly external investigations, OLAF is situated at the centre of a very complex institutional environment that involves daily interaction with several EU bodies, the national authorities of EU and non-EU countries, the beneficiaries of development aid, donor agencies, diplomatic representations as well as with other international investigators. Alas, the fact that there are so many actors involved also increases the risk of delay.

Another important issue is the need for OLAF to market itself in order to ensure co-operation. To this end OLAF provides training for both EU officials and for colleagues posted to EU Delegations in countries receiving EU aid and is also actively building wide partnership networks. However, it must be recognised that administrative investigations are not the same as those conducted by national law enforcement. OLAF investigators do not have the same coercive powers and their investigations can only result in a recommendation of sanctions or remedial action. They depend on co-operation and compliance with contractual arrangements. At the same time, it is possible for OLAF to support those national authorities with evidence as well as with expert information and expertise that a national authority could not be expected to know, or even to acquire easily. In the end, OLAF protects the financial interests of the European Commission against fraud, wherever those finances are used, invested or donated and that means that it also safeguards the interests of EU citizens who pay their taxes and are, ultimately, the real victims.

Chapter 6

Balancing political and practical interests

The SECI Center[1]

Mitja Močnik

Co-operation in international law enforcement cannot be separated from the political and economic environment in which it operates. The countries of south-east Europe have always had a distinct personality and been blighted by a volatile history. However, out of the instability that followed the disintegration of the Soviet Union and the former Socialist Federal Republic of Yugoslavia, the region has now emerged with an even stronger regional identity, not only in terms of trade and economics, but also in terms of law enforcement challenges and opportunities.

Improving national legal frameworks and restructuring law enforcement infrastructures are primary challenges but, in many cases, national developments in this area are only viable thanks to the direct support, guidance and, especially, finance provided by bodies such as the UN, the EU and the OSCE as well as from generous national donors such as the USA. Although greatly needed and gratefully received, this aid has not been offered entirely out of philanthropy; local security issues pose a wider threat than just to the countries of the region and addressing them at an earlier stage before they impact at home makes good commercial as well as law enforcement sense for the donors.

International co-operation is a huge challenge and a measure of its importance is reflected by the way that so many national groupings have sought to build their own co-operation frameworks. Whether this is the result of strong local motivation or because of disenchantment with existing methodologies is not known. However, a common view on how to streamline these many different efforts is definitely lacking.

The Southeast European Cooperative Initiative (SECI)[2] Regional Center for

1 This review is based on the author's personal experience in managing the SECI Center as well as on international documents and analysis of security sector reform in south-eastern Europe, the SECI Center, EU documents, assessments and political statements. It does not purport to offer a complete or exhaustive account of security-sector reform initiatives in the region or of all international organisations involved.

2 The Center actually began as one component of the SECI Initiative the seat of which is in Vienna. See www.secinet.info.

Combating Trans-Border Crime (The SECI Center) is one such framework. It is an international organisation with its offices in Bucharest, but with a regional perspective and participation. It is separate and distinct from the EU (although five of its 12 members are also EU Member States and are therefore also members of Europol[3]) and this allows the Center to act as a bridge between EU Justice and Home Affairs policy whilst offering an expert and informed insight into the challenges, issues and activities in south-east Europe which is unavailable elsewhere.

The need for trust and confidence has been explored elsewhere in this book, but one of the main achievements of the SECI Center has been to offer a neutral working environment where representatives from these particular countries (many of whom were recently at war with each other) can work together on an equal footing. Before the SECI Center there was almost nothing in the way of multilateral law enforcement co-operation in the region but it has now succeeded in opening the door.

As with all other similar organisations, the chief mission of the SECI Center is to improve co-operation in combating trans-border crime. Something that is not so explicit in other organisations is the equal status given to customs and police authorities. The advanced case-management system developed by the Center, also means that the SECI Center serves as a facilitator or 'service provider' for both aspects of law enforcement by offering a forum for the secure exchange of information. Member countries can audit and link the information exchanged using this system, but their information and input is encrypted to international standards so that it remains private and confidential to the national liaison officers using it.

POLITICAL CONTEXT

Recently the international security debate has refocused away from purely defence and military security towards a more complete concept involving discussions on transnational crime. This inevitably has repercussions for national priorities and perceptions on how to develop law enforcement networks. Almost all countries in south-east Europe share recent experience of transition into democracy, and to some extent are still finding their feet as single players in the international law enforcement arena. They face similar challenges and naturally find it comforting to share developments and co-operation activities with neighbours and others from a similar background and who are familiar with

3 The SECI Center members are currently: Albania, Bosnia and Herzegovina, Bulgaria, Croatia, Greece, Hungary, Moldova, Former Yugoslav Republic of Macedonia, Romania, Serbia, Slovenia and Turkey. It is likely that most of these will remain outside the EU for a considerable time to come.

the problems, even if they find themselves in disagreement in certain areas. The SECI Center has been a useful means for expressing this, but it was more than a desire to imitate the institutions on its western flank that led to its creation. It was apparent to all that standards in law enforcement and criminal justice generally would have to improve if the region was to meet European standards and to demonstrate suitability to join the EU club (something that the EU has made clear through its various national assessments and evaluations).

At the moment the pan-European security model lacks an international 'crime map' for the whole of continental Europe. Such a map would undoubtedly reveal south-east Europe to have an importance in terms of the origin, transit and targeting of organised trans-border crime groups in inverse proportion to its economic stature. For example, during 2005 more than 300,000 illegal migrants were detected at SECI country borders and more than 60 tons of drugs were seized in the region, of which 10 tons were heroin from Afghanistan. Very little of this contraband was destined for south-east Europe. The EU has created an EU Organised Crime Threat Assessment, but its insight into this region in its own backyard is limited.

Over the past 17 years, south-east Europe, perhaps more than anywhere else, has played host to an enormous growth in opportunities for trans-border organised crime and it is no secret that some national governments in the region have struggled to impose the rule of law needed to compete effectively against such criminal enterprise. Illegal immigration and trafficking in human beings, drugs, proliferation of small arms and smuggling of highly taxed goods such as cigarettes and stolen vehicles are all prominent criminal activities. South-east Europe is also host to many crime groups specialising in financial and computer frauds. In fledgling market economies, such as those of the region, financial crimes in particular can have serious repercussions that undermine public confidence in the legitimate payment system and in destabilising national economies. A significant trend over the past six years has been the more intense focus and activity against illegal immigration in south-east Europe. This has clearly been in response to events and priorities in other parts of Europe. More recently radical groups and other forms of extremism have been quietly fermenting within south-east European boundaries and national participation in the fight against terrorism of most of these states has raised the spectre of local terrorist attacks. This has helped countries to reassess their priorities in terms of international co-operation and resource allocation in favour of security issues.

Since the changes in the regional political structure in the late eighties and nineties, development in all south-east European countries has shown significant progress, but there are still unsolved problems in some areas, such as corruption and judicial capacity, that are likely to influence or impact on the future security situation and trans-border organised crime. Outstanding jurisdictional and sovereignty issues in the region, in Trasdnistria and Kosovo, will also need to be resolved in order to establish effective law enforcement coverage. It is a sad fact that, in the wake of the break-up of the former regimes, national, social, political and legal controls collapsed. Organised crime and corruption, among the most serious obstacles to development, have damaged the stability of democratic institutions by eroding the rule of law, violating fundamental rights and undermining the trust and confidence of citizens in the fairness and justice of public administration.[4] It is also possible to suggest that the growth of organised crime in today's south-east Europe has been partially facilitated by inadequate mechanisms for the transition from community ownership to mass privatisation (including poorly invigilated procedures for tenders, trade sales and management-employee buy-outs). This created a criminal sector with significant political influence and economic (purchasing) power, but a weakened capacity for law enforcement which has taken time to address.

BENEFITING FROM A REGIONAL CO-OPERATION CENTRE

The SECI Center became operational in 2001 and now has 12 member countries with 17 observers.[5] For many of these countries, the SECI Center represented a first:

- the first experience of having their own liaison officers posted abroad;
- the first experience of co-operating within a permanent information sharing and operational framework; and
- the first time in which customs and police services have been represented as equal partners (in the past customs services have not always had investigative powers).

The 'SECI Agreement', a memorandum of understanding signed between the founding members, established the organisation and represented a significant achievement in itself. Unlike in western Europe there was very little experience of any form of cross-border working in the region. Suddenly, 12 countries were committed to developing a common approach to serious and organised crime, but finding an approach that was acceptable to all was not without teething problems – not least because of the national scepticism that there would be a willingness to co-operate with each other.

The Center is now recognised as a vehicle for disseminating information, best practice, training and standards under a collective banner, but it has been a slow process with the SECI Center still working to establish itself. Nevertheless,

4 Media reports throughout the region relate how the influence of powerful firms and individual figures has shaped the legal, policy, and regulatory environments in their own interests.

5 Observers participate in activities and meetings, but may not vote. Italy and the USA have a permanent presence at the Center through the representatives of the Italian Police, Guardia di Finanza, the US Department of Justice, FBI, DEA, and the US Secret Service.

despite the initial scepticism, member countries have now developed a sense of ownership and responsibility for the regional co-operation process.

In negotiating the SECI Agreement, the member states favoured the approach of keeping the administration limited to that necessary for providing essential support for the liaison officers (who act as the vehicle for operational activity). As time has moved on, it has become clear that the SECI Center needs a more comprehensive legal basis reflecting its maturity and extended areas of activity. Operational activities have increased from around 300 cases in 2001 to over 2,000 in 2006 (in which year over 6,000 requests for assistance were transmitted and more than 10,000 operational messages exchanged). Liaison officers alone can no longer be expected to manage the wide variety of services increasingly demanded by the national authorities.

As already mentioned, one of the challenges for the SECI Center was to promote joint working where none had previously existed and where there was considerable national resistance to change. In the space of only four years the SECI Center has co-ordinated 24 successful region-wide operations, but when the idea of such operations was first proposed it was not at all clear if, given the current state of co-operation, they were even feasible. This success and acceptance has been partly achieved by the formation of teams of countries to focus on particular crime issues (each under the leadership of one of the member states). A further innovation in this regard has been the involvement of local prosecutors in the planning and execution of these operations.

In 2005, 142 persons were prosecuted directly due to SECI Center operations (with 93 being prosecuted during the first half of 2006). An example of a successful operation arose in January 2006 when information was provided by Romanian Customs about a suspicious cigarette consignment legally declared for export to Montenegro. The information was disseminated to all SECI countries and national alerts were issued. An operation was co-ordinated between Romania and Greece, which led to the seizure of 37 million cigarettes and four arrests whilst the consignment was being illegally unloaded in Greece.

Although such operations are concentrated in south-east Europe, they can also involve countries from further abroad including Austria, Germany, the Netherlands and the USA.

A unique activity conducted by the SECI Center is its special witness programme. This is a prime example of the organisation being responsive to a specific concern voiced by its membership. Trafficking in human beings for sexual purposes is recognised as being prevalent in the region, but convictions have been difficult to achieve. One of the problems has been arranging for victims (who have already returned to their countries of origin) to attend court in the country in which the traffickers are being prosecuted and to do so in a way that protects the victims from intimidation. Although the details of the programme are sensitive and cannot be discussed here, all activity is co-ordinated with the law enforcement and judicial authorities of the member countries concerned in order to arrange safe and expedited passage for the witness. Despite the fact that the programme only started in 2003 (when two witnesses were assisted), during 2006, 16 witnesses participated in trials in different SECI member countries thanks to the scheme.

A further benefit provided by the SECI Center to its members derives from the strategic analysis and situation reports on task force activity and regional crime issues released every six months.

CONSENSUS

One of the main concerns for any international organisation (and particularly in south-east Europe) is the changing political and security situation either in the region as a whole or in certain strategically placed member countries. International organisations are, after all, subject to the decisions taken by its membership under whatever voting arrangements exist. Where unanimous decisions or consensus are required, the strategic direction of an organisation can radically alter. Linked to this is the question of funding. Where funding is dependent on just one or two donors, national changes in priorities or disillusionment with organisational performance can result in unwelcome financial pressures. This means that, any international organisation that is not aligned to a fixed political grouping, must always seek out new sources of funding. It also means that long-term commitments or projects need to be carefully assessed against the risk of loss of financial support.

Consensus rather than majority decision-making can also lead to difficulties in getting agreement on priorities. Different countries have different national considerations which do not always coincide. It is always necessary to find the best possible agreement (as opposed to the lowest commonly acceptable solution). In terms of the SECI Center, these issues are especially important because of the need to reach agreement on new services demanded by the national authorities, but to ensure they have adequate funding from the ministries and other third party donors. Benefits must not be allowed to be warped in favour of one country at the expense of other less affluent members, but there are financial considerations and members should equally not be allowed to receive a benefit if they themselves do not provide their fair share of resources.

Where its member countries lack financial resources, as is often the case in south-east Europe, an international organisation must appeal to other sources of funding to supplement membership fees. This inevitably compromises independence.

TARGETING CHANGE

Today there are a number of international, governmental and non-governmental initiatives aimed at reducing trans-border crime in south-east Europe. Their projects are mostly oriented towards the establishment of training academies and staff development, on the promotion of good practice, on the adoption and implementation of a more 'European' legislative and institutional framework, and towards consolidating criminal justice in partnership with civil society (historically criminal justice in the region emphasised military-type philosophies rather than policing with consent). Indeed, the whole region has become the focus of attention for so many different external programmes that it has become saturated by well-meaning, if duplicated, efforts vying against one another for influence and donor support. Unfortunately, this has resulted in the general impression that there is a lack of co-ordination with international actors being only marginally aware of other initiatives, but too busy promoting single issue agendas to consider how their individual efforts could jointly support a comprehensive regional strategy. It is, of course, not easy to identify all the weaknesses in and opportunities for law enforcement across such a diverse region, but neither is it impossible and it could be greatly aided by harnessing an organisation such as the SECI Center which is associated and deeply involved with all of the countries concerned.

Contrary to the adverse influence of criminal activity, most governments of the region have, with international support, individually been making progress towards adopting legislative reforms and national plans of action against serious and organised crime. However, the real challenge lies in their implementation.[6] The solution, it is suggested, will not be found in further and further fora for political debate (particularly where these are based in a political perspective external to the countries of the region themselves), but in the targeted use by practical bodies such as the SECI Center as a vehicle for change. The SECI Center as a regional organisation co-operates with Interpol as well as with the World Customs Organization. Indeed, the association with both of these has been long and fruitful and their help and advice have proved invaluable. Co-operation with Europol is also now increasing since Europol was requested by the EU to develop closer co-operation with the SECI Center as a matter of priority. Such associations could be utilised as vertical channels for delivering real enhancements to national capacity by regionally harmonising the development programme instead of offering piecemeal solutions on a country-by-country basis.

It is important for any new international initiative to respect and to benefit from experience already gained by other agencies operating in the same field. It is equally important to learn from their mistakes but, for obvious reasons, established international organisations can be reticent and guarded about revealing any deficiencies. They can also be representative of partisan lines of

6 Kosovo for example represents a significant geographical gap in terms of a regional approach to combating trans-border crime. There are no specific projects in this field and it seems that the fight against such crime is not on top of the Kosovo priority list.

thinking or strategic approach that may adequately reflect the joint interests of their own membership, but be less than relevant to any new set of circumstances. Independence is essential for an international organisation to have credibility. This is especially important when the main activity of an organisation relies on the manipulation of sensitive material and on the confidence of the member countries, but exclusivity in sources of funding can render any attempts at independence suspect. Unfortunately, in south-east Europe (as in other parts of the world) the economic power lies beyond the region and local empowerment is not always viewed as an acceptable alternative. The use of an international organisation, such as the SECI Center, based locally, can make it more so. Independence is also an important attribute in a region where political strife and divisiveness have, until recently, undermined its social and economic potential and where nationalities and ethnic groups overlap across political borders. To make sense of the trans-border crime picture will also require an acknowledgement of such human and cultural bonds and regional organisations should not only reflect that fact, but also be able to translate it into action. This is a unique quality of the SECI Center and part of its mission.

Chapter 7

Overseas Liaison Officers

Neil Bailey

Despite the enhanced and expanded liaison facilities available through Interpol, and the creation of new regional co-ordination mechanisms such as Europol, the growth of bilateral liaison postings has continued. Variously known as Drug Liaison Officers (DLOs), Crime Liaison Officers (CLOs), Legal Attachés or Law Enforcement Liaison Officers they have become a vital element of international co-operation at both the regional and global levels.

In order to appreciate the role of Overseas Liaison Officers (OLOs), it is helpful to understand the history of these extensive and expensive networks, and most importantly to understand how they can complement and not compete with other communication channels.

Until relatively recent times, most international law enforcement co-operation was centred on the gathering of evidence to support the prosecution of criminals, for crimes that had already been discovered or detected. To facilitate such co-operation, a combination of rogatory letters and police to police responses through Interpol was considered sufficient.

Although the advent of affordable travel in the 1960s meant that inevitably the number of minor crimes with an international dimension requiring the exchange of information between jurisdictions increased, it was only the rapid emergence of international drug trafficking as a major crime threat that highlighted the need for a radically different form of co-operation.

In order to interdict major consignments of drugs, and prosecute those responsible for the trafficking, co-operation needed to be in place well before arrests and seizures were contemplated. The simultaneous involvement of agencies in multiple jurisdictions was required, and liaison was not necessarily most effective if routed through Interpol National Central Bureaux. Seeking to obtain information or intelligence by rogatory letter before a prima facie case had been established was fraught with the risk of premature disclosure, and in any event such a process was too slow and cumbersome for many active investigations.

Attachés posted to overseas embassies already covered co-operation in military and trade spheres, so an extension of this to law enforcement was a comparatively simple step. The creation of the Drug Enforcement Administration

(DEA)[1] in the USA with a clear remit to handle international co-operation in respect of drug trafficking provided an opportunity to establish a network of DEA agents around the world, in both source and transit countries. The benefits of such a network were quickly realised by the Royal Canadian Mounted Police (RCMP), the Australian Federal Police (AFP), closely followed by many EU countries (including France, Germany and the Netherlands), and despite the establishment of several new conduits for exchanging information (for example Europol) and a much improved and more responsive Interpol network, the growth of Liaison Officer Networks has continued unabated during the last three decades.

Although OLOs are now accepted as a legitimate conduit to and from the countries to which they are posted or accredited (usually referred to as 'Host' countries), this recognition was not achieved overnight, and the concept of Liaison Officers was initially treated with a degree of suspicion and hostility.

There is no 'typical' Liaison Officer, but they are normally recruited from the ranks of established law enforcement agencies, and remain in post for around four years. They are expected to converse in the language of the country in which they are based, and are usually accredited as members of the appropriate diplomatic mission, usually an embassy or consulate.[2]

It is important to understand that OLOs have no powers to conduct investigations in the countries in which they are based or accredited,[3] and are only able to liaise with local law enforcement agencies and request assistance. This ability 'to request' may often become translated as 'to suggest' but it can never become 'to demand'.

Although OLOs have many varied roles and responsibilities, there are broadly two primary roles for them:

- Referred cases: the facilitation of assistance by host country law enforcement agencies, to ongoing investigations that originate in the country posting the OLO. These investigations are probably not known to law enforcement agencies in the host country until brought to their attention by the OLO.
- Discovered cases: discovering links from host country operations that could be developed internationally, especially those that involve the country posting the OLO. These investigations are probably not known to

1 Founded in 1973 from the Bureau of Narcotics and Dangerous Drugs (US Department of Justice), www.usdoj.gov/dea/agency/genealogy.

2 In postings amongst EU countries, such diplomatic accreditation is not always considered necessary, and the OLOs may be posted directly to law enforcement agencies in the host country, but such examples are still the exception rather than the rule.

3 Often a Liaison Officer will be accredited to several countries in the region that he or she is based.

the country posting an OLO until he or she reports back to his or her parent service.

In referred cases, Liaison Officers are most effective when involved at the earliest stage of an investigation, which obviously requires the lead investigating agency to share intelligence freely with them, and they need to be kept abreast of day-to-day developments as the investigation progresses. There needs to be an acceptance that in order to obtain the full co-operation of local agencies, there will need to be full sharing of the intelligence available – and that requirement to share intelligence with foreign agencies, known only to the Liaison Officer, is often a difficult concept for others to grasp. The temptation is always to share the minimum possible intelligence and to work on the 'need to know' principle. Whilst, given the background and training of most OLOs this is understandable, without a full and frank sharing of intelligence with the appropriate agency, trust cannot be established effectively, and host agencies are unlikely to maintain co-operation in the longer term. It is equally important that the OLO does not try and deceive his or her colleagues in host law enforcement agencies, as it is inevitable that such deception will be discovered. By way of example, several years ago an OLO was handling a referred case that involved the smuggling of drugs by boat, and approached the appropriate host law enforcement agency to request assistance in maintaining surveillance on suspects visiting it. He told his host interlocutors that he 'believed' from information that he had received that the boat was located in a particular yachting marina. He did not tell his interlocutors that the previous day he had driven through the marina, confirmed that the suspect vessel was moored there, and, posing as a tourist, had taken a photograph of it, which he had sent back to his service. Co-operation was forthcoming, and several months later the boat set sail, was tracked and subsequently challenged. A substantial quantity of drugs was seized, and several arrests made. When the prosecution papers were being collated, the photograph taken by the OLO was included with the rogatory letter of request, and sent to the 'Host' country as part of the evidence gathering process. It then became apparent that the OLO had not 'believed' the boat to be in the marina, but had known it for a fact. To compound his error he had conducted unauthorised surveillance by taking a photograph, and had deceived his hosts. Fortunately in this instance, trust was re-established and the OLO was not asked to leave, but the example serves to illustrate the risks of clandestine unauthorised activities.

There needs to be a high level of mutual trust between the OLO and those tasking him, and with the host law enforcement agencies, if maximum benefit is to be gained. Unfortunately, it is often extremely difficult to persuade the tasking agencies, which usually believe that they 'own' all the intelligence, of the need to share. Many of them still work to the old maxim 'intelligence shared is advantage lost', but in the sphere of international co-operation there can be no place for such an insular view.

Discovered cases require the OLO to have established a strong relationship with all the law enforcement agencies in the host country responsible for investigating crimes at an international level. Those law enforcement agencies should ideally think of contacting the OLO as soon as a potential link to his or her country is established and, provided that a position of mutual trust has been established, then invite the OLO to share all the intelligence that they hold. Such links are most frequently discovered during host country operations that involve telephone interception ('wire tapping') of suspected criminals. Interception will often reveal that a suspect is in contact with co-conspirators overseas, often contacting the ultimate recipient of a consignment of drugs for example. Rapid consultation with the OLO will usually enable him or her to ensure that a parallel investigation is commenced by his own service and, by sharing intelligence as the operation progresses, decisions can be made jointly on the future path of the investigation and when and where arrests should be effected. Subsequently the gathering of evidence to support prosecution will have to be obtained through the judicial process (for example rogatory letters), but the pooling of intelligence prior to arrests being made will ease this process considerably.

There are however two particular areas of difficulty for OLOs in respect of drug trafficking cases that present a challenge to the principle of a full exchange of intelligence. The first of these is where the host country still retains the death penalty for drug trafficking. If the OLO is made aware that a courier is travelling to the country in which he or she is based, any request for co-operation with host law enforcement agencies carries the risk that they may have to arrest the courier at some point, and that if convicted the death penalty could be imposed. Over the last 30 years, many drugs couriers, often claiming not to be aware that they are carrying drugs, have been young people of previous good character. If it became known that the OLO had been involved in the passing of information that led to the arrest and subsequent imposition of the death penalty, there would be significant public concern. There is not a universal solution to this problem, but it clearly moves from the law enforcement to the political sphere and there have been several instances of bilateral agreements designed to prevent the situation occurring. For example, it may be possible to have an intergovernmental agreement to the effect that if country A passes information in respect of one of its citizens to country B, the death penalty would not be imposed by country B. In the absence of such an agreement, such cases will always prove challenging to OLOs.

Another potential area of difficulty concerns the sharing of intelligence with host agencies in respect of controlled deliveries. In theory, every country that has ratified the 1990 UN Convention has to have legislation in place that permits controlled deliveries. The reality is sometimes different,[4] as in several

4 Over the last 20 years, the UNODC and its predecessor agencies have been very effective in persuading governments to address this issue in order to permit controlled deliveries

countries police officers effectively swear an oath that they will always act to apprehend a criminal in the process of committing a crime. This can put the OLO in a quandary – if he tells the host agency about the arrival of a courier, and requests surveillance assistance, there is a risk that if the surveillance is compromised the courier will be arrested. The alternative is simply not to inform the host agencies and to effectively endorse an 'uncontrolled delivery', but such deception is almost certain to be discovered at some stage, with the consequent risk to good relations between the participating countries.

An extension of this scenario that can also present difficulties is when the courier is in fact an undercover officer. In such cases, an undercover officer should never be allowed to travel to the host country until the OLO has obtained formal approval of the course of action proposed, and this will often have to be agreed at the highest level – sometimes at ministerial level.

The role of the OLO in respect of the recruitment and running of informants is another area that can be fraught with difficulty, as in some countries such activity is specifically forbidden, in others it can only take place with the prior authority of a host law enforcement agency, and in the remainder the position is often ambiguous. Most OLO postings have to be initially approved through an agreement with the host countries Ministry of Foreign Affairs (MFA) and it is at this stage that ground rules need to be agreed. OLOs are not secret agents engaged in espionage and their relationship with host law enforcement agencies must always be transparent – unlikely to be the case if they are meeting nationals of the host country and receiving details of criminal activities or conspiracies without the prior knowledge of the appropriate host country law enforcement agency.

In certain source countries, it is not uncommon for a local citizen to appear at the doors of an embassy, requesting to speak to the Police or Customs Liaison Officer. These individuals, known colloquially by OLOs as 'walk-ins', then proceed to explain that they have been asked to carry drugs out of the country, and seek a financial reward to do so. The difficulties that follow such an approach are not confined to the host country, and every case needs to be considered carefully. As far as the host law enforcement agencies are concerned, they would inevitably be interested to learn who had approached the 'walk-in' in the first place, and what other information was available that could lead to arrests and seizures locally. If there was to be an agreement that the 'walk-in' could depart the host country as a courier with a consignment of drugs, the problem then shifts to the OLO who has to ensure that the 'walk- in', now effectively a 'participating informant', will be granted safe passage through the countries that s/he will transit (usually but not always by commercial aircraft), and that both s/he and the drugs will always be in a controlled situation. Given the difficulties of converting such theory into practice, a solution favoured in some jurisdictions is for the drugs to be carried separately by a law enforcement officer, and reunited with the participating informant at the ultimate destination. Difficulties do not end there, as any subsequent prosecution can be dogged by accusations that the participating informant was essentially an 'agent provocateur', the identity of the participating informant may not be capable of protection in the subsequent judicial process, and any payments made to him will inevitably call his motives and integrity into question.

Although the above 'walk-in' scenario is a good example of the problems of international law enforcement co-operation, it is an equally good example of the value of an OLO. Having an officer available locally to assess the risks and benefits of the proposed course of action and to be able to discuss the issue directly with local host country agencies is invaluable, and it is doubtful if any such cases could ever be progressed without the engagement of an OLO.

Over the 30-plus years since OLOs were established, their roles and responsibilities have evolved, partly through precedent and experience and partly by a framework of intergovernmental agreements. The OLO networks have certainly proved their worth, which is why this most expensive liaison conduit continues to expand, but there are still rivalries between the various organisations also tasked with international law enforcement co-operation. Although it is clear that OLO networks are now well established and successful, there is still a belief in some quarters that Interpol or Europol could perform the same role, but this is misguided, and often due to confusion or ignorance of the unique role of the OLO.

Countries posting OLOs can help reduce rivalries and improve co-operation and co-ordination by clarifying the roles of each liaison channel, and most importantly by providing a single National Unit, through which all incoming and outgoing requests for international assistance are channelled. It is then the clear responsibility of that National Unit to determine the most appropriate channel to deal with each request. It may well be the case that as an operation moves through different phases, different liaison channels will be used, but it is essential that all the intelligence gathered is channelled through one point. Such a system was envisaged by the architects of the Europol Convention, but even in the EU there are countries where the reporting base for OLOs, the Europol National Unit and the Interpol National Central Bureaux are in different departments or ministries.

It is particularly difficult for an OLO if he discovers that an enquiry he is progressing has also been passed to another agency in the host country, and too often this is because the originating agency has decided to try and short circuit established procedures. A strong National Unit can counter this, but governments need to ensure that the routing of requests through it is mandatory and not merely recommended. Such a system ensures that the OLO is only handling requests that are appropriate to his role, and eliminates the duplication of effort that inevitably follows from unregulated contact with agencies overseas.

The success of OLO networks, especially in the field of drug trafficking, has been increasingly significant over recent years, and it is only the high cost of the networks that has limited further expansion. The idea of OLOs covering a group of adjacent countries (rather than one) has been advanced in an effort to share costs but there appears to be little enthusiasm for this course amongst the countries with large established OLO networks. It therefore appears that OLO networks will continue to expand and evolve for the foreseeable future alongside established organisations such as Interpol and Europol, and the need for close co-operation between them will be vital.

Chapter 8

Liaising in international organisations

Vladimir Gilca

There are two broad scenarios for international co-operation that may involve liaison officers: the appointment of a 'police' or 'customs' envoy to a diplomatic mission abroad, or the posting of liaison officers to an international organisation where they work together under commonly agreed rules. In the first role, a law enforcement attaché to an embassy, in addition to being a representative for his or her country's agencies, has a support and advisory role for the ambassador. Where such a role exists, it will normally be the primary channel for bilateral co-operation, but many countries do not have the resources to fund this kind of liaison officer or are only able to do so on a limited basis.

Multilateral co-operation, on the other hand, will often be channelled through an international organisation. Interpol, the largest and best established of these, does not use liaison officers and information exchange is sent directly between different national bureaux in the different member countries but, increasingly, other organisations with a more regional focus, such as Europol and the SECI Regional Center for Combating Trans-Border Crime (SECI), bring representatives of national law enforcement together in a central location where they can work together face to face. Such institutions also have an important function in promoting standards of efficiency and disseminating knowledge about international crime. They extend the geographical range of national law enforcement and provide facilities on a shared basis that many individual countries could not afford alone. It is this latter type of co-operation involving liaison officers posted to international organisations that is the main focus for this chapter.

International organisations are all based on some kind of legal document by which the member countries recognise its international status and role and any liaison officer working within that framework is obliged to work in accordance with those provisions whilst, at the same time, respecting the rigours of national law. Therefore it is important for any legal framework to be clear about both the range of responsibilities and the limits imposed on a liaison officer's powers as well as the type, level and complexity of crime with which s/he is expected to deal. Europol, for instance, can currently only concern itself with serious international organised crime that affects two or more EU Member States, but SECI can deal with any serious crime involving a trans-border component.

SHARING INFORMATION

Good liaison officers promote and generate cross-border co-operation and need to be permanently and continually in touch with their colleagues at national level: offering advice on how to prepare better documentation for initiating an international request; helping them to identify international priorities; and suggesting which channel of co-operation is more appropriate for a particular case. In order to offer the best advice, liaison officers also need to become experts in the systems, procedures, regulations and facilities available to their colleagues from other jurisdictions.

The kinds of information exchange handled by a liaison officer can range from a one-off message relating to a single event or target (requiring a simple yes or no response) to an extended dialogue spread over a period of months in pursuit of a long-term investigation that grows in complexity and shifts in focus as the investigation develops. When a message is first received, it is always impossible to predict where it will lead or how complex the outcome will turn out to be and, consequently, a liaison officer cannot afford to be complacent about any of the messages s/he receives.

However, a liaison officer is not merely a post box and in order to achieve the full potential of the role a liaison officer must conduct research, both in terms of 'environmental scanning' (namely what is happening generally in the field) and on specific cases of international crime. Where appropriate, the liaison officer must try and determine the full facts of such crimes before communicating the information to the relevant colleagues. To do this, a liaison officer has to be aware of what is going on and s/he will be greatly assisted by uninhibited access to his national colleagues, to national databases as well as by access to open sources on the internet. This may seem obvious, but such advantages are not always permitted or provided.

A liaison officer should not become overly preoccupied with the micro-level, but should also consider the macro-level and try to acquire an ability to interpret world events in terms of its impact at home. Analysis of such developments at an early stage can allow domestic agencies to adjust their resource allocation and strategies in preparation for future threats – if the political levels of law enforcement are prepared to listen and respond appropriately.

In addition to the primary function of forwarding information and intelligence there are a number of other activities that a liaison officer will undertake on a regular and routine basis. Liaison officers will often be asked to provide assistance for a prosecution or to otherwise support court proceedings (usually under the authority of rogatory letters[1]). This can include:

1 See Chapter 10.

- locating and arranging for the arrest of suspects;
- identifying and interviewing witnesses;
- collecting new or corroborating evidence;
- support for extradition proceedings;
- contacting and arranging travel for international witnesses.

Failure to use rogatory letters in accordance with accepted international procedure can lead to frustrating, but completely preventable, results. For instance, in July 2007, a terror suspect was detained in Australia attempting to return to his native India on a one-way ticket. When an Australian investigator from the Australian Federal Police arrived in India to make local follow-up enquiries, he came up against a brick wall. The Indian Criminal Investigation Bureau refused to share information without a properly constituted rogatory letter signed by an appropriate Australian authority. While the Indian authorities may have been castigated in the media, they were simply following established and normal legal procedure with which the Australian authorities were supposed to have complied.[2] This refusal by the Indian police was later vindicated when charges against the terror suspect were dropped in embarrassing circumstances.[3]

MORE THAN MEETINGS

A liaison officer in an international organisation also has a representative function. She or he may have to host visitors from home, give presentations on his or her work at conferences or attend various other meetings. Some international organisations have in excess of 100 meetings a year and the costs involved in their attendance can be prohibitive for smaller countries with lower budgets. Although these meetings may be given a variety of names (such as, conferences, seminars, training, working groups, etc.), they come in two basic categories: operational and strategic.

Strategic meetings have the main purpose of looking at transnational trends, sharing new ideas, disseminating good practice and establishing and consolidating personal networks. Operational meetings, on the other hand, look at a particular, active investigation. Representing agencies at specialist meetings can be a little difficult; for example, the topic of the meeting may not be within the expertise of the liaison officer and he or she may have been delegated simply because there are no funds to send a specialist from home. On the other hand, under such circumstances the liaison officer can only be expected to participate

2 'Australia-India Terror Suspect Case Stalled' ABC News, www.abc.net.au/ra/news/stories/s1976485, accessed 12 July 2007.

3 'Errors lead to dropping of Haneef charge', www.abc.net.au/news/stories/2007/07/27/1990249, accessed 27 July 2007.

on a limited basis. She or he cannot make any decisions or offer any significant contribution beyond the instructions he or she has been given in advance.

A JOINT INVESTIGATION IN PRACTICE

Joint investigations between counties have been successfully conducted for many years throughout the world. They are not exclusive to international organisations nor to the participation of liaison officers, but their co-ordination does fit well under the neutral umbrella of such an organisation. This can best be illustrated by example.

Acting on information received concerning illegal migration and the trafficking of human beings, officers from the Austrian Criminal Intelligence Service had conducted exhaustive national inquiries. They had interviewed victims, organised surveillance and wiretaps on key targets and collected as much information as possible at the Austrian end of the criminal enterprise. However, the investigation had disclosed extensive links abroad and they knew that, unless the roots of the network were eradicated, even if they arrested their suspects it would not be long before the network regrouped and reasserted itself not only in Austria, but also in the other countries involved. Thus they approached the management of the SECI Center in recognition of the fact that this was the most inclusive forum within which they could effectively collaborate multilaterally with the other countries concerned.

Their reasoning was as follows:

1. The target criminal network was spread across a territory covered by member and observer states belonging to the SECI Center.
2. The required scale of response was beyond the available national resources and it would have been impractical to use a series of bilateral agreements.
3. The operation required concerted and simultaneous action in different countries.
4. The SECI Center provided a convenient venue for all concerned.

The target network was highly organised and was transporting people from Moldova and Ukraine through Romania, Hungary and Austria to countries in Western Europe (mainly Germany, Italy, Portugal and Spain). In the first instance, the SECI Center management approached the liaison officers of the relevant countries who then, in turn, consulted their national agencies responsible for dealing with such crimes. National consent for initiating an international joint operation was received and the SECI Center arranged a first meeting at which Austrian officers briefed the others on what was known about the target crime group. The meeting also identified roles and key tasks for each of the participants, established channels for exchanging information and nominated the place and date of future meetings. It is important to note that, in terms of operational structure, this joint investigation was, in fact, a matter of law enforcement agencies in four countries conducting parallel investigations but collaborating and sharing information through their liaison officers.

During 2005 there were five further meetings at which knowledge was shared and compared and the progress of the individual national investigations was reviewed. Finally, it was felt that sufficient information and evidence had been gathered and during simultaneous operations in Romania, Hungary and Austria, 96 suspects were detained.

The operation utilised a number of techniques including:

- analysis of the information shared by the different countries;
- extensive victim interviews;
- physical surveillance;
- fixed line and mobile telephone interception (including translation from Russian and Romanian into English);
- informants;
- financial investigation.

Debriefing and post-operational analysis led to proposals for enhancing future tactics and for amendments to existing laws and regulations by which future co-operation could be facilitated, whilst press conferences and the marketing of results, jointly and at national level, have helped to emphasise the value of combined working.

THE SPECTRE OF CORRUPTION

Others have emphasised the importance of a culture of trust in sharing information. Unfortunately, the spectre of corruption has always haunted criminal justice and a major reason for the suspicion and secrecy that surrounds police inquiries is the fear that an investigation will be corrupted by the influence or interference of external forces.

The need to recruit persons of high integrity speaks for itself, but the creation of secure methods and procedures for handling and transmitting sensitive data is equally important (both for objectively protecting the information and in defending the liaison officer from unwarranted accusations). Such methods and procedures can either be specified in the agreements on which liaison activities and international organisations are based or as secondary protocols. However, the challenge is to establish methods which are strictly applied not just to the international exchange of data but also to the domestic handling of those data once they have been exchanged. This will be of no concern where co-operation partners share a similar well-structured approach to information management but can be difficult where the culture of following security procedures is less well developed. The use of security software can be used both to protect and detect deliberate or negligent failures in information handling but is only useful where data are being handled electronically and in many countries access to computers is still limited on the national level. Strong and well-supervised procedures for hard copies and paper files are, therefore, equally important.

Although a rare circumstance, and not encountered by the author, there is a further potential implication of being a liaison officer that is often forgotten, but must be acknowledged: the fact that, as the gatekeeper for passing information from one country to another, s/he is a likely target for criminals who want access to that information. This means that there must be a special emphasis on safeguarding the integrity of liaison officers. They must be properly trained and equipped to prevent this from happening.

LEARNING TO LIAISE

In building co-operation, the concluding of a legal instrument is not the end of the process but the beginning. Co-operation will not happen just because there is a legal document allowing it. A good deal of the responsibility lies with the liaison officer him- or herself. The greatest asset of a liaison officer is credibility and this is only achievable where s/he possesses (or takes steps to acquire) relevant knowledge, experience and an enthusiasm for teamwork. If a liaison officer can cultivate a reputation for openness, friendship and remaining calm under pressure, colleagues will be more prepared to co-operate and go the extra mile in offering assistance. The liaison officer can then exploit this goodwill, but must always remember that reciprocation is the currency of co-operation. Without an adequate or timely response to requests for assistance, the liaison officer's reputation will suffer and information flows will soon dry up. Nor should the personal touch be underestimated in networking with colleagues; interacting on a social level can lead to a deeper understanding of the personalities involved and allows one to have a better understanding of colleagues and of the personal and professional challenges they face at home.

BARRIERS AND BENEFITS

Sometimes convincing management at a national level that a certain investigation is worth supporting can be difficult. National managers need to allocate their limited resources and budgets wisely and an investigation which may be very important for colleagues abroad, might have limited relevance to domestic crime priorities. This is when the importance of reciprocity (for national interests) needs to be emphasised.

One of the fundamental failures in co-operation is the lack of implementation by agencies on the national level of the legal frameworks agreed internationally. Co-operation between liaison officers of different countries can sometimes actually be better than that between different national agencies. From time to time, colleagues may need to be reminded that defeating international crime not only has mutual benefits and rewards but is also a common obligation.

In part, the professional side of police culture is similar in most countries because the tasks and responsibilities are similar. On the other hand, a large part is also embedded in, and deeply influenced by, the respective national culture. Any emerging international ethic for law enforcement co-operation should emphasise the similarities and minimise potential conflict. As international law enforcement develops, a new international police tradition will evolve but a conscious effort to develop intercultural understanding now, whilst it is still in its infancy, will not only speed the development of an international police culture but also ensure that it embraces the most important common values. The liaison officer has a role in this development that should be recognised by managers at the national level. S/he is a rich source of knowledge, understanding and practical experience on which they would do well to capitalise.

Chapter 9

Legal Attachés and liaison

The FBI

Sandra L. Fowler

The Federal Bureau of Investigation (FBI) has had a long and interesting history in the arena of international co-operation and investigation. Beginning in 1940 with the first assignment of FBI personnel at the US Embassy in Mexico City, to the 71 offices and sub-offices of today, the FBI has dedicated significant personnel and financial resources to the development and maintenance of its international relationships which do so much to enhance FBI investigations.

According to FBI Director Robert S. Mueller, III:

> The globalization of crime – whether terrorism, international trafficking of contraband and people, and cyber crime – absolutely requires us to integrate law enforcement efforts around the world. And that means having our agents working directly with their counterparts overseas on cases of mutual interest – not only to solve crimes that have been committed, but to prevent crimes and acts by sharing information in real time.[1]

The mission of the FBI's International or Legal Attaché Program is to facilitate the progress of domestic FBI investigations through a worldwide network of co-operative relationships with foreign law enforcement and intelligence services. In addition, in the aftermath of the terrorist events of 9/11, the mission was enhanced to include the extensive development of intelligence information relating to threats against US interests both in the US and worldwide.

This chapter will look at the FBI's International Program and will examine the position of the Legal Attaché (Legat) and Assistant Legal Attaché (ALAT) at embassies throughout the world, the way they work, the internal structure of the Program and how it is managed.

Unlike the US Department of State (the diplomatic arm of the US Government) and other US agencies such as the Central Intelligence Agency, the FBI is not a foreign service agency. The FBI has no mandate under US law to conduct

1 www.fbi.gov/contact/legat/legat.htm, accessed 16 April 2007.

investigations outside the USA. It is a domestic US law enforcement and counter-intelligence agency, and maintains an international network of liaison personnel solely to facilitate FBI investigations being conducted in its 56 domestic field divisions and to develop intelligence information regarding threats against US interests at home and abroad.

The FBI does not work on behalf of other US federal, state, or local law enforcement agencies either at home or abroad. Because of their limited jurisdiction it is unlikely that a state or local service would routinely be involved in matters requiring the co-operation of foreign law enforcement services; however, in the event they have an inquiry which needs to be forwarded to a foreign service they would use the Interpol channel. Many of the federal services, like the Drug Enforcement Administration and the US Secret Service, maintain their own international liaison networks, and the FBI Legal Attaché will work co-operatively with the representatives of those services.

HISTORICAL DEVELOPMENT

With the broadening of the FBI's jurisdiction to include espionage, sabotage and other subversive activities in 1939, and a Presidential Directive issued on 24 June 1940 ordering the FBI to take on responsibility for examining Axis movements in the Western Hemisphere, the FBI's International or Legat Program was born and by mid-1941, Special Agents were posted to Santiago, Chile; Rio de Janeiro, Brazil; Caracas, Venezuela; and Mexico City, Mexico. By November 1942, offices had been opened in all of the US embassies in Latin America with the exception of Honduras and Panama, and Legat offices had also been opened in London, Ottawa, and Bermuda.

By 1988, only Mexico City and Bogotá remained of the original Legal Attaché offices in Latin America (the others having been either closed or consolidated into a new office at the embassy in Montevideo, Uruguay), but new offices had been opened in Panama City (1945), Paris (1945), Tokyo (1954), Rome (1954), Bern (1961), Hong Kong (1965), Canberra (1972), Bridgetown (1988), Manila (1988), and Brussels (1988), bringing the total number of Legat offices to 15 in the first 28 years of the Program. Between 1988 and today an additional 45 Legal Attaché and 11 sub-offices have been opened around the world. Two new Legal Attaché offices are scheduled to be opened in 2007, and two sub-offices are scheduled to be replaced by full-scale Legal Attaché offices.

Although the number of employees assigned to permanent overseas positions has grown to almost 340 (including both Agent and Professional Support personnel), the total number remains insignificant when compared to the nearly 31,000 total FBI employees today. As a domestic US law enforcement and counter-intelligence agency, the FBI does not recruit employees with a view to international assignments. This lack of a world view, for want of a better term, may adversely impact the FBI's ability to staff international positions and may result in misunderstandings regarding the way non-US national law enforcement and intelligence services work. The enormous number of US law enforcement agencies at the state and local levels (nearly 18,000[2]) and the federal law enforcement agencies all work in a manner very similar to that of the FBI, so it is natural for FBI employees to assume that foreign services work in a similar way.

From the beginning until the early 1980s the Legats were mainly tasked with gathering counter-intelligence information which could be used in the USA to identify persons engaged in espionage or other subversive activities. However, under the guidance of former Director Louis J. Freeh in the 1990s, the FBI's international commitment was reevaluated, and an ambitious programme of expansion was begun and the mission was expanded to include a more broadened approach to supporting criminal investigations in addition to gathering counter-intelligence information.

Following 9/11 the mission of the Legal Attaché Program was again modified to include an expanded mandate for developing intelligence information which would enable the FBI to make more meaningful analyses of threats against the USA and its overseas interests. In order to better develop the needed intelligence information, mainstream FBI employees who heretofore had no international experience were suddenly reassigned to international terrorism investigations. They needed to develop a quick understanding of international operations, and learn how Legat offices operated. Many volunteered (or were volunteered) for temporary duty assignments in such places as Islamabad, Pakistan; Riyadh, Saudi Arabia; Sana'a, Yemen; and Abu Dhabi, UAE. In any given week it was not uncommon to find hundreds of FBI employees assigned to these temporary positions outside the USA, and many were serving in locations where there had never before been an FBI presence. Not only was the FBI staffing temporary offices in these remote locations, there were also large cadres of employees temporarily assigned to existing Legat offices such as Berlin where investigations conducted in the FBI's domestic field offices resulted in the development of information the FBI was able to pass to their colleagues in Hamburg, Germany. This information formed the basis for investigations which ultimately enabled the German authorities to prosecute peripheral members of the 9/11 plot.

THE INTERNATIONAL PROGRAM AND THE DEPARTMENT OF STATE

The US Government relies on the Department of State to act as its diplomatic arm in the foreign environment. Because of its authority to represent the US

2 US Department of Justice, Bureau of Justice Statistics, Census of State and Local Law Enforcement Agencies, 2000, www.ojp.usdoj.gov/bjs/abstract/csllea00.htm, accessed 2 July 2007.

Government overseas, the FBI's International Program works with the support of the Department of State and at the pleasure of the ambassador, and FBI personnel are viewed as support resources for the embassy who work for the ambassador.

The Department of State supports the FBI Legat office by providing certain services and facilities for which the Office of International Operations is billed. Such services include office space, furniture, equipment, telephone service and other assistance required for business purposes. The issue of office space within the embassy can be a stumbling block in the establishment of a new Legat office since most, if not all, embassies are overcrowded and space is at a premium. The negotiations and subsequent build-out of the space may take several months or even years. During this interim period the Office of International Operations may elect to staff temporary space in the embassy with temporary duty (TDY) personnel rotated through the position on 60–90 day cycles pending the selection and deployment of permanently assigned employees.

STRUCTURE

In the early days management of the FBI's International Program was conducted in the Office of Liaison, later renamed the Office of Liaison and International Affairs (OLIA), at FBI Headquarters in Washington, DC, which reported directly to an Executive Assistant Director, who in turn answered only to the Director. OLIA's placement this high in the FBI's organizational structure guaranteed the Legat Program a significant degree of elitism and distance from the day-to-day operations in which most FBI personnel were routinely engaged. Legat personnel were often moved from one international assignment to another, frequently spending the majority of their career outside mainstream domestic operations. This meant that they were essentially unknown to their US-based colleagues who understood little if anything about the FBI's work in the international environment.

Today the International Program is managed by the Office of International Operations, headed by an Assistant Director, who is directly responsible to the Executive Assistant Director for the Criminal, Cyber Response and Services Branch. Within the Office of International Operations there are two sections, each managed by a Section Chief and Assistant Section Chief, and nine Units where oversight of the Legat offices is handled, each headed by a Unit Chief who is responsible to one of the Section Chiefs. Overall the Program is much more connected to the organization than it was in the past. International experience is valued as a desirable skill for career advancement, and an enormous number of FBI Special Agents have participated in international assignments and/or investigations.

The majority of Legat offices are staffed by the Legal Attaché and an Assistant Legal Attaché (ALAT), both Special Agent positions, along with one or two Legat Operations Specialists/Assistants.[3] Many Legat offices are responsible for vast territories encompassing many countries, and there may be sub-offices within the territory staffed with an ALAT and an Operations Specialist. Legat offices which are responsible for relations in extremely large countries such as Mexico and Canada may also have one or more sub-offices staffed with ALATs but managed by the Legal Attaché in the capital city. The size of the staff in a particular office is dictated by the investigative demands and the size of the territory as well as the strength and depth of the liaison relationships. Some offices with enormous workloads, such as London, Mexico City, Ottawa, Baghdad, and Bogotá, are staffed with several ALATs in addition to the Legat, and several Operations Specialists or Assistants.

The 60 Legal Attachés today are responsible for establishing relationships with all of the countries with which the US Government maintains diplomatic relationships. Many of the Legat offices cover large territories of countries where there may be only a little work during the course of the year. Nonetheless, the Legat is responsible for ensuring that appropriate relationships have been established with the host country law enforcement and intelligence services, and for establishing solid relationships within the embassy.

METHODOLOGY

The methodology of work varies greatly from one foreign nation to another throughout the Legat network. In one nation the government may permit Legat personnel to participate directly in resolving the requested investigation, while in other countries such participation may be strictly prohibited. Each Legat is obliged to determine the parameters of permitted participation and must advise headquarters and field divisions when and under what conditions such work can be allowed.

While the Legats and ALATs maintain the law enforcement and intelligence connections in the international arena which are vital to the success of FBI domestic investigations, they work solely at the behest of their US-based FBI counterparts, and their success at supporting domestic investigations flows from the quality and strength of their relationships with the host country authorities on which they rely for information. The Legat Program, as a support network for enhancing FBI investigations and federal prosecutions, is fully matrixed into the overall structure of the FBI.

Legal Attaché personnel do not initiate investigations nor do they independently conduct them with a view to US federal prosecution. They rarely, if ever, have the full view of any case, and, while they may make significant

3 Akin to secretaries, but with additional job responsibilities including tracking and managing the paper flow in the Legat office.

contributions to a case, they do not control it or make any decisions regarding potential investigative avenues to be pursued. However, any case involving an international connection will have involved a Legat either directly in the obtaining of information from the foreign authorities or in facilitating the travel and introduction of FBI personnel to the foreign authorities.

To illustrate this, let us take the hypothetical example of a terrorism investigation conducted by the FBI field division in Indianapolis, Indiana. During the course of this investigation a routine review of telephone toll records of the target's telephone in Indianapolis reveals that he/she has had contact with other telephone toll numbers in California, New Jersey, the UK, Germany and Saudi Arabia. The FBI agent responsible for the investigation would send a communication directly to the domestic field divisions in California and New Jersey where the telephone numbers originate, and also to the Legal Attachés in London, Berlin and Riyadh, requesting that the owners of the telephone numbers be identified. This communication would also ask that the local police be requested to provide any available information regarding the owners of the telephone numbers in question. In the foreign environment the Legat might also consider asking the intelligence services of the host country for whatever information is available regarding the owner of the number.

Mutual Legal Assistance Treaties (MLATs), treaties entered into between the US Government and a foreign government, are the foundation for obtaining investigative assistance which may be used as testimony in court or which may become a matter of public record, such as the statements of witnesses, co-conspirators, and individuals/institutions which provide documentary evidence such as bank records or physical evidence such as computer hard drives. MLAT requests are timely, quickly resolved and easily tracked. The MLAT permits direct requests between the foreign Ministry of Justice and the US Department of Justice's Office of International Affairs and eliminates the need for a letter rogatory, a formal diplomatic instrument requesting judicial assistance. In those countries where there is no MLAT in place the only method available for obtaining information for use as testimony in court is a letter rogatory, which is transmitted between the US Department of State and the foreign Ministry of Foreign Affairs or its equivalent. This process is, unfortunately, cumbersome, exceedingly drawn out and time consuming, and does little to encourage or enhance co-operation on matters of mutual investigative interest.

Extradition treaties ratified by the US Government and foreign governments control the way fugitives from justice may be returned to the US or the foreign country. For example, in December 2000, Eric Franklin Rosser[4] was the first child predator placed on the FBI's Ten Most Wanted Fugitives List. He had been charged with the production, distribution, receipt and transportation of child

4 www.news.findlaw.com/hdocs/docs/rosser/rosserindict.pdf, accessed 30 July 2007.

pornography. Rosser fled the USA, and travelled to the Netherlands, England, France, and then to Thailand, where he was ultimately arrested by the Thai authorities at the request of the Legal Attaché.[5] Pursuant to the extradition treaty between the USA and Thailand, Rosser was eventually returned to the USA. Legal Attachés in the Netherlands, France and the UK all co-ordinated extensive investigations with their host country colleagues in an effort to locate Rosser.[6] Absent an extradition treaty Rosser could not have been returned to the USA.

In countries with highly developed law enforcement services and well-established co-operation procedures it is often possible to simply forward a request and await the response. However, in those countries where the relationship is less well established or where co-operation is new and untested, it may take several personal meetings and significant advice from the Legat staff before the same task is accomplished.

Legal Attachés are held to the same service standards as those which are set forth for all FBI employees. Leads designated as 'Routine' must be forwarded to the appropriate services within 10 days, leads which are 'Priority' must be transmitted with two days, and leads which are 'Immediate' must be transmitted within two hours. While this is well-established FBI procedure, it is impossible to control the amount of time it takes to receive a response from the outside service. An 'immediate' lead might be transmitted to the foreign service within the mandated two hours, but the response might not be received for two or three weeks despite numerous calls and discussions emphasising the urgency of the request. Once the requested information has been received from the local service, a responding communication will then be prepared by the Legat staff and transmitted to the requesting FBI agent, and the request for assistance, or 'lead', is closed in the Legat office. On a practical level, a Legat can always call the field agent with any urgent information as soon as it is received and then follow it up with a written communication, but realistically everything is transmitted electronically in real time from the Legat's desk directly to the requesting agent in the USA. All Legat offices are linked electronically to the FBI network and all communications to or from the Legat, to or from the host country services, and to or from the domestic field divisions are individually retrievable through the FBI's information management system. More importantly, they can also be researched through the system using text searches. Although there are some exceptions based upon classification or 'need to know', all information in the FBI's network is transparent within the organization.

5 www.fbi.gov/libref/factsfigure/fugitives.htm, accessed 30 July 2007.
6 Based upon author's personal experience as Legal Attaché.

EXTENDING THE NETWORK

Decisions regarding where and when to open a new Legat office may be influenced by a number of factors, both positive and negative. Considerations or factors within the FBI, the Department of Justice or the Office of Management and Budget (where all federal budget submissions are reviewed) regarding the role and importance of the International Program, or the personal interest of Congressional representatives, may impact on the FBI's intention to open new offices.

In considering where and whether to open a new Legal Attaché office, the Office of International Operations continually monitors a wide variety of factors such as:

- increases in the number of investigative requests (sometimes referred to as 'leads') sent by domestic field divisions for a specific territory;
- changes in the complexity of investigation requested (for example obtaining telephone subscriber information versus extensive labour-intensive bank record examinations and interviews of witnesses);
- increases in the number of requests for FBI assistance received from the host government or law enforcement services; and
- training needs in the host territory.

In addition to the above information accumulated by the Office of International Operations, the Legal Attaché with current responsibility for the territory will routinely be asked to identify personnel needs for the future which may dictate the need for another Legat office within that territory (for example the Legat in Pretoria may identify personnel needs in Namibia which could ultimately become part of the justification for a new office in Windehoek). Keeping in mind that the budget planning is completed two years in advance of expenditure, the Legat must be able to forecast increases in workload, identify potential new demands on FBI resources, and analyse changes in the host country services which could impact on the FBI's local relationships.

The one overriding factor which can derail the establishment of a Legat office is world events which may overtake the best laid plans of any organization. These events can, and do, render all prior analyses and evaluations redundant. For example, the embassy bombings in East Africa in 1998 caused program managers at FBI headquarters along with their counterparts in Congress to immediately prioritize the creation of a Legat office in Nairobi (East Africa was then covered by the Legat office in Rome) despite the fact that none of the prior analysis suggested a law enforcement need for a Legat office in that region of Africa. The realization that terrorist organizations were targeting US interests in East Africa and other African nations forced the FBI to amend its strategy in response to world events. From today's perspective it seems clear that there was a need for an FBI presence in East Africa, but hindsight is always 20/20, and from this vantage point it is easy to second-guess decisions made or not made.

THE IDEAL LEGAL ATTACHÉ

Director Mueller has repeatedly stated that he views international experience as a significant enhancement to the skill-set necessary for all high-ranking managers in the FBI, and he has made it a priority to ensure that international experience is valued in the organization as a criterion for advancement. The process of selecting the best-qualified Special Agents for the Legat and ALAT positions, along with support personnel who can succeed in the foreign environment, is critically important to the international police co-operation mission of the Office of International Operations and enhances the development of well-qualified managers within the FBI. Errors made during the selection process can have an adverse impact on liaison relationships with the host country authorities; thus it is critically important that sufficient consideration be given to selecting the best candidates for these sensitive positions.

Policy changes implemented during the past 10 years seek to ensure that a wide range of employees become involved in the International Program. Overseas tours are now limited to five years unless exigent needs for the skill-set of a particular individual exist, and while this limitation results in the continual rotation of productive Legat employees back to domestic assignments, it ensures that individuals remain current with FBI policies and procedures and that they reconnect with the mainstream of the organization. A concerted effort is made by the Office of International Operations to lobby for the promotion of returning Legat employees to higher positions in other components within the FBI's hierarchy in order to ensure that both the Legat and ALAT positions are viewed as career enhancing.

Ideally the person selected for the Legat position should have all of the following basic skills:

- a minimum of five years' broad-based investigative experience;
- a specialty of investigative experience in the crime problem generally identified with the particular territory (for example financial crime experience for the candidate selected for Bern, Switzerland);
- a proven ability to work without direct and continual supervision (an independent work ethic);
- a minimum of two years' supervisory experience, either at FBI headquarters or in a field division;
- language fluency in the language of the country in which they will be resident;
- excellent interpersonal skills; and
- excellent liaison skills.

With the exception of management experience, the basic skills are the same for the ALAT position, although ALAT candidates with management experience are generally viewed as more qualified than their counterparts without management experience. Candidates who possess all of these skills are more likely to succeed, and will ultimately be a positive force for international police co-operation than those who do not have the full range of basic skills.

Unfortunately, not all international assignments generate the same level of interest. The Department of State characterizes some posts as 'hardship' locations where limitations on the length of the tour of duty and limits or prohibitions on the presence of family members/spouses may make one location much less desirable than another. Most of the posts with such prohibitions are those locations where there is the greatest turnover in the Legat and ALAT positions and where there are the fewest number of candidates applying for the jobs. In order to encourage a spirit of volunteerism and to address staffing shortages in some of the highest threat/hardship Legat offices, the Office of International Operations has proposed various incentives (such as increased promotional opportunities or transfers to another more 'desirable' Legat office upon completion of a tour in a hardship post) to increase the pool of qualified applicants for those offices. Director Mueller approved a variety of incentive packages in 2006 and these packages, coupled with shorter tours in the most difficult posts to fill, have increased qualified applicant interest appreciably.

As already mentioned above, the FBI is a domestic agency which has not previously identified foreign language ability as a desirable skill during the recruitment process. As a result, the agency has struggled with the ranking of language skills among the various criteria for selection for the Legat and ALAT positions. From time to time it has seemed more important to select personnel with the appropriate language skills, particularly when there was a need for rare and unusual language ability, rather than the full range of the qualities mentioned above. Inevitably this has led to difficulties for both the employee in the foreign environment and for program managers at FBI headquarters. Today, candidates for an overseas posting are selected more than a year in advance of deployment, and, for those who lack the necessary language skills, instruction is provided either through language instruction offered by the Department of State at the Foreign Service Institute, or commercial language instruction, such as Berlitz.

Other training programmes to familiarize the selected employees with the country they will be assigned to and with life in an embassy are offered. Moreover, some of the specialized training will involve the candidate's spouse in order to ensure that the family is able to acclimatize to life in a foreign country. Courses may include area studies classes offered by Department of State, security and safety overseas, defensive driving, and a wide range of training designed to familiarize the candidates with the operation of a Legat office. Some candidates, particularly those who will be responsible for opening a new office, may be offered the opportunity to travel to other Legat offices in order to observe how a fully operational office functions. Once at post, the FBI continues to pay for language training for both the employee and his/her spouse in order that they may further develop their language skills which will enable them to more readily adapt to life in the foreign environment.

From time to time, the Office of International Operations may also conduct training programmes for the Legal Attaché in co-operation with other federal agencies with an international presence in order to maximize the effectiveness and efficiency of the Legats where there is overlapping jurisdiction or where there may be competing interests for the same information. In the post-9/11 environment, positive co-operation with the other federal law enforcement agencies with a contingent of personnel either at post or in the region has complemented the Legat's ability to develop intelligence relating to threats against US interests at home and abroad.

GET ALONG TO GO ALONG

Not only is co-operation with the foreign authorities vital to the productivity of the Legat office, but co-operation in the embassy with the other US agencies can enhance the Legat operation and will contribute to the overall success of the mission. The Legat staff may encounter other federal law enforcement agencies, such as the Drug Enforcement Administration (DEA), the Immigration and Customs Enforcement Service and the US Secret Service at post. The overseas relationship between the FBI and the DEA is governed by a mutual agreement which makes the DEA the *only* contact for drug investigations outside the USA. Thus, the Legat is required to forward all leads received from domestic FBI offices which ask for investigation in drug-related matters to the local DEA Country Attaché for handling. The Legat and the DEA Country Attaché normally work closely together to resolve the requested investigation, and their positive working relationship complements the FBI investigative efforts in international drug-related investigations.

Since 9/11, in co-operation with local customs authorities, new initiatives regarding the pre-screening of containerized shipping destined for the USA (the Security Container Initiative) have become operational and a large number of Homeland Security (Immigration and Customs Enforcement) personnel may be assigned to the embassy to support this mission. While these Customs Enforcement Officers are assigned to the embassy staff, they are not generally housed at the embassy since their duties require them to be active at the shipping ports (which are generally not in close proximity to the embassy locations). In addition to these Customs Enforcement Officers, a small team of Customs Special Agents is also assigned to selected embassies worldwide. In these locations they may interact with host-country authorities on a variety of issues relating to the illegal importation of goods or contraband into the USA.

All of the federal law enforcement agencies at post must co-operate in an effort to maximize their effectiveness when working with the host-country authorities. It is not uncommon for the Legat to take the DEA Country Attaché, Customs Attaché or Secret Service Attaché out to meet his/her contacts in the local foreign services, and vice versa; nor is it unusual for them to meet together with their local colleagues to reinforce US interests to the host-country government components. Embassies are small communities, and it is extremely difficult to keep personality or jurisdictional conflicts secret, and even minor conflicts may be brought to the attention of the ambassador resulting in strained relations between the agencies and within the embassy.

CONCLUSION

The world is getting smaller, travel is easier, and borders are more porous. The European continent is united through the EU which has brought forth a finely developed concept of trade and travel. Where borders once existed between each country, it is possible today to travel throughout the Schengen Zone without ever taking your passport out of your pocket. While an excellent resolution to the movement of goods within a part of the EU, it has also enabled the criminal elements to travel and even relocate within this vast territory. Likewise, the porous nature of the US borders between Canada and Mexico and the ease of movement through the US makes it easy for criminal elements to move with impunity through the vast North and Central American territory.

Throughout its nearly 70-year history, the FBI's International Program has enhanced the mission of the agency by developing the international network vital to the success of FBI investigations and the development of crucial intelligence. It is true that the majority of the FBI's investigative interests are domestic and that most FBI employees will never participate in international matters but, when such contacts are needed, they are well-established and firmly grounded in the foreign environment. There is a Legal Attaché assigned responsibility for developing contacts with the law enforcement and intelligence services of every country in the world with which the US Government maintains diplomatic relations. While there may not be a Legat or ALAT in permanent residence in each country, the foreign government components should know who to call if they need the assistance of the FBI, and the Legat staff should be known in every embassy and to every ambassador throughout the world.

During a press conference on 11 April 2007, reported by the Daily Times of Lahore, Pakistan,[7] Thomas V. Fuentes, the current Assistant Director of the Office of International Operations, commented, 'The US would like to base an

7 K. Hasan, 'For FBI Pakistan is in the Middle East', 12 April 2007, www.dailytimes.com.pk/default.asp?page=2007%5C04%5C12%5Cstory_12-4-2007_pg7_11, accessed 21 July 2007.

FBI office in every country of the world, eventually.' Whether or not such an ambitious undertaking will ever come to pass, it is clear that the future of the Legat Program will be one of further growth and development. It is likely that some offices like Ottawa and Mexico City will continue to expand, while offices or sub-offices in other locations may be closed, consolidated or relocated due to such factors as a reduction in workload or shortfalls in appropriated staffing levels. Continual adjustments will need to be made in order to maintain the high efficiency and effectiveness of the International Program. And, as Fuentes went on to say in the same interview, 'We work in partnership with host governments and help when such help has been asked for.' The mission of the International Program to facilitate FBI investigations and intelligence-gathering will remain the same into the future and the methodology used to successfully fulfill that mission will continue to be to work in partnership with host-country governments throughout the world.

Chapter 10

No hiding place

How justice need not be blinded by borders

Kimberly Prost[1]

Note: Any views expressed are those of the author and are not attributable to any government or organization.

INTRODUCTION

With advances in technology, and the ease of global travel, the world we live in has become, in many ways, as Canadian author Marshall McLuhan predicted 'a global village'. This has had a dramatic impact on many aspects of life and society and law enforcement is no exception.

Globalization, fuelled by technological development and the opening of economic markets, has altered radically the framework for the interaction of nations politically, socially and economically. While many benefits have resulted, these have been accompanied by the negative by-products which historically always accompany progress. Perhaps the most notable developments in this respect have been the growth of transnational crime in its many forms.

Organized crime has expanded rapidly both with an increase of traditional forms such as drug and arms trafficking, and the rise of new threats from human trafficking, alien smuggling, cybercrime and money laundering. While with us from times of antiquity, we have seen corruption offences of staggering proportion which have shaken the democracies and economies of nations and which centre on the abuse of international markets and financial industries. And of course, the ever present dangers of international terrorism have become a deadly reality for all nations. One must also remember that even crimes committed within national borders – fraud, murder, sexual offences – increasingly have an international component to them which makes the gathering of evidence, as well as detection and apprehension, all the more difficult. All of these developments and the response of the international community to them,

1 Judge, International Criminal Tribunal for the Former Yugoslavia.

has created many new challenges, not the least of which fall to be met by law enforcement authorities the world over.

In a 1989 case, *United States of America v Cotroni*, the Supreme Court of Canada, made the following statement:

> The investigation, prosecution and suppression of crime for the protection of the citizen and the maintenance of peace and public order is an important goal of all organized societies. The pursuit of that goal cannot realistically be confined within national boundaries. That has long been the case, but it is increasingly evident today.[2]

What has unfolded in the nearly 20 years since that pronouncement, has evidenced that it was not only a prophetic declaration but perhaps an understated one. The challenge for law enforcement authorities in every nation is that sovereignty, a fundamental principle which grounds the relations of states, is also a major tool in the armoury of the criminal element in our societies. Criminals depend heavily upon the barriers of sovereignty to shield themselves and evidence of their crimes from detection. Organizations which orchestrate transnational crime and which then disperse and conceal the proceeds of their illicit activities the world over have no regard for national borders. In fact, by structuring their organizations to span borders, they are better able to protect their interests and organizations. They are positioned to take advantage of the differences between legal systems, the clash of bureaucracies, the protection of sovereignty, and, at many times, the complete incapacity of nations to work together to overcome their differences.

International co-operation in criminal matters – mutual assistance and extradition – are means which can be used to overcome the barriers of sovereignty and allow the international community to 'fight back'. Such co-operation measures are 'about' countries building bridges to overcome the differences in their legal systems and assisting each other in law enforcement matters. Driven by the necessity of our times, the last twenty years has seen a great expansion in the use of these legal tools and some important improvements and developments in their application. More and more successful investigations and prosecutions are dependent upon effective use of these measures. In essence, international co-operation in criminal matters has on a practical level come of age.

But despite the tangible progress, there remain many obstacles and challenges to effective co-operation amongst investigative, prosecutorial and judicial authorities the world over. The purpose of this text is to provide a brief overview of the world of international co-operation as it relates to judges, prosecutors and law enforcement authorities generally. The intent is to give a brief 'snapshot' of where we have been, where we are and the future challenges that we face.

2 *United States of America v Contronì* (1989) 48 CCC (3d) 193 at 215.

Two important caveats are necessary. The term 'international co-operation in criminal matters' is a broad one which encompasses many measures including everything from law enforcement exchanges and co-operation, agencies and facilities such as Interpol, as well as legal measures such as extradition, mutual assistance, transfer of sentenced prisoners, transfer of proceedings, and co-operation in the restraint and confiscation of proceeds of crime.

This chapter will focus strictly on legal measures and will address the three perhaps most common aspects of those which most directly impact on the work of judges, prosecutors and law enforcement – extradition, mutual assistance and co-operation in the restraint and confiscation of proceeds of crime.

Second, there can be no question that some of the most dramatic and significant developments in the world of international co-operation have arisen within the community of the EU. The adoption of measures such as the European arrest warrant and the concept of mutual recognition in evidence gathering are undeniably changes that few would have envisaged even as recently as ten years ago. However, these measures are of such a nature so as to merit an examination within a separate paper. More significantly, while important developments they are of restricted use and application at this time. The vast majority of nations still must rely on traditional measures for legal co-operation, including states within the EU in terms of their interactions with states outside that community. For these reasons, while the relatively new tools within the EU will be referred to in the course of the text, no attempt will be made to consider their operation in detail. Rather the chapter will focus on the challenges in international co-operation generally which constitute the reality for the vast majority of states.

PURSUING THE SUSPECT – EXTRADITION

Extradition is the surrender by one state, at the request of another, of a person who is accused or has been convicted of a crime committed within the jurisdiction of the requesting state.[3]

Extradition is the best known and certainly the oldest component of international co-operation in criminal matters. It is a concept which originated in ancient societies such as the Egyptian, Chinese, Chaldean, and Assyro-Babylonian.[4] As is often noted, the first recorded extradition treaty dates from circa 1280 BC when Ramses II, Pharaoh of Egypt, signed a peace treaty with the Hittites which expressly provided for the return of persons sought by each sovereign, who had taken refuge on the other's territory.[5]

3 A. W. LaForest, *Extradition to and from Canada* (3rd edn, Aurora: Canada Law Books, 1991).

4 M. Cherif Bassiouni, *International Extradition, United States Law and Practice* (3rd edn, New York: Oceana Publications, 1996), p. 1.

5 Ibid., p. 3.

While extradition has long been a component of the relations between states, its role and purpose has been altered radically through the ages. In ancient times and in fact up until the early 1800s, extradition was directed almost exclusively to the return of fugitives sought for political or religious offences. Extradition was viewed as a means to protect the political order of states.

In modern times, particularly the last 150 years, the focus of extradition has changed completely to common serious crime, which in many ways has replaced political offences as a major challenge to the stability of nations. In fact, quite ironically, political offences, the original focus of extradition have been, until very recently, generally excluded from extradition regimes.

Despite its long history and ancient roots, the practice of extradition has seen its most radical development in the last 50 years. Driven by the intersection of amazing advancements in global travel and the rise of criminality spanning borders, extradition, particularly between countries with vastly different legal systems, has changed substantially. The further enhancement of extradition relations and practices has become a priority for many countries and a number of international organizations.[6]

The basis for extradition

The first issue an investigator, prosecutor or investigating judge faces when a suspected or accused person in one of their cases or dossiers is located in a foreign state, is whether it is even possible to have that person extradited to face trial.

While historically controversial, it is the generally accepted view at international law that there is neither a legal nor moral duty upon states to extradite, in the absence of a specific binding agreement to that effect.[7] Because of this principle, many states, in particular those of a common law tradition, originally adopted legal regimes which did not allow for extradition in the absence of treaty. While civil law countries are not generally as restricted in principle to treaty-based extradition, there has been a general tendency to govern extradition relations on the same basis, often influenced by the need of a partner country to have in place such an instrument for extradition to proceed.

The result is that most countries have at least some bilateral extradition treaties and this remains the predominant and still, for many states, the exclusive basis for extradition.[8] However, considering the ever-expanding list of

6 See for example: 'Recommendations of the P8 Senior Experts Working Group on Combating Transnational Organised Crime', G7/P8 Summit, Lyon, 1996 www.uncjin.org/Documents/6comm/21_1e.pdf; 'Report of the Intergovernmental Expert Group on Extradition', Siracusa, 10–13 December 1996 as presented to the Commission on Crime Prevention and Criminal Justice, Sixth Session, Vienna, 28 April–9 May 1997; 'Resolution of the Ninth Congress on the Prevention of Crime and the Treatment of Offenders', A/Conf.169/16.

7 I. A. Shearer, *Extradition in International Law* (Manchester: Manchester University Press, 1971), p. 24.

8 Ibid., pp. 28–35.

nations, it is safe to say that the number of bilateral extradition treaties is clearly insufficient to address the growing need for extradition relations. This combined with growing pressure within the international community for improved international co-operation and general availability of extradition, especially for serious crime, has led to a trend toward alternative bases for extradition. The following is a brief overview of the network of instruments that ground modern extradition, as well as alternative approaches to treaty based relations.

Bilateral extradition treaties

As noted, many states have traditionally based their extradition relationships on bilateral treaties. Even today, there continues to be a vast web of bilateral extradition instruments particularly flowing from the traditional commitment of the UK, other Commonwealth states and the USA to treaty-based relations.

By example, in the 1800s, the UK negotiated several extradition treaties which were applicable to many of its realms and territories. For many years, even as those colonies attained independence, they continued to rely on the old imperial treaties for extradition relationships with many states. Some still do so today. Similarly, the USA has long required a treaty for extradition and thus has developed a broad network of bilateral instruments to govern extradition relations.

While other legal systems may not have evidenced the same strong commitment to bilateral treaty, many civil law states also have in place a broad web of bilateral extradition treaties with other states. The result is that bilateral treaties still dominate extradition practice, although there is an increasing tendency for states to consider alternatives because of the practical and political realities, and the problems of negotiating individual instruments to govern extradition relations with an ever-expanding world community.

Regional and other agreements or arrangements

With the inherent difficulties of negotiating bilateral instruments and yet the clear advantages of having some form of instrument upon which to ground extradition relations, there has been increasing resort in the second half of the twentieth century to regional agreements and schemes for extradition. These have become a popular alternative for many states.

While some arrangements have historic roots, for example, rendition amongst British possessions, such agreements and schemes saw a particular period of growth in the 1950s and 1960s. Generally the common bond for these instruments is the geographical location of the participant states but there are also those which are dependent upon common legal traditions. In some instances they reflect both geography and common legal tradition.

The following is a brief survey of existing regional agreements and schemes.

The European Convention on Extradition[9] *(European Convention)*

Perhaps the best success story in extradition, the Convention signed on 13 December 1957, in force on 18 April 1960, has served as an important instrument for the harmonization of extradition relations and practice amongst European states. The Convention serves as an actual basis for extradition and, until recent times,[10] was the most commonly used extradition instrument within Europe. As one of the first multilateral instruments for extradition, it reflects many of the fundamental principles recognized as general concepts adhered to by most states in extradition practice.

Commonwealth Scheme[11]

Commonwealth states, from the legal tradition of the common law, have adopted an alternate approach in the form of the *Commonwealth Scheme for the Rendition of Fugitive Offenders*, renamed in 2002 as the *Scheme for Extradition within the Commonwealth*. The scheme has its roots in the system for rendition between British possessions that was governed originally by an 1843 Imperial Statute[12] and subsequently the 1881 Fugitive Offenders Act.[13]

The scheme was adopted at the 1966 Meeting of Commonwealth Law Ministers, with subsequent amendments in 1986, 1990 and 2002. Unlike the European Convention, the scheme is not an actual instrument for rendition or now extradition. Rather it is a set of agreed recommendations, intended to guide Commonwealth governments in regulating their rendition relations with other Commonwealth states. Generally the scheme will be implemented within the relevant states through legislation and administrative action. The goal of the scheme is not to prescribe uniform legislation but rather to encourage the adoption of national legislation and practices amongst member states which will afford a high level of co-operation. Importantly, if properly implemented, the scheme allows for extradition to proceed between the 53 member states of the Commonwealth without the requirement for any form of underlying treaty. In essence the extradition is carried out on the basis of the legislation of the two relevant states. With some exceptions, most Commonwealth states have properly implemented the scheme such that the potential for extradition does exist,

9 European Treaty Series No. 24, 12 December 1957; Second Additional Protocol, 17 March 1978; European Treaty Series No. 98; First Additional Protocol, 15 October 1975, European Treaty Series 86.

10 See below, discussion of European arrest warrant.

11 Scheme Relating to the Rendition of Fugitive Offenders within the Commonwealth, 1966, now entitled The London Scheme for Extradition within the Commonwealth, www.thecommonwealth.org.

12 See An Act for the Better Apprehension of Certain Offenders, 1843, 6 & 7 Vict. ch. 34.

13 See Fugitive Offenders Act, 1881, 44 & 45 Vict. ch. 69.

albeit there are numerous practical challenges which may prevent its actual effective operation.

The Inter-American Conventions

There is a long and complex history of inter-American extradition conventions. Beginning in 1899 with the Montevideo Convention, subsequent conventions were adopted in 1911 and 1928. In 1933 the Second Montevideo Treaty was adopted, which was subsequently revised in 1940 and 1957.[14] On 7 February 1973 the Organization of American States proposed a new Draft Inter-American Convention on Extradition. With a number of intervening resolutions, this history ultimately cumulated on 25 February 1981 in the adoption of the Inter-American Convention on Extradition. While the convention entered into force in 1992, 30 days after the second ratification, as of 2007, only six[15] of the 35 member states are parties to it, with 10 others having signed but not ratified. As such, its effectiveness as an instrument for extradition is limited in scope.

The Benelux Extradition Convention[16]

Adopted by Belgium, Luxembourg and the Netherlands on 27 June 1962, the Convention on Extradition and Judicial Assistance in Penal Matters is an excellent example of how states which are closely related and limited in number will tend to develop more permissive relations with respect to extradition. While mirroring in many respects the provisions of the European Convention, some of the substantive articles in this Convention clearly reflect close ties of the State Parties.[17] Again recent developments within the practice of the EU have impacted on the application of this instrument

The Nordic States Scheme[18]

In 1962, Denmark, Finland, Iceland, Norway, and Sweden adopted the Nordic Treaty for Extradition. Similar to the Benelux agreement it reflects the close relations of the member states. Of particular note in the agreement is the recognition of 'juridical equality' of these states' citizens.

14 Op. cit., Cherif Bassiouni, fn 4, pp. 14–15; Op. cit., Shearer, fn 7, pp. 61–62.

15 The six parties are Antigua and Barbuda, Costa Rica, Ecuador, Panama, St Lucia and Venezuela.

16 See Bart de Schutter, 'International Criminal Law in Evolution: Mutual Assistance in Criminal Matters Between the Benelux Countries', Netherlands Journal of International Law, 14 (1967), pp. 382–410.

17 Op. cit., Cherif Bassiouni, fn 4, p. 12.

18 Ibid, p. 15.

The Arab League Extradition Agreement

The Convention was approved by the Council of the League of Arab States on 14 September 1952 and was signed by Egypt, Iraq, Jordan, Lebanon, Saudi Arabia, and Syria. However only Egypt, Jordan and Saudi Arabia have ratified it and thus it has been in force since 24 August 1958 but only in relation to these three states. The Convention, while a 'stand alone' basis for extradition, contemplates the existence of bilateral arrangements between State Parties.

Africa

In 1961, 12 of France's 14 former Equatorial and West African colonies formed the Union Africaine et Malagache. On 12 September of that year these states signed a convention on judicial co-operation at Tananarive.[19]

On 6 August 1994, 16 member states of the Economic Community of West African States signed a convention on extradition which will enter into force upon ratification of nine signatory states.

Multilateral Conventions

In the mid-twentieth century, in the face of crimes with effects of international proportion, a new approach to extradition developed in the form of multilateral conventions, directed at particular crimes, which included articles specifically relating to extradition.

Genocide and War Crimes Conventions

The earliest of such conventions, the Geneva Conventions,[20] which provide for basic principles of humanitarian law in the context of armed conflict, placed an obligation on states to either prosecute or extradite alleged offenders, applying the principle of *aut dedere aut judicare*. Thus State Parties to the Conventions are obligated to bring alleged offenders before their courts or hand them over to be tried by another party.

The subsequent Genocide Convention[21] while imposing an obligation on a territorial state to prosecute allegations of genocide, does not impose the *aut*

19 Ibid.

20 'Geneva Convention for the Amelioration of the Condition of the Wounded and Sick in the Armed Forces in the Field', 12 August 1949, 6 U S T 3114; 'Geneva Convention for the Amelioration of the Condition of Wounded, Sick and Shipwrecked Members of Armed Forces at Sea', 12 August 1949, 6 U S T 3217; 'Geneva Convention Relative to the Treatment of Prisoners of War', 12 August 1949, 6 U S T 3316; 'Geneva Convention Relation to the Protection of Civilian Persons in Time of War', 12 August 1949, 6 U S T 3516.

21 'Convention on the Prevention and Punishment of the Crime of Genocide', 9 December, 1948, 78 U N T S 277.

dedere aut judicare principle. However, Article VII of the Convention does provide that genocide and other acts covered by the Convention shall not be considered 'political offences' for the purpose of extradition.

Anti-terrorism Conventions

The 1971 Hague Convention for the Suppression of the Unlawful Seizure of Aircraft, was the first of a series of conventions, often described as 'anti-terrorism' agreements, which contained detailed articles on extradition. The Convention and several others which have followed[22] obligate states to take jurisdiction over the relevant convention offences and in the face of allegations, extradite the person or submit the matter to competent authorities for the purpose of prosecution. In addition these conventions provide:

(a) that the convention offences shall be deemed to be included as extraditable offences in any treaty existing between contracting states;
(b) if extradition is conditional on treaty and no treaty exists between two contracting parties, the convention may, in the discretion of the requested state, be considered as a treaty for extradition purposes; and
(c) if extradition is not conditional on treaty, the parties shall consider the convention offences extraditable.[23]

The advent of these multilateral conventions has meant an expansion of the base for extradition as between many states, at least with respect to these particular offences. The significance of the instruments has increased as well because of the surge in state ratifications spurred by the events of 11 September 2001 and the encouragement for such ratification set out in UN Security Council Resolution 1373.[24] Interestingly, and illustrative of the changes in policy arising from the growth of international terrorism, the latest conventions

22 The other relevant conventions containing similar provisions on extradition are as follows: 'Convention for the Suppression of Unlawful Acts against the Safety of Civil Aviation, 1971'; 'Convention on the Prevention and Punishment of Crimes against Internationally Protected Persons including Diplomatic Agents, 1973'; 'International Convention against the Taking of Hostages, 1979'; 'Convention on the Physical Protection of Nuclear Material, 1979'; 'Protocol for the Suppression of Unlawful Acts of Violence at Airports Serving International Civil Aviation, 1988'; 'Convention for the Suppression of Unlawful Acts against the Safety of Maritime Navigation, 1988'; 'Protocol for the Suppression of Unlawful Acts against the Safety of Fixed Platforms Located on the Continental Shelf, 1988'; 'International Convention for the Suppression of Terrorist Bombing, 1997'; 'International Convention for the Suppression of the Financing of Terrorism, 1999'.

23 See for example: 'Convention on the Prevention and Punishment of Crimes Against Internationally Protected Persons, Including Diplomatic Agents', 14 December 1973, 13 ILM 41 (1974); 'International Convention Against the Taking of Hostages', 18 December 1979, 18 ILM 1456 (1979); 'Convention Against torture and Other Cruel, Inhuman or Degrading Treatment or Punishment', 7 December 1984, 23 ILM 1027 (1984).

24 S/Res/1373 (2001), para. 3(d).

adopted on terrorist bombing and terrorist financing contain a provision which excludes the application of the political offence exception to the offences governed by the Conventions.

Crime Conventions

One of the most important multilateral instruments not only for extradition but also for related measures of mutual assistance and asset confiscation was the 1988 United Nations Convention against Illicit Traffic in Narcotic Drugs and Psychotropic Substances[25] (1988 Drug Convention). This instrument not only brought about significant advancement in extradition and other forms of co-operation with respect to drug trafficking and proceeds of drug trafficking offences but it served as the impetus to the development of subsequent conventions of this nature.

Article 6 of the Convention is dedicated to extradition and, *inter alia*, imposes a prosecute or extradite obligation on states where extradition is refused on the basis of nationality or because the offence was committed on the territory of the requested state. It also imports such an obligation where a state has, in its discretion, taken jurisdiction over offences committed extraterritorially and extradition is refused for other reasons.[26] The Convention also mirrors the various 'deeming' provisions found in the earlier 'anti-terrorism' conventions and provides for the Convention to operate as an extradition treaty if the requested state so decides in its discretion. With 183 State Parties, close to universality, this Convention provides a potential extensive base for extradition in relation to drug offences.

In December 1998, 10 years after the adoption of the 1988 Drug Convention, the UN General Assembly adopted a resolution establishing an open-ended intergovernmental ad hoc committee for the purpose of elaborating a comprehensive convention against transnational organized crime and discussing the elaboration of instruments addressing specific manifestations of such crime.[27] The work of the committee led to the adoption of the United Nations Convention against Transnational Organized Crime (TOC Convention), which was signed in Palermo, Italy in December 2000 and came into force on 29 September 2003. The Convention was accompanied by three protocols each addressing specific criminality of concern in the context of organized crime namely; Protocol to Prevent, Suppress and Punish Trafficking in Persons Especially Women and Children (Trafficking Protocol); Protocol against the Smuggling of Migrants by Land, Sea and Air (Smuggling Protocol) and Protocol against the Illicit Manufacturing and Trafficking in Firearms, Their parts and Components and

25 19 December 1988, 28 ILM 493 (1989), www.unodc.org.

26 See Article 6, para. 9.

27 General Assembly Resolution 53/111. 9 December 1998.

Ammunition (Firearms Protocol). The Trafficking Protocol came into force on 25 December 2003, the Smuggling Protocol on 28 January 2004 and the Firearms Protocol on 3 July 2005.[28]

The TOC Convention contains provisions on extradition which mirror those of the 1988 Drug Convention with only slight modification.[29] Thus for the offences covered by the convention and the protocols, as well as serious offences (punishable by four years' imprisonment or more) involving organized crime, there is once again a potential extended base for extradition under these instruments. With 135 parties to the main convention, 114 for the Trafficking Protocol, 107 for the Smuggling Protocol and 64 for the Firearms Protocol, the potential for extradition is quite significant.

Finally, there is the most recent in the serious of crime conventions, the United Nations Convention against Corruption (Corruption Convention)[30] which came into force on 14 December 2005 and has some 95 parties to it. With a series of obligatory and discretionary offences, the Convention further extends the possibilities for extradition in this subject area.

National legislation

The negotiation of bilateral, regional and multilateral treaties is a time consuming and resource intensive exercise. As well, it is simply unrealistic for any state to have a complete set of extradition instruments applicable to every nation in the world. For that reason, several countries have adopted an alternative approach; extradition without treaty on the basis of national laws, with or without a requirement for reciprocity.

By way of example, relatively new laws in both Canada and the UK contemplate extradition on the basis of bilateral treaty, as well as pursuant to multilateral instruments, the designation of a country on a schedule to the act or an ad hoc or case specific arrangement.[31]

While models vary, the concept is essentially the same. One of the central advantages of this approach to extradition is that it provides for a broader base for extradition, placing countries in a much better position to respond to the

28 Convention and Protocol, www.unodc.org.

29 As the Convention refers to four specific offences (participation in an organized criminal group, money laundering, corruption and obstruction of justice) and also relates to serious offences carrying a penalty of at least four years' imprisonment, the scope of the extradition provision is slightly modified from the 1988 Drug Convention. Under Art. 16 of the TOC Convention, the extradition provisions relate to the four specific offences and to any serious offence involving an organized criminal group and where a person sought is located in another State Party, provided there is dual criminality. The extradite or prosecute obligation is limited to cases where extradition is refused on the basis of nationality.

30 www.unodc.org.

31 See Canada Extradition Act, SC 1999, c18; Extradition Act 2003, Chapter 41, UK.

particular situations that may arise, where extradition is a necessity. It is also an approach of particular value to developing states and smaller jurisdictions where resources for treaty negotiation and legislative amendments are extremely limited. By adopting one flexible piece of extradition legislation which allows for a broad range of possibilities, the state will be in a position to address the various situations that may arise with a minimum use of resources.

It is interesting to note that expert working groups which have considered extradition practice have consistently recommended that countries consider the adoption of extradition regimes which allow for a flexible base for extradition.[32]

UN Model Treaty on Extradition

On the recommendation of the Eighth Congress, in 1990 the UN General Assembly adopted the Model Treaty on Extradition.[33] While it is not an actual instrument for extradition, it is an important document which can be used by states in the development of bilateral or multilateral extradition instruments. The Model, along with the manual[34] prepared as a guide for it, provide a detailed outline of the provisions of an extradition treaty and how best to implement the same.

Conclusion

While there is much discussion and debate in the international community about the benefits and drawbacks of these different approaches to grounding extradition, the good news for judges, prosecutors and other law enforcement practitioners is that there are simply more possibilities. Today, it is more likely that a prosecutor will find some basis for extradition, than existed five or 10 years ago. In that simple fact, there is progress.

Extraditable offences

The extradition process is a difficult and complex one which traditionally has not been available for all crimes but rather reserved for the most serious offences. Thus, there has long existed a concept of an 'extraditable offence' which signifies those crimes for which extradition has been available. This is another area of extradition which has seen considerable progress in recent times. In line with the development of criminal activity, the number and type of crimes for which extradition may be granted has been extended and, more

32 Op. cit., 'Report of the Intergovernmental Expert Group on Extradition', fn 6. 'Report of Informal Expert Working Group on Effective Extradition Casework Practice', Vienna 2004.

33 UNGA Res 45.116, www.un.org/documents/ga/res/45/a45r116.htm.

34 International Review of Criminal Policy, Nos. 45 and 46 available in printed form from UNODC at www.unodc.org.

importantly, the process for defining and determining extradition crimes is becoming more pragmatic. The progress has been twofold.

Non-list approach

Most extradition treaties developed in the late 1800s to the early to mid-1900s, defined extradition crimes by reference to a list of offences. The conduct involved had to be considered a crime in both states, which constituted one of the offences listed in the relevant treaty. The problems with that approach are legendary. New crimes would develop and the treaties, generally stagnant for many years, would not cover them. Terminology would change making it difficult to bring the alleged offences within the treaty list. The differing definitions and classifications of offences within states would make it difficult to bring specific kinds of conduct within the offences as described in the treaty list.

The 'new' approach to extradition, incorporated in most modern treaties and extradition laws, eliminates the list approach and substitutes a conduct and penalty test for defining an extradition crime. Specifically the conduct involved must constitute an offence punishable in both states, by a period of incarceration, as defined by the two states. For example, the Commonwealth Scheme provides that offences punishable by two years' imprisonment or a greater penalty will be extraditable. The European Convention includes offences punishable by one year's imprisonment or a more severe penalty. Similar formulas are incorporated into bilateral instruments and national laws.

For those charged with pursuing extradition in practice and who have struggled to bring criminal conduct within antiquated lists, the progressive amendment of extradition laws and instruments to reflect this approach is a much welcome relief.

Dual criminality

The second development, which parallels the first, is the employment of a relaxed test for dual criminality. The concept of dual criminality is a fundamental aspect of modern extradition law. For extradition to be possible the act in question must be a crime in both the requesting and requested states. While a seemingly simple requirement, in practice establishing dual criminality can prove to be one of the most challenging issues in an extradition case. The problems flow from the technical differences in how states define, name and prove criminal offences. For example, what may be called theft in one state may be larceny in another. While the conduct of the alleged offender may include all of the elements of fraud, as it is defined in both states, the definition of the offences might differ.

The result is that extradition cases have failed because of a technical approach to dual criminality. However, the modern test for dual criminality, incorporated in many extradition treaties and instruments, focuses not on technical terms or definitions but on the substantive underlying conduct.[35] Thus, the test is whether the conduct alleged against the fugitive would constitute a criminal offence in the requested state, regardless of whether the offences in the two states carry a different name or have different elements to them. The challenges posed by these differences have led to the development of principles for approaching a dual criminality determination. Those principles have arisen through case authority and can often now be found in bilateral treaties on extradition and in domestic law.[36] The United Nations Model Extradition Treaty describes these principles as follows:

> In determining whether an offence is an offence punishable under the laws of both Parties, it shall not matter whether:
>
> (a) The laws of the Parties place the acts or omissions constituting the offence within the same category of offence or determinate the offence by the same terminology;
> (b) Under the laws of the Parties the constituent elements of the offence differ, it being understood that the totality of the acts or omissions as presented by the requesting state shall be taken into account.[37]

These principles take the test for dual criminality away from an analysis of the legal classification of the offence to a consideration of the fundamental issue – would this be criminal here. The name of the offence, whether it is classified in the same manner or under the same type of statute or its description are not relevant considerations.

This leads to the most essential element of the modern dual criminality test, as it is applied in many jurisdictions, which is that it is a 'conduct-based' test. This development has greatly simplified and improved extradition practices and constitutes an excellent example of effectively bridging the differences between legal systems.

Practical issues in extradition for prosecutors

The practice of extradition is replete with problems, from the simple question of proper channels of communication, to the complex issue of the proper role of the political offence exception in modern day extradition. It is not possible to review this myriad of issues in a global overview of international co-operation.

Instead, it is perhaps most useful to focus on two issues which most often impact on the practice of extradition from a prosecutor or investigating judge's perspective. I would identify, those as:

35 See for example op. cit., United Nations Model Treaty on Extradition, Art 2, fn 33.
36 See for example Canada Extradition Act, SC 1999, c18 s 3(2).
37 Op. cit., United Nations Model Treaty on Extradition, Art 2(2), fn 33.

(a) evidentiary requirements; and
(b) the non-extradition of nationals.

Evidentiary requirements

Any criminal law authority seeking the extradition of an accused person for trial, after concluding that there is a basic extradition relationship between the states involved, will face the fundamental question of what material must be provided to the foreign state in support of the request.

While a seemingly simplistic question, this issue has been and remains a critical problem in extradition, particularly extradition as between civil and common law countries.

For civil law states, the issue of a warrant of arrest within a requesting state evidences that a judicial authority, within that state, has determined that there is sufficient evidence in the case. On that basis, the authorities in the requested state should be able to accept and rely on that determination and not look behind it to reassess the underlying basis of the decision. The warrant itself, along with a summary of facts sufficient for a determination of dual criminality and extraditable offence, with proper identification material, should be enough to ground extradition.

Traditionally, common law states have required, in addition to the warrant, the submission of evidence by the foreign state sufficient to meet a prescribed domestic standard. Many such states have also demanded that the evidence be adduced in a form consistent with the law of the requested state before extradition will be granted. This secondary requirement generally involves a requirement that statements of witnesses be provided which respect the common law rule that excludes so called 'hearsay' evidence. This means that each of the critical witnesses must provide an individual statement that recounts, with few exceptions, only that which the witness can give a first-hand account of, devoid of any reference to things he or she was told by others.

Meeting those demands for evidence often proves to be one of the greatest challenges in the extradition process. The problem is simple; the solution is not. When evidence must be adduced to meet an unknown standard, in a completely foreign format, it can prove to be an insurmountable hurdle to extradition. To meet this burden the requesting authorities are forced to generate an entirely separate package of evidence that they would not normally produce, which cannot be used in any ultimate domestic trial process against the particular accused. For the investigating magistrate or prosecutor in a non-common law state, the requirement for evidence is unquestionably the major challenge in pursuing the extradition of a suspect. And the problem is not solely an irritant as between systems of different legal tradition, but can arise between countries with the same general traditions but differing rules of evidence and differing approaches to extradition. Further, even if the systems are similar if not identical, common law authorities, while familiar with the domestic standards and evidentiary rules, still struggle to amass a sufficient amount of evidence in the extradition packet. This is increasingly the case with complex fraud, money laundering and terrorism cases where the amount of material required to meet the relevant standard in an admissible form can be staggering.

Historically, the result has been that many fugitives have escaped justice or found safe haven because it was impossible for countries to generate the level of material required in the form sought. It is no understatement to identify evidence as the most significant issue for investigative and prosecutorial authorities and in many instances the most significant issue for the extradition relations between many states.

Fortunately, there is a notable exception to these onerous requirements. The USA employs a lower threshold of proof that must be met and will accept evidence adduced in a summary form, without requiring that it meet the normal evidentiary standards of the requested state.[38] In addition, in recent times, several common law countries have eliminated the requirement for evidence in prescribed circumstances.[39] One other important development has been the adoption of an intermediate approach to the extradition standard in some countries which have before now employed the traditional requirements. This is the use of the 'record of the case', the essence of which is reflected in Clause 6 of the Commonwealth Scheme as an optional alternative approach to evidence requirements.[40]

Under this approach, the foreign state must still meet the domestic standard with the evidence adduced,[41] but there is no requirement for evidence to be submitted in a form that complies with domestic rules of evidence. Most importantly, there is no longer a requirement to submit first person statements which respect the hearsay rule. A summary of the evidence in the case will suffice. All the material submitted, whatever its format, can then be considered to determine if the relevant standard has been met.

To date few states have adopted this approach[42] but it remains a useful option for a jurisdiction that does not wish to maintain the strict traditional approach to evidence but for constitutional or other reason may not be able to adopt a pure 'no evidence' standard.

At the same time however there remain a number of common law states that have yet to modify their process.

38 The test is that employed for the issuance of a search warrant, whether there is sufficient 'probable cause'.

39 See for example UK Extradition Act 2003, Chapter 41, www.opsi.gov.uk; Australia Extradition Act, 1988, www.comlaw.gov.au.

40 See para. 6 of the London Scheme, www.thecommonwealth.org.

41 The standard is generally that of a *prima facie* case, which is the standard employed in a domestic context to determine if an individual will be committed to stand trial.

42 See Canada Extradition Act, SC 1999, c18, ss 31–34; see Statutes of the Republic of Trinidad and Tobago, Act No. 12 of 2004, 2 April 2004, ss 8, 9.

To the extent that there are states which require the submission of evidence, in a form admissible under domestic law, one of the central challenges in extradition practice is to develop ways and means of reducing the detrimental effect of evidentiary requirements. As with many problems in international co-operation, a critical component of the solution is enhanced communication between the relevant authorities in the different states that will increase understanding and knowledge about the demands of diverse legal systems.

Practitioners should check for relevant websites that might assist in understanding the requirements to be met. Individual countries and international organizations often maintain such sites which provide descriptive information as to what must be submitted in terms of evidence in support of a request.[43] While these can be extremely helpful, perhaps the most effective means of overcoming the obstacles is to endeavour to make informal contacts and initiate discussions with the proposed requested state, in advance of submitting formal documents. In the absence of any direct routes being available, relevant authorities can look to international organizations and associations to assist in identifying relevant contacts.[44] In addition some countries have liaison authorities which may be of great assistance in the preparation of extradition request material.

Before leaving this area it is useful to make reference to the developments within the EU which relate to this topic of evidentiary requirements. On 13 June 2002, the EU Council of Ministers adopted the Council Framework Decision on the European arrest warrant and the surrender procedures between Member States. By virtue of this decision, which was to be implemented by Member States through domestic law by 1 January 2004, a concept of a European arrest warrant valid throughout the Union has been established. The arrest warrant is founded on the principle of mutual recognition of judicial decisions.[45] It means that a decision by the judicial authority of a Member State to require the arrest and return of a person should be recognized and executed in other member countries.

While this approach eliminates requirements for the production of evidence, unlike the developments discussed above, this European arrest warrant does not bring about changes to an existing extradition process. Rather it replaces extradition with a mutual recognition and execution procedure. It differs

43 See for example Organization of American States, www.oas.org; UK Home Office, www.police.homeoffice.gov.uk/operational-policing/extradition-intro/, accessed 24 August 2007.

44 For example the United Nations Office on Drugs and Crime, www.unodc.org; Commonwealth Secretariat, www.thecommonwealth.org; Council of Europe, www.coe.int; Eurojust, www.eurojust.europa.eu; International Association of Prosecutors, www.iap.nl.com.

45 The arrest warrant is one means by which the principle of mutual recognition is being implemented; similar initiatives are underway with respect to judicial orders related to evidence gathering.

substantially from extradition procedures in several important respects including the elimination of dual criminality requirements for the most serious offences and of any political component to the process, as well as removal of the bar on the extradition of nationals.

Non-extradition of nationals

In many states, particularly of civil law tradition, by their constitution, law or practice, the extradition of nationals is prohibited. In most instances, countries which do not extradite nationals will have domestic jurisdiction to prosecute their citizens for offences committed in the territory of a foreign state.

Thus, many extradition treaties reflect the principle that, where extradition is refused on the basis of nationality, the case should be referred to competent authorities in the requested state with a view to prosecution.[46] These articles reflect the *aut dedere aut judicare* principle and are intended to ensure that a criminal will not escape and find safe haven on the basis of nationality.

However, it is increasingly evident that domestic prosecution of offences committed outside the country is a process replete with problems. The following description is taken from the report of a UN expert working group on extradition:

> It was noted that the use of the principle *aut dedere aut judicare* would in theory be an alternative to the extradition of nationals and had on some occasions proved effective. There were, however, several significant practical problems in its application, including the low priority assigned to such prosecutions by overburdened requested states. The difficulty and costs of obtaining evidence from the requesting state, and the serious burdens imposed by such trials on the victims, witnesses and other persons, were cited as examples. These problems significantly impeded the effectiveness of this alternative to extradition.[47]

Because of the litany of practical problems, it is no longer possible for states to ignore the growing problems associated to the non-extradition of nationals. And this reality has led some countries to critically examine their extradition practice in relation to nationals. Some states, particularly in Latin America where extradition of nationals has traditionally been prohibited, have in recent times altered this position and allowed for the extradition of nationals either generally or for particular offences.[48] It should also be noted that the introduction of the European arrest warrant constituted a major step forward in terms

46 See for example op. cit., United Nations Model Treaty on Extradition, Art 4(a), fn 33.

47 Op. cit., Report of the Intergovernmental Expert Group on Extradition, fn 6, para. 19.

48 See for example Argentina, Colombia and Mexico.

of the extradition of nationals. As noted above, at least amongst EU Member States, nationals must now be surrendered to other states despite long traditions within the region to the contrary. While restricted to a very limited context, one can also view the surrender of nationals to international tribunals and the International Criminal Court as further movement away from the traditional position.

Short of abolishing the prohibition, other alternatives are also being developed. One encouraging example can be found in the Treaty on Extradition between the Netherlands and the United States. In this treaty, both parties have agreed to the extradition of nationals provided that the two states are also bound by a prisoner transfer treaty, which would allow for the return of the person for service of any sentence imposed. Such an approach and variations thereof[49] have been recommended in various international fora and have been incorporated into international instruments as alternative means of meeting the prosecute or extradite obligation.[50]

However, it is not realistic to expect dramatic change in domestic policies on the issue of non-extradition of nationals overnight. In many instances, the principles are deeply entrenched and in some countries are constitutionally enshrined. Thus, practitioners will continue to face situations where the extradition of nationals will not be possible. For those cases, there are many challenges for judges, prosecutors and investigators, who wish to see the alleged offender brought before a court for an effective trial. Initially, the prosecutor in the requesting state will have to make a decision whether to press for prosecution in the foreign state or await an opportunity for circumstances where extradition might be possible (for example if the fugitive travels to another state). If prosecution is to be pursued in the foreign state, the relevant authorities in both jurisdictions will have to consider how best to ensure the transmission of evidence to the prosecuting state. And as long as the non-extradition of nationals remains a reality, it will be critical that the challenges in these cases be met. For without solutions that bring the fugitives to justice in some forum, safe haven for nationals will be the reality.

PURSUING THE EVIDENCE – MUTUAL ASSISTANCE IN CRIMINAL MATTERS

Every justice system in the world requires some form of evidence for use in the adjudication of criminal culpability for an alleged offence. Whatever the system for determining guilt or innocence, be it free evaluation of all relevant

49 e.g. the temporary transfer of a person for trial only.

50 See op. cit., Recommendations of the P8 Senior Experts Working Group on Combating Transnational Organised Crime, fn 6; TOC Convention Art 16, para. 11; op. cit., Corruption Convention, Art 44, para. 12, fn 30.

information or consideration of only that which meets specified rules of accessibility, the criminal justice process functions on the basis of an assessment of evidence. Evidence then is the focus point for investigators, prosecutors and judges. It is what they need to do their jobs.

Mutual assistance[51] in criminal matters is a process by which states seek and provide assistance in gathering evidence for use in criminal cases or in the restraint and confiscation of proceeds of crime.

In earlier times, most law enforcement and prosecutorial authorities would go through their entire career, without ever having to obtain evidence from outside national borders. Today there are literally thousands of requests transmitted between states seeking assistance in evidence gathering and most investigators, judges and prosecutors will have at least one case where they will need to obtain evidence from a foreign state for use in a prosecution. And it is for that reason that mutual assistance has become the fastest growing business in the criminal justice field.

Background

Countries have long assisted each other in gathering information and evidence for criminal investigations and prosecutions. There are well established police-to-police channels through which much essential information has been and continues to be shared. These channels range from direct relationships between police officers and police forces, the posting of police liaison personnel in foreign states, to the auspices of Interpol. All of these measures remain critical to co-operation in evidence gathering and have not been replaced by the more formal process of mutual assistance.

But the reality is that there are types of assistance which cannot be provided between states, through police or informal channels. The most obvious is where the type of assistance sought will require resort to the legal process within the requested state, where some type of judicial order or compulsory measure must be applied to produce the desired information or evidence in an acceptable form.

For example, where a country is seeking the production of bank records or the search of a residence, there is need for a judicial process through which the appropriate authorization can be obtained for those records to be obtained or the search carried out.

For many years, states were required to rely entirely upon traditional letters rogatory submitted through diplomatic channels to gain access to such evidence.[52] However, in our modern age, this method has become insufficient

51 Also referred to as Mutual Legal Assistance.

52 A letter rogatory is a letter emanating from a judicial authority in one state seeking assistance from a judicial authority in another state. While many civil law countries will also call requests for assistance submitted through a mutual assistance process 'letters rogatory', this is simply because the request in such jurisdictions emanates from a judicial authority.

to meet the growing demand for speedy and effective assistance in evidence gathering.

Letters rogatory did not provide for the scope of assistance required, nor were they efficient enough to allow for the production of the evidence within a reasonable period of time. As well, because of fundamental differences between investigative authorities and process in civil and common law states, letters rogatory were in many instances ineffective between states of a different legal tradition. The problem was particularly acute for common law states where judicial authorities have limited involvement during the investigative phase when evidence from other states may well need to be obtained.

In the second half of the twentieth century, the need for alternative methods of evidentiary assistance was apparent. The identifiable gaps, combined with the rise of terrorism and transnational organized crime, combined to spur the development of mutual assistance in criminal matters, a new concept for co-operation in evidence gathering. Mutual assistance was 'an idea whose time had come'.

The features of mutual assistance

Mutual assistance in criminal matters is a mechanism of co-operation which allows for a wide range of assistance between states in the production of evidence, in a direct and efficient manner. Generally rendered on the basis of bilateral or multilateral treaty, though increasingly on the basis of national laws,[53] mutual assistance provides a means for one state to obtain evidence from another state for use in a criminal investigation/prosecution.

One of the major advantages of this form of co-operation is that it covers a broad range of assistance including *inter alia*, taking evidence from or statements of persons, search and seizure, the provision of documents or evidentiary items, the service of documents, and the temporary transfer of persons to assist an investigation or appear as a witness. As well, assistance can be rendered at any stage of a criminal process from investigation to appeal. Mutual assistance is also used in order to obtain the restraint and confiscation of proceeds and instruments of crime, a topic which will be addressed in more detail in the next section.

Generally mutual assistance can be rendered directly between competent authorities in the two states, often justice ministries. This is one of the features of mutual assistance which makes it an effective and efficient mechanism of co-operation: the direct channelling of requests without necessity, for use of diplomatic or other channels.

53 In some countries, mutual assistance is provided for on the basis of domestic legislation which is either applied generally to all states or to designated states on the basis of reciprocity. See for example Switzerland and the UK.

The instruments of co-operation

Over the last decade great strides have been made in the development of a framework of instruments for the rendering of assistance.

The first significant instrument for mutual assistance was the European Convention on Mutual Assistance in Criminal Matters, developed by the Council of Europe, entered into on 20 April 1959, in force 12 June 1962.[54] It was an important achievement of its time in its recognition of the necessity for specific instruments for co-operation in evidence gathering. However, like all new instruments, it had limitations. Perhaps the most notable in this instance was that the Convention was designed to operate amongst states of like legal tradition, the civil law states of Europe, and it therefore did not address perhaps the most significant challenge to effective mutual assistance, bridging the differences between legal systems.

Similarly, within the Commonwealth, in 1986 law ministers in Harare, Zimbabwe, adopted a scheme for mutual assistance.[55] It is a non-treaty-based scheme, like the London Scheme for extradition considered above, which depends upon states enacting domestic legislation to permit the rendering of assistance in criminal matters. However, it too is based on the commonality of systems.

In between the creation of these two multilateral instruments of co-operation, individual states began to develop treaties on a bilateral basis, to allow for the provision of assistance and most notably the provision of assistance between states of different legal traditions. The oft-cited example of the first breakthrough instrument is the treaty between the USA and Switzerland which came into force in January 1977.[56] Since then, there has developed a network of bilateral instruments between states of similar or different legal tradition. Those agreements are further supplemented by domestic legislation within some states which allows for assistance to be rendered on the basis of reciprocity, designation or administrative arrangement.

Similar to extradition there has also been an increasing development of regional agreements for mutual assistance. Some recent examples include the Inter-American Convention on Mutual Legal Assistance in Criminal Matters,[57] and the Economic Community of West African States Convention on Mutual Assistance in Criminal Matters.[58]

Another advancement in the field of mutual assistance came with the adoption

54 European Treaty Series No. 30, Strasbourg: Council of Europe, www.conventions.coe.int.

55 Scheme Relating to Mutual Assistance in Criminal Matters within the Commonwealth, Commonwealth Secretariat, London, LMN (86) 13, www.thecommonwealth.org.

56 Lionel Frei and Stefan Freschal, 'Origins and application of the United States – Switzerland Treaty on Mutual Assistance in Criminal Matters', Harvard International Law Journal, 31 (1990), pp. 77–79.

57 Canada Gazette, Part I, Vol. 130, No. 35, p. 2483.

58 Signed July 1992.

by the UN General Assembly of the Model Treaty on Mutual Assistance.[59] The Model Treaty provided an excellent guide for nations wishing to develop mutual assistance treaties and for the first time it allowed for the fundamental principles underlying the process to be elaborated and agreed upon by member states of the UN.

However, without question, the most important instrument for the advancement of mutual legal assistance was the 1988 Drug Convention. The inclusion of a 'stand alone' provision on mutual assistance within the Convention has often been referred to as the adoption of a mini-treaty within a treaty. In addition to its practical effect, it also constituted recognition of the integral role mutual assistance plays in combating crime, in this instance drug trafficking. That message has been reinforced with respect to transnational organized crime generally within the international community in various statements arising from international fora.[60] It has been further concretely recognized with the inclusion of similar extensive articles on mutual legal assistance within the subsequent TOC Convention and the Corruption Convention.

What is important about the inclusion of these detailed mutual assistance articles is that, unlike the provisions relating to extradition, they do not operate on a discretionary basis. That is, unless there is a bilateral agreement between the two parties, State Parties to these conventions are obligated to render mutual assistance in respect of the relevant offences on the basis of the Convention provisions. In addition, if it will be beneficial the parties can also agree to use the convention in place of an existing bilateral instrument. Given the number of State Parties to the various conventions, this means that there is a broad basis for the rendering of mutual assistance at least with reference to drug, organized crime and corruption offences.

While the provisions in the anti-terrorism conventions are not of a detailed nature, there is an argument to be made that they also place an obligation on State Parties thereto to render mutual assistance to other parties in respect of terrorism offences. This position is bolstered by UN Security Council Resolution 1373 which obligates states to provide the greatest measure of assistance with respect to terrorism investigations.

Central authorities

One of the key components of the mutual assistance process, identified above, is the direct channelling of requests between relevant authorities be it justice

59 General Assembly resolution 45/117, UN GAOR 45th Sess., Supp No. 49A at 215.

60 See 'Naples Political Declaration and Global Action Plan' adopted at the World Ministerial Conference on Organised Transnational Crime, November 1994; 'Report of the Oxford Conference on Mutual Legal Assistance', 5–9 September 1994, Christ Church, Oxford (London: Commonwealth Secretariat, 1994); op. cit., Recommendations of the P8 Senior Experts Working Group on Combating Transnational Organised Crime, fn 6.

ministries, prosecution offices or other similar bodies. These authorities through which the process operates are often referred to by the term of art 'central authority'. Most bilateral and multilateral instruments include a provision calling for the establishment or designation of a central authority responsible to present and receive requests for mutual assistance. While envisaged originally as the bodies which would speed up the process for transmission by allowing for direct communication, experience has shown that central authorities have a far more critical role to play in effective mutual assistance.

A good central authority will be much more than a post box for requests for assistance. If properly staffed with experienced and trained personnel it will operate as a critical resource point for both foreign and domestic authorities. Thus, the relevant investigative and prosecution authorities, both foreign and domestic, will be able to contact the central authority to obtain advice and information in relation to requests. As well, the central authority will be responsible to either promptly see to the execution of requests or transmit them to executing authorities and encourage prompt execution.

Central authorities also have an important role to play in following up on the requests that have been sent to other states. Delay is a significant problem in mutual assistance. One often hears tales of requests being submitted and no reply being received for months or even years. While such delay justifies complaints with reference to the requested state, they also highlight deficiencies within the central authority of the requesting state. No request can be left without follow-up for such an extended period of time. A good central authority will be a persistent, even pesky one, which seeks follow-up information on its requests.

What is clear from experience is that the difference between the success and failure of a mutual assistance programme is often directly linked to the effectiveness of the central authority. For this reason, the importance of a central authority has been stressed in several multilateral fora and the functions of the optimum authority have been highlighted in various documents and instruments.[61]

One other point needs to be highlighted with regard to these authorities. Effectiveness of a central authority is not dependent on its size. While the authority needs proper resources to function, what that will entail will vary depending on the domestic context and considerations such as the volume of requests and the nature of the jurisdiction. A good central authority can range

61 See 'Report of the Oxford Conference on Mutual Legal Assistance', 5–9 September 1994, Christ Church, Oxford (London: Commonwealth Secretariat, 1994); op. cit., 'Recommendations of the P8 Senior Experts Working Group on Combating Transnational Organised Crime', fn 6; 'Report of the Expert Working Group on Mutual Legal Assistance and related International Confiscation', Vienna, 15–19 February 1993 and 'Report on Mutual Assistance Best Casework Practice', Vienna, 2001, both available at www.unodc.org; see also op. cit., Corruption Convention, Art 46, para. 13, fn 30.

from a large office such as the US Office of International Affairs within the Department of Justice to a smaller unit or even just one or two people within an office who are designated as the responsible officials for mutual assistance.

Practical issues for prosecutors

Effective implementation

The framework of international instruments for the rendering of assistance is an impressive one. As well, increasingly there is recognition that the principles of mutual assistance are such that agreements are not a necessary pre-requisite for it. More and more states are looking towards the adoption of flexible legislation which will allow for the seeking and obtaining of such assistance without the need for underlying treaties or agreements. Therefore relevant authorities will find more and more opportunities available to them for assistance in evidence gathering.

However, no matter how complete the network of agreements may be and regardless of how well-crafted the instruments of co-operation are, none of that is of much value, if it is not possible to present a request for assistance and receive evidence in an acceptable form, in an effective and timely fashion.

Unfortunately, in a great number of cases, despite the existence of an applicable instrument, evidence is not forthcoming; it arrives in a form such that it is not useful to requesting authorities; or it is provided so late as to be of little practical value.

The critical problem is lack of or inadequate programmes and procedures for effective implementation of mutual assistance programmes and the provision of evidence on a practical, case-by-case, level. Admittedly, significant progress in the effective implementation of mutual assistance obligations the world over can be achieved through state action. Governments must enact the relevant legislation, negotiate the necessary instruments and establish some form of administrative framework for the processing of mutual assistance requests and apply sufficient resources to implement requests.

But effective implementation is not limited to legislation and administration. It runs far deeper than that. A country may have an excellent legislative and treaty scheme for mutual assistance and an established administrative process and it still may be virtually impossible to provide or receive effective assistance because the best designed system is only as good as the people who operate it on a practical level. In many instances, success in mutual assistance is dependent on the knowledge and most critically – the flexibility – of the authorities requesting and, even more importantly, providing the assistance.

It is quite understandable that authorities raised within a particular legal tradition have a natural bias for the approach and practices of that legal tradition. As well, in providing foreign states with access to compulsory process within a given state, there will be, whether by virtue of constitutional or legislative requirements, constraints on what measures are available and in what circumstances.

However, one of the most important goals of mutual assistance is the bridging of differences between legal systems. This goal can be realized only if the authorities entrusted with execution approach mutual assistance requests with a view to overcoming the differences and not entrenching them.

The governing philosophy for mutual assistance must be to provide the widest scope of assistance possible and to provide that assistance in a useable form for the requesting state. For mutual assistance to succeed, the operative principle must be that requests will be executed in accordance with the law of the requested state and, to the extent not prohibited by that law, will be provided in the manner sought by the requesting state. In other words, while authorities in a requested state must always meet the standards prescribed by domestic law, unless the rendering of assistance in the form sought would constitute a violation of that law, it should be provided. If that principle does not govern at the operational level, mutual assistance will fail. This is unquestionably the central challenge that practitioners face each day. The importance of this point is perhaps best illustrated by example.

Generally in common-law legal systems, police and prosecutors are responsible for the questioning of witnesses. At the investigative stage, police or, in some systems, prosecutors will gather witness statements. During the trial process, it is the prosecutor and defence counsel who will conduct the examination and cross-examination of each witness. While a judge may occasionally ask a question during a trial, by the law of those states, judges do not gather the evidence of witnesses nor conduct examinations before the court. In contrast, many civil-law systems have investigating judges who will take witness statements and include or summarize evidence in the preparation of their files or 'dossiers'.

If an investigating judge seeks to interview a witness in a common-law state, strictly speaking, it would be 'inconsistent' with the law of the requested state for that judge to conduct the interview. It would not however be a violation of domestic law if the judge were allowed to conduct the interview. In this instance, success or failure depends entirely on whether the authorities in the requested state allow the evidence to be gathered in an appropriate form for the requesting state, even where it is inconsistent with the normal process employed in the requested state.

A similar example arises in the reverse scenario. In a civil-law system very often an investigating judge hearing a witness will prepare a summary or 'proces verbal' of what the witness said. In the common law, when a witness is examined and cross-examined before the court his or her evidence must be recorded verbatim. A summary or 'proces verbal' is not admissible. If a request is made by common-law authorities to take the evidence of a witness in the foreign state and to record the evidence verbatim, once again that process would be inconsistent with the practice of the requested state. However, the foreign authorities would not be violating the law by allowing a verbatim record. Again, it is a question of flexibility and the philosophy employed in the requested state.

The need for flexibility is not limited to authorities called upon to execute a request for assistance. Requesting authorities too must strive to submit materials which will meet the requirements of the requested state and which will be workable and useful to authorities in a state of a different legal tradition. Submitting a request which meets all of the requirements of the domestic law of the requesting state but none in the requested state does little to facilitate the provision of assistance.

While the proper choice in these examples may seem incredibly obvious and simple, in reality, there are a multitude of examples of instances where mutual assistance requests are frustrated because of a rigid adherence by authorities to their own domestic practices. Unless requesting and executing authorities recognize and employ a flexible approach, mutual assistance will fail.

Sufficient information

As in extradition, a great deal of the frustration in mutual assistance flows from the differences between legal systems, with a resulting lack of understanding as to what information must be included in a request for assistance, in what detail and in what form. Clearly, it is not possible to cover in a single chapter what each system demands by way of information to support a request. However some general recommendations are possible.

When faced with seeking assistance from a foreign state, the obvious 'first source' to consider is any applicable treaty or other instrument which should outline the information to be included in the request. In the absence of a treaty or often in addition to it, authorities will want to consult with the central authority (if there is one) within his or her own state. And finally, in many instances, only discussions between authorities in the two states will produce adequate information. Once again, for this, the existence of central authorities within the two relevant states will greatly facilitate the transmission of relevant information.

Practical tips

Without attempting to address the substantive requirements of legal systems, which will vary from one state to another, the following are five basic general tips on the content of requests that would appear to be applicable for all states.[62]

62 See also 'United Nations Manual for the Model Treaty on Mutual Assistance in Criminal Matters', *International Review of Criminal Policy*, Nos. 45 and 46, p, 41.

Non-system-specific language

Every legal system has its own terminology. For example, an 'affidavit' may have meaning in Malta but not in Switzerland. As a request for assistance is addressed to and intended for a foreign authority, system-specific terminology should be avoided. Instead the request should describe what is sought, rather than referring to a term. For example, rather than 'affidavit', the request should refer to a statement which is sworn or affirmed to by the person providing it.

Relevance

While the test that must be met before a compulsory order will issue can vary from state to state, in almost every legal system the relevance of the evidence sought to the investigation or prosecution will have to be established. Every request for assistance therefore should address that issue (namely there should be a clear description of why or how the evidence in question is relevant to the investigation or prosecution).

Specificity

In most legal systems 'fishing expeditions' are not permitted. All requests for assistance should be specific as to the assistance sought. For example, if the requesting authorities are seeking bank information they will need to provide an indication, if not of a specific bank account, at least sufficient information for the relevant bank to be identified in the requested state. The type of information needed from those accounts and the time period should also be indicated.

Form of evidence

In preparing a request, prosecutors should focus not only on the evidence sought but the form or manner in which the evidence must be provided for it to be admissible at trial. Those requirements as to form and procedure must be set out in detail in the request and be included from the very beginning. For example, if a country requests bank documents, it may be necessary to obtain an accompanying certificate for the documents to be admitted at trial. If that is the case, the certificate should be provided with the request to avoid unnecessary duplication of work in the requested state.

Time constraints

Requests for assistance take time to execute. While urgent situations and emergencies may arise, investigations and prosecutors should strive to submit requests on a timely basis, with reasonable deadlines that take into consideration the resource constraints in a requested state.

Conclusion

Mutual assistance has come a long way in a very short period of time for an instrument of international co-operation. The challenge for the future lies in the effective implementation of the instruments of co-operation which have been developed. The success or failure of mutual assistance rests not only with governments but with competent authorities, such as prosecutors, who seek and render the assistance on a practical level.

PURSUING THE PROFITS – CO-OPERATION IN THE RESTRAINT AND CONFISCATION OF PROCEEDS OF CRIME

It is a twentieth-century reality that crime is big business. Recent estimates indicate that the illegal drug trade alone involves billions of dollars. The figures related to offences in cases of 'grand corruption' are staggering. And the list goes on and on. From fraud to human trafficking, on a small scale or large, money makes the crimes go on. And with the lucrative nature of economic-based crime it is evident that many criminals have come to consider prison sentences as simply a necessary cost of doing business.

In our modern world, to effectively combat any economic-based crime it is critical to attack that which motivates individuals to commit the crime – profit. To that end, co-operation in tracking, restraining and confiscating the proceeds of crime has become a major component of international assistance.

While the concept of the state taking 'ill gotten gains' away from criminals has been, in some way, reflected in legal systems for many years, the encouragement and development of a large scale, internationally recognized effort to remove proceeds of crime from criminals is a relatively recent phenomenon.

Instruments and methods of co-operation

1988 Drug Convention

The most significant milestone for the advancement of co-operation in this field was the negotiation and coming into force of the 1988 Drug Convention. For the first time, pursuit of the proceeds of criminal activity was given a 'starring' role in an international instrument intended to combat crime. The motive behind the Convention measures, which are directed at the restraint and confiscation of proceeds of crime, are well described in the preambular paragraphs to the Convention:

> ... Aware that illicit traffic generates large financial profits and wealth enabling transnational criminal organizations to penetrate, contaminate and corrupt the structures of government, legitimate commercial and financial business and society at all its levels ...
>
> Determined to deprive persons engaged in illicit traffic of the proceeds of their criminal activities and thereby eliminate their main incentive for so doing ...

The Convention obligates State Parties to, *inter alia*, create an offence for 'money laundering'[63] and, subject to constitutional or other basic concepts of the applicable legal system, to criminalize the knowing acquisition, possession or use of property derived from the convention offences.

In addition, and perhaps most significantly, the Convention requires State Parties to create mechanisms in domestic law which would allow for the tracing, restraint (freeze or seize) and confiscation of the proceeds of drug related crime. And, in recognition of the transnational dimension of this criminal activity, State Parties also must be able to respond to requests presented by other states, seeking the tracing, restraint and confiscation of the proceeds of drug offences committed in a foreign jurisdiction.

The latter requirement is critical because experience demonstrates that sophisticated criminal organizations launder and distribute the proceeds of their activities, through many countries using a vast array of businesses, institutions and organizations. The reality is that without the assistance of other states, no country can successfully investigate, restrain and confiscate the profits of a sophisticated criminal organization. It is not enough that each country has its discrete domestic scheme for restraint and confiscation. There must be a developed network for fast and effective international co-operation, which allows for cross-border action. At the same time, that process must respect the rights of individuals: those whose property may be improperly restrained and innocent third parties. This area of international co-operation presents perhaps the most significant challenge for investigative, prosecutorial and judicial authorities the world over.

Council of Europe Convention

As mentioned, the 1988 Drug Convention marked the first recognition internationally that any efforts to pursue the profits of crime require the

63 'The conversion or transfer of property, knowing that such property is derived from any offence or offences established in accordance with sub-paragraph (a) of this paragraph, or from an act of participation in such offence or offences, for the purpose of concealing or disguising the illicit origin of the property or of assisting any person who is involved in the commission of such an offence or offences to evade the legal consequences of his actions.' (UN Convention against Illicit Traffic in Narcotic Drugs and Psychotropic Substances 1988, Art. 3(1)(b)(i)).

co-operation of states. An important instrument adopted shortly after was the 1990 Council of Europe Convention on Laundering, Search, Seizure and Confiscation of the Proceeds from Crime.

This Convention, which established an elaborate scheme for co-operation in tracing, restraint and confiscation of proceeds, was of particular note at the time because it established a regime of co-operation applicable to criminal offences generally which generate proceeds of crime. It was not restricted to drug or any other particular type of offence. As such it served to foreshadow developments in the late 1990s with respect to proceeds of crime work.

Financial Action Task Force

While not involving any actual instruments of co-operation, other noteworthy achievements have arisen from the work of the Financial Action Task Force on Money Laundering (FATF).[64] Established in 1989 by the then G7 at their summit in Paris, the FATF is an intergovernmental body whose purpose is the development and promotion of policies to combat money laundering.

The FATF currently consists of 34 countries and two international organizations. Its membership includes the major financial centre countries of Europe, North America and Asia. It is a multidisciplinary body, which brings together the policy-making power of legal, financial and law enforcement experts. The Forty Recommendations of the task force were originally drawn up in 1990. In 1996, those recommendations were revised to take into account the experience gained over the six-year period and to reflect the changes which had occurred in the money-laundering problem. In 2001, nine Special Recommendations on Combating the Financing of Terrorism were adopted. In 2003 the original Forty Recommendations were further revised in light of developments to date. The work of the organization now also has resulted in the establishment of six FATF-style regional bodies, which focus on policy development and implementation relevant to the particular regions.

These recommendations address measures to be taken in the legal, financial and administrative spheres and include a section focused on the enhancement of mutual assistance, extradition and other methods of co-operation in money-laundering investigations. The recommendations and their adoption and implementation in participant states, have contributed significantly to increased awareness and understanding of the issue of money laundering, as well as improvement in the development of mechanisms for combating the problem.

64 www.fatf-gafi.org.

TOC and Corruption Conventions

As in the case of extradition and mutual assistance, the adoption of both the TOC Convention and the Corruption Convention has brought about important advancements in the context of cross-border co-operation in the restraint and confiscation of proceeds of crime. The TOC Convention provisions mirror the obligations contained in the 1988 Drug Convention requiring member states to have money laundering and proceeds offences and to have in place mechanisms for domestic and cross-border restraint and confiscation. But importantly, the convention extends the application of these measures to the broad range of crimes covered by it – the four core crimes, as well as serious offences. The practical result has been the extension of proceeds of crime and money-laundering legislation beyond the realm of drug trafficking to either a range of designated offences or, in some countries, to all crimes.

Last, but certainly not least, of the important multilateral initiatives in this sphere is the recently adopted Corruption Convention. While built upon the 1988 Drug Convention and the TOC Convention, this instrument includes important new provisions particularly relating to the ultimate question of the disposition of assets in corruption cases, where those assets are recovered through international co-operation. Some of the key innovations include:

- Article 52 – detailed provisions on preventing and detecting the transfer of proceeds of crime;
- Article 53 – incorporation of principles on the direct recovery of assets through the initiation of civil actions, orders of restitution upon conviction and recognition of claims in confiscation proceedings;
- Article 54 – introduction of specific mechanisms that can be used to facilitate recovery of property including the use of money-laundering offences as a basis for confiscation and allowing for confiscation in the absence of a criminal conviction in appropriate cases;
- Article 57 – for the first time sets a principle for the return of assets to affected states depending upon how closely the assets are linked to the requesting state.

Because of these various innovative instruments, assistance in the restraint and confiscation of proceeds of crime, more than any other form of co-operation, is most frequently rendered on the basis of multilateral, as opposed to bilateral, agreements or at the least on the basis of laws which have been enacted in the implementation of such instruments. In essence, implementation of the 1988 Drug Convention, the FATF recommendations and now the TOC and Corruption Conventions has led to the adoption in many states of domestic regimes for restraint and confiscation which apply to the proceeds of both foreign and domestic offences; that is, proceeds of criminal activity located in a state will be subject to restraint and confiscation even if the underlying or 'predicate' offence through which the profits were generated took place elsewhere.

In addition, many countries have made assistance with the restraint and confiscation of proceeds of crime, a component – in some instances a central component – of their mutual assistance treaties. Thus, there also exist bilateral instruments which provide a basis for co-operation between states in the restraint and forfeiture of proceeds of crime.

In many ways while co-operation in 'proceeds matters' is the newest form of international co-operation, the network upon which such assistance is rendered is much more complete than any other.

Practical issues for prosecutors

At the same time, international co-operation in tracing, restraining and confiscating the proceeds of crime is the area most replete with difficult legal and practical issues and the one which poses the greatest challenge, particularly for those authorities who must bring these cases before the courts.

As the newest form of international co-operation, it remains a relatively unknown concept even amongst the authorities who may be called upon to respond to requests for assistance. Many investigators, prosecutors and judges are simply unfamiliar with and unaccustomed to the restraint and confiscation of property and assets. This makes the pursuit and rendering of assistance both difficult and time consuming.

Asset confiscation regimes

What also makes this form of assistance incredibly complex is the diversity of schemes for asset restraint and confiscation. It is no exaggeration to say that no two states have adopted the same legislative regime, unlike the kinds of similarity that can be found in extradition and mutual assistance, at least amongst states of similar legal tradition. In confiscation there are a wide range of general approaches and each country has a different 'twist' to its scheme. Here it is only possible to touch on some of the main areas of difference between approaches, in order to highlight the maze that must be navigated in seeking assistance.

To begin with there are essentially three approaches to the confiscation of proceeds of crime – administrative, criminal conviction confiscation and non-conviction-based confiscation.

Administrative confiscation

Administrative confiscation is often employed in the context of customs legislation. Generally administrative forfeiture occurs without judicial order as it arises by operation of law, as a result of the occurrence of a prohibited event in relation to the property. Again in general terms, under such a system, where property is seized by authorities in accordance with applicable legislation, upon service of relevant notices, the property will be confiscated unless a challenge is brought before a court. Thus in the context of administrative confiscation, it is for the claimant to establish that the property should not be confiscated. As this form of confiscation has limited application it will not be given further consideration here.

Criminal conviction confiscation

The most important and familiar form of confiscation is conviction based. Most states still employ this approach exclusively to implement the relevant international conventions. As is evident from the title, with such an approach conviction is a prerequisite to confiscation proceedings. That is, upon a criminal conviction being entered, consideration may be given to the confiscation of proceeds or instruments related to the offence.

Non-conviction-based confiscation

The most recent development in confiscation, which has brought about important improvements and at the same time added to the complexity, is the adoption by some states of non-conviction-based regimes, often referred to as civil confiscation or civil recovery. Long in use in the USA, such systems are being implemented in several jurisdictions to augment criminal conviction confiscation and provide for a more effective regime to aggressively pursue the proceeds and instruments of crime. Distinct from conviction-based confiscation, a non-conviction or 'civil' confiscation regime involves the government launching court proceedings to recover property, on the basis that the property is alleged to constitute proceeds or instruments of crime. While the models vary, most involve *in rem* proceedings where the action is aimed at the property itself. Obviously, the important distinction from criminal conviction confiscation is that there is no requirement for an underlying conviction of any person. What must be demonstrated generally on the 'civil' standard, for confiscation to occur, is that the property constitutes the proceeds or instrumentality of unlawful or criminal activity.

Several common-law jurisdictions have now adopted such legislation including Australia, Canada, Ireland, the UK and South Africa.

While fewer countries of a civil-law tradition have moved towards such a system, Italy and Colombia have both instituted some powers for such confiscation. Ireland and South Africa represent two jurisdictions which have used non-conviction confiscation aggressively to combat corruption and organized crime.[65]

65 See Proceeds of Crime Act, 1996, No. 30 1996 (Ireland); Prevention of Organised Crime Act 1998, Act 121 of 1998, South Africa Gazette No. 19973.

The challenges

Variation of conviction-based systems

As mentioned, the most common type of measure introduced by states to fulfill the obligations under the relevant international conventions is confiscation post conviction. However, while the concept is uniform, the way in which such confiscation is carried out can vary considerably. While time does not permit an in-depth consideration of the various models, some examples of key distinctions should illustrate the diversity.

One important distinction is whether the criminal confiscation orders relate to specific assets or are 'value' based or both. While the scheme was altered with the adoption of the Proceeds of Crime Act 2002, the old UK model, which has been replicated in several Commonwealth jurisdictions, is perhaps the best example of a purely 'value'-based system. In summary, if a person were convicted of an offence, the court could calculate the 'benefit' to the defendant from that offence. Having determined the accrued benefit, the court would then assess the defendant's ability to pay or, in other words, the value of the amount that might be realizable from the defendant's assets. On the basis of these calculations, the court would make a 'confiscation' order, in the amount of the benefit or the realizable assets, whichever was less. In the case where the defendant had been convicted of two or more offences, or if the conviction related to drug trafficking, certain assumptions would come into play in relation to the calculations to be made by the court.

While the order in this system was referred to as a 'confiscation order' in fact nothing was confiscated. Rather the court would order the person to pay a specified sum of money. The order was enforceable like a fine but in addition the court could appoint a receiver to collect and sell the defendant's assets in its satisfaction.

In direct contrast, Canada employs a 'tainted property' approach which is dependent upon the establishment of a link between the crime and the assets in question. Under this system, upon conviction, the sentencing judge may order forfeiture if the court is satisfied, on a standard of balance of probabilities, that the property is proceeds and the offence for which the conviction was obtained was committed in relation to those proceeds. Even if not satisfied that the property relates to the specific offence, the court may also order forfeiture of property if satisfied beyond reasonable doubt that the property is proceeds of crime.

Australia employs a mixed system whereby the court may make either or both a forfeiture order relating to specific property or a pecuniary penalty order reflecting the benefit accruing to the person from the commission of the offence. The law also provides for the use of deeming provisions with respect to property found in the possession of the accused, at the time of, or immediately after the commission of the offence.

One can envisage immediately, in looking at these differing approaches, the complications when such systems must intersect in the context of cross-border confiscation requests.

Direct/Indirect enforcement of foreign orders

Unfortunately the complications do not end with the varied approaches to domestic confiscation. There are, as well, distinct methods for dealing with foreign requests and orders for confiscation and restraint.

This particular problem originates with the international criminal law conventions starting with the 1988 Drug Convention. While this instrument, along with those that have followed it, has done much to enhance international co-operation and asset confiscation laws on a global basis, it is not without difficulties in terms of practical application. In the mid-1980s when the concept of asset confiscation was a relatively new one, understandably there was much caution used in the drafting of the first convention obligations. States were particularly concerned to guard against abuse of powerful tools which allowed for the removal of individual property by the state particularly when it arises at the behest of a foreign state. There were also constitutional concerns that had to be taken into consideration. As a result, while agreement was reached that states would be obliged to respond to foreign requests for restraint and confiscation, considerable flexibility was imported into the text as to how the states would go about meeting this obligation. Specifically, the 1988 Drug Convention recognized alternative methods that may be used to respond to a request from another state for restraint or confiscation of assets on the basis that they constitute the proceeds or instruments of crime. In summary the systems envisaged are:

- 'direct enforcement' where, subject to relevant prerequisites being met, a foreign order for restraint or confiscation is registered in the requested state and executed like a domestic order; or
- 'indirect enforcement' where information and evidence submitted by the requesting state is used to support an application for a domestic order for restraint and confiscation, with the domestic regime being applicable to proceeds or instruments generated from domestic or foreign crimes.

These two broad alternative approaches have been replicated both in the TOC Convention and the Corruption Convention. And naturally, states have proceeded to adopt legislation in accord with one or other or both of the optional methods. The result is problematic in two respects. First again one encounters differing approaches depending on the jurisdiction. Second, the latter option of 'indirect enforcement' is fraught with problems such that it is difficult if not impossible for practitioners to use it effectively for cross-border restraint or confiscation. While time does not permit a thorough consideration of the matter, some of the challenges can be immediately identified.

Given the different types of confiscation regimes, the evidence gathered by a requesting state to substantiate the basis for restraining or confiscating the funds may not be at all sufficient to meet the requirements of the system in the requested state. For example, if a state with a tainted-property regime seeks confiscation it will generate evidence to show the link between the property and the crime but not necessarily all the assets of the individual. If the state to which the request is to be presented however employs a 'value' approach, the important evidence for the requested state would be that which demonstrates a connection between the property and the accused or convicted person and not to the crime itself.

Further, if the requested state is using a conviction-based system it may not have a means to properly commence proceedings for confiscation. That is, even though the legislation extends to proceeds of foreign crimes, there will be no conviction in the requested state to trigger the operation of the confiscation regime.

In addition to these broader conceptual differences in approach, authorities seeking assistance through an indirect system face a multitude of procedural variations as well. For example, in some legal systems, before a state will seek the restraint of assets, it will require the requesting state to produce evidence to establish the necessary factors for confiscation. Other systems will accept a description of that evidence and still others a simple summary, without reference to available evidence. The variations are endless as is the frustration for police, prosecutors and judges.

It is for this reason that despite the existence of the optional approaches under the Conventions, states are being encouraged to implement a direct-enforcement regime whereby a restraint or confiscation order issued in a foreign state can be registered and enforced as a domestic order. While such systems require discretion and safeguards to protect against abuse, they provide a far more effective mechanism for cross-border restraint and confiscation. The direct enforcement regime is also far more pragmatic for small and developing states as the alternative indirect mechanism is very resource intensive.

Co-operation in non-conviction-based confiscation cases

There is compelling evidence to support the conclusion that only with a complete armoury, including conviction- and non-conviction-based measures, can a state effectively take the profit out of crime. By example, in grand corruption cases, death, immunities and safe havens often make criminal prosecution impossible and stolen assets unreachable. For this reason, there is an important and growing trend towards the introduction and use of non-conviction-based confiscation, as highlighted above. But it will be a considerable period of time before such systems constitute the norm and as a result those authorities who investigate and bring cases forward under such regimes face their own unique challenges in cross-border cases.

First and foremost, the regimes and procedures for non-conviction-based confiscation are civil in nature. The cases are commenced and carried out without any underlying or related criminal proceeding, and civil procedures are employed in their adjudication. As a result, the existing regimes for international co-operation in evidence gathering – mutual legal assistance schemes, treaties and laws – are by and large inapplicable to these investigations and proceedings. While informal law enforcement mechanisms can be used and various creative techniques are sometimes employed to overcome this legal lacuna, this particular deficiency is increasingly posing an obstacle to effective asset confiscation.

On a related note, even for countries that have adopted direct-enforcement regimes for the execution of restraint and confiscation orders, it is not clear that the provisions can be applied to orders obtained under a non-conviction-based regime. Unless there is an express provision to that effect, it is likely that the enforcement mechanism would be restricted to an order obtained post-conviction. This too will increasingly constitute a major impediment to taking the profit out of crime.

Practical measures

Obviously the ultimate key to more effective asset confiscation lies in the adoption of flexible legislation which incorporates a range of measures including both conviction-based and non-conviction confiscation and allows for direct enforcement of foreign orders. Unfortunately however this is not the reality in the vast majority of jurisdictions so that it falls to the relevant authorities to find practical solutions for the current challenges.

The following are a few suggestions for practitioners who must endeavour to overcome the odds in pursuing the profits of crime internationally.

Be informed

Authorities making a request for assistance must be informed as to the law and the requirements in the other state. While true in respect of all forms of co-operation, in no other context does it carry the same level of importance. While in mutual assistance a request submitted without advance knowledge of the system in the requested state might still succeed, in asset restraint and confiscation it is bound to fail.

Before proceeding with a request it is critical to determine at the very least what asset confiscation regime is in place, whether there is direct enforcement available, and if non-conviction confiscation is an option. Only armed with this basic information will you be in a position to determine whether to make a request and if so what kind of information to provide.

Be detailed

Whatever the system, restraint and confiscation orders cannot be obtained or enforced without precise and detailed information on the assets involved. Before any request is drafted law enforcement or other appropriate channels should be used to gather as much detail as possible to identify the relevant assets in the requested state. Vague requests will go unheeded and unexecuted.

Be thorough

For those receiving requests, especially if domestic law does not provide for any direct enforcement, it is equally important to communicate with the authorities in the requesting state to draw out as much relevant information as possible. As the absence of a criminal proceeding in the requested state is the fatal problem in many cases, it is important to think about the use of money laundering, possession of proceeds of crime or even possession of stolen goods offences in order to ground an effective confiscation action. This is not to say that criminal charges should be pursued without basis, but it is the rare case where the presence of proceeds of crime does not involve a series of criminal violations in both the requesting and requested state.

Be creative

While cross-border confiscation is difficult, the most challenging component is restraining assets in a foreign case. In such actions, time is always of the essence. Everyone knows that assets can be moved in an instant, with the touch of a computer key. In the face of these realities, it is important to be creative and to make full use of legislative provisions relating to money laundering and proceeds of crime. For example, sometimes assistance in restraint can be obtained simply by relaying intelligence or information about the existence of potential proceeds of crime within another state through informal police or other channels for domestic use and action. The authorities in the receiving state can use that information to develop a sufficient evidentiary basis to seek a domestic restraint order without the necessity of invoking some of the formalities of a mutual assistance request. As most domestic legislation provides for restraint in relation to proceeds of foreign or domestic crimes this is a legitimate application of the proceeds of crime legislation. Similarly, in the case of assets held in financial institutions, authorities may wish to consider the transmission of information regarding suspect accounts to the relevant institution. This can result in the institution taking action to at least temporarily freeze the assets by virtue of the obligations on the organization under anti-money-laundering laws. While such measures are not the optimum solution, particularly in the context of urgent restraint matters, they may be the only means to ensure that assets are secured pending formal requests for confiscation via a mutual assistance request.

Ask and assist

Finally while perhaps a trite statement, the key to effective co-operation lies in frank and open communication. Particularly in this developing area of asset confiscation, it is always worth asking another state for assistance. There are many situations where the laws of one state may be effective enough to overcome deficiencies in the laws of another jurisdiction. There is a growing trend amongst states and the practitioners who work in this field to view cross-border asset confiscation as a joint undertaking as opposed to a matter to be dealt with as a requesting and requested state. Many states with experience in the field are prepared to help their counterparts in the tracing of assets, in the drafting and presentation of requests and even in preparing cases for courts. So the message is: be prepared to ask and be prepared to assist.

CONCLUSION

There can be no illusions about international co-operation in criminal matters. The criminals are far more skilled in using national borders to protect themselves and the evidence and profits of their crime from detection than law enforcement is in overcoming the barriers of sovereignty in order to pursue them.

But if one considers where we have been and where we have come in co-operation matters in the last 50 years, there is much reason to be optimistic. There should be no doubt that, with the continued efforts of the world community, its effectiveness in combating transnational crime will continue to increase, as will the security of our global village. In the end, justice need not be blinded by borders.

Chapter 11

Extradition

Croatian experiences relating to war criminals

Josip Cule

INTRODUCTION

We live in times in which the criminal knows no boundaries. Criminal acts are planned in one country, the logistical means are obtained in the territory of another, the offences themselves are committed in the territory of yet another country, whilst the proceeds of crime end up in the financial institutions of yet further countries (often with exotic sounding names). Detection and investigation of the perpetrators, of criminal acts and their proceeds is therefore somewhat difficult even though we may be dealing with crimes, such as terrorism and drug trafficking, the suppression of which is of interest for the entire international community.

In the Republic of Croatia exactly the same challenges present themselves when dealing with the perpetrators of war crimes committed during the war between 1991–1995. It is often the case that such acts were committed in Croatia, while the perpetrators are located elsewhere, or that the perpetrator resides in the Republic of Croatia, whilst the criminal offence was committed abroad.[1] When this is the case, the only recourse is to international co-operation. In Croatia, war crimes are regarded as having an exceptionally high priority. Bearing in mind the severity of the crime, the vast number of perpetrators who have fled the jurisdiction and the need for the interests of justice to be satisfied, this chapter, will focus especially on extradition. It will examine the problems in achieving extradition and propose possible solutions.

In the past 10 years, the countries of the EU have established completely new mechanisms of judicial co-operation which represent considerable progress in developing international legal assistance. They advocate certain basic principles such as:

- real-time and direct communication between judiciary authorities;

1 For example, in Bosnia and Herzegovina.

- fast-track extradition procedures for offenders to face trial in the jurisdiction in which the criminal act was committed;
- independence from political influence and from the direct engagement of the executive in judicial decisions.

Several EU instruments have been developed in support of these principles, such as the European Arrest Warrant[2] (which provides for a simplified extradition procedure) and the European Evidence Warrant, and a number of new institutional mechanisms providing channels for legal assistance from 'liaison magistrates' to the 'European Judicial Network' (also known as 'the Judicial Atlas') and culminating in 'Eurojust'.[3]

European countries that are not members of the EU have individually been unable to keep up with those advances and still remain governed by the earlier European Convention on Mutual Legal Assistance of 1959[4] (with many countries reserving their position on particular provisions, especially in respect of extraditing their own citizens), or by mutual bilateral agreements. Conscious of the fact that desirable changes to the legal framework would take many years, it was necessary to find a method of interstate co-operation that would stay within the boundaries of existing law and, at the same time, be compliant with the legal requirements in those countries requesting assistance.

INTERNATIONAL CO-OPERATION IN CRIMINAL PROCEEDINGS

Whenever an alleged offender is outside the jurisdiction and cannot be directly prosecuted, there are a range of common forms of judicial co-operation available that attempt to overcome the obstacles. These include (but are not exclusive to):

- extradition;
- various forms of low-level mutual legal assistance;
- the transfer criminal proceedings to the offender's country of residence;
- trial 'in absentia';[5]

2 www.europa.eu/scadplus/leg/en/lvb/l33167, accessed 5 May 2007.

3 www.ec.europa.eu/justice_home/news/laecken_council/en/eurojust_en.htm, accessed 5 May 2007.

4 European Convention on mutual legal assistance in criminal matters, Strasbourg, 20 April 1959.

5 In the Republic of Croatia there is a possibility of conducting a trial *in absentia* (Criminal Procedure Act, Art 305, para. 5). However, since 2000, the Attorney General's office of the Republic of Croatia has, as a matter of policy, not proposed such trials. However the courts still retain the right to allow them without the Attorney General's consent.

- the domestic enforcement of foreign judicial verdicts; or
- the transfer convicted persons to their country of citizenship.

Experience has shown that such forms of international co-operation are often insufficient for the successful conduct of criminal proceedings related to war crimes. Where the perpetrator cannot be found or placed in custody, low-level international co-operation is of little value. The transfer of criminal proceedings is also not possible because this is prohibited under the provisions of the Croatian International Legal Assistance in Criminal Matters Act[6] (for offences with a maximum prison penalty longer than 10 years) and existing bilateral treaties do not provide for such a possibility.[7]

Extradition remains the only available option.

EXTRADITION

It is a matter of fact that the perpetrators of war crimes committed within the Republic of Croatia are usually Croatian citizens, citizens of Bosnia and Herzegovina, or of the Republics of Serbia and Montenegro.

Where suspects are resident outside of Bosnia and Herzegovina, the Republic of Serbia, or the Republic of Montenegro, the classical procedure is applied to extradition requests; the authorised court applies to the Ministry of Justice of the Republic of Croatia, which the forwards an official letter of request to the prescribed bodies of the country in which the perpetrator is located. Certain petitions are filed, for arrest, pre-trial detention and extradition. This procedure is usually lengthy, and the outcome is unpredictable. There are countries that have been known to deny extradition but where war crimes are concerned most will usually comply with such a request.

However, there are difficulties where those suspected of war crimes committed in Croatia are found in Bosnia and Herzegovina, the Republic of Serbia or the Republic of Montenegro and are citizens of those countries. In the same way that the constitution of the Republic of Croatia[8] does not permit the extradition of its own citizens, the constitutions of these other countries have the same regulation and it matters not how grave their offence or its severity; they will not be submitted to any kind of criminal proceedings.

To change this situation would require changing the national constitutions of

6 International Legal Assistance in Criminal Matters Act ('Narodne Novine'), Art 65, para. 2, The Official Gazette of the Republic of Croatia, No. 178 dated 16 December 2004, in force on 1 July 2005.

7 I.e. bilateral international treaties between the Republic of Croatia and Bosnia and Herzegovina and with the Federal Republic of Yugoslavia (now the Republic of Serbia and Republic of Montenegro).

8 Constitution of the Republic of Croatia, Art 5.

each country and this is not an easy task.[9] The inability to change the constitution could result in a failure to prosecute serious crimes and put at risk the application of the *aut dedere aut judicare* principle.[10] There are no statutes of limitations for these crimes but, whilst this situation prevails, suspects need only remain in their home countries, protected by their own citizenship, to escape trial.

A POSSIBLE SOLUTION

The impossibility to extradite one's own citizens results in the paralysis of the legal systems in war-crime proceedings in Croatia as well as in other neighbouring countries. In general, the country in which the crime has been committed is the country in which most of the evidence will be available, including the witnesses and victims, and it is not in the interests of justice to try to prosecute the case in another country (it should also be noted that the option of trial *in absentia* is only available in Croatia).

For the reasons stated above, the Attorney General's office of the Republic of Croatia suggested the negotiation of memoranda of understanding with the State prosecutor's offices in these other countries with the goal of allowing the transfer of evidence. The memorandum with the office of the Public Prosecutor of Republic of Montenegro was signed on 28 June 2006 and the memorandum with the office of the Public Prosecutor of Serbia on 12 August 2006.

Such transfer provides the State prosecutor's office of the country concerned with the necessary evidence for charging the suspect. The prosecutor's office, having received this specifically prepared package of evidence, independently reviews the file for sufficiency of evidence for bringing a prosecution and then decides on which criminal offences are disclosed under national law. The prosecutor's office transferring the evidence has no right to participate in the review or to influence in any way the proceedings in the receiving country, but will be later informed of the outcome both of the review of the case file and of any subsequent trial.

The advantage of this process is that it creates a moral obligation on the receiving authority to consider the evidence as part of their national duties and responsibilities but without requiring them to take any action. If the Attorney General's office in the sending country is not content with the decision of the prosecutor's office or the court in that other country, nothing really changes: the grounds for prosecution still exist in the original country and the status of the case remains the same in that the suspect is beyond reach. However, where

9 Changing any part of the constitution in Republic of Croatia requires two thirds of the vote in Parliament.

10 I.e. 'surrender the suspect or judge them'.

the outcome is satisfactory and has led to criminal trial in the receiving country, the case in the sending country can be closed

However, this mechanism has to be handled responsibly. The package of evidence must be of high quality and should only be transferred if the accusation is fully supported. Otherwise, the review of the receiving office will be negative, the alleged perpetrator will go free and confidence in the process will be undermined. For this reason the policy on implementation has been to begin with a very limited number of cases and to test the potential for this co-operation process.

As stated above, memoranda already exist with Serbia and Montenegro. Time will tell whether a similar memorandum will be signed with Bosnia and Herzegovina and the results and success of co-operation under existing memoranda will be of great influence in future negotiations.

A separate case in 2005 involving informal co-operation with Bosnia and Herzegovina demonstrates how, given the right relationship and common goals, suspects can nevertheless be brought to book. The case involved a suspect for war crimes committed in Bosnia and Herzegovina. He held Croatian citizenship and was currently resident in the Republic of Croatia. Although he had been detained in Croatia under an international arrest warrant, it was not possible to transfer him to Bosnia and Herzegovina for the legal reasons given above. To overcome this, the Republic of Croatia initiated criminal proceedings in the Croatian courts on the basis of the international arrest warrant. However, the evidence supplied with that warrant was not enough. At first Bosnia and Herzegovina was reluctant to supply further evidence. Consequently, the proceedings were adjourned. However, upon the later receipt of evidence from the State Prosecutor in Bosnia and Herzegovina, the Attorney General's office in Croatia was able to resume the prosecution.[11]

RESULTS SO FAR

Despite only recently coming into force, the memoranda have already led to a number of examples of co-operation. In the first test of the process, a request was made to establish whether known suspects, already indicted in the Croatian courts, were located either in Serbia or in Montenegro. Once the presence of the suspects had been confirmed, the complete case files were provided to the Attorney for War Crimes in Serbia (four cases involving five suspects) and to the Supreme Prosecutor for Montenegro (one case involving 10 suspects) and have already resulted in the raising of criminal indictments in Serbia.

11 The case described here relates to the trial in the county court in Split against the defendant Miroslav Anic (alias 'Firga') for war crimes against civilians under the Criminal Code of the Republic of Croatia, Art 120.

This new approach to the sharing and exchange of evidence has meant that one more loophole has been closed for those seeking to escape justice by avoiding extradition. It has an especial significance given the large number of war-crimes suspects known to be living in these countries. In the Republic of Croatia we are currently dealing with approximately 1,200 persons (at various stages in the judicial process). In Bosnia and Herzegovina, it is estimated that there may be up to 13,000 persons wanted for war crimes, and in the Republic of Serbia perhaps even more. The only thing for sure is that a very large number of suspects are involved. Of course, it is not to be expected that all such persons are guilty; they are just suspects but, even so, the numbers reflect a vast number who fall through the net of the classical extradition and mutual legal assistance framework.

CONCLUSION

While preparing the prosecutions of suspects for war crimes it became clear that existing international co-operation mechanisms were inadequate and lacked the necessary teeth to bring these suspects to trial (let alone justice). Often the countries involved do not have the legal basis for extraditing their own citizens even for the most heinous and savage crimes.

Give the legal impossibility of extradition, or of the transfer of criminal proceedings, the Republic of Croatia embarked on an initiative to conclude memoranda of mutual co-operation between prosecutor's offices. These memoranda provided for the complete exchange of evidence to ensure a successful charge and prosecution in the suspect's country of residence and fully support the principle of *aut dedere aut iudicare*.

At this moment in time, memoranda have been concluded between the General Attorney's office of Republic of Croatia and the office of the Public Prosecutor of the Republic of Montenegro as well as with the Republic of Serbia. Concluding these memoranda, or by transferring evidence, creates no formal treaty obligation – the judicial authorities are required only to act as they would when normally confronted with evidence of a crime. However, they do impose a moral obligation to conduct their work using their best intentions and, once they have made their decision, to provide full information to the other side. If the country forwarding the evidence is satisfied with the outcome, it will suspend proceedings against the same defendant in its own jurisdiction but, if not, there is nothing to stop the reinstatement of the prosecution should the suspect become available to the legal process at a later date.

Part III

The mechanics of communication

Chapter 12

Getting the message across

Information exchange as a communication chain

Steven David Brown

In earlier chapters it was explained how working in international law enforcement has a good deal to do with exchanging information, so let us now take a closer look at the actual mechanics involved for an officer who wants to pass messages across international boundaries to colleagues in other countries.[1] These messages will typically consist of (a) a dialogue of questions and answers relating to a specific case or enquiry, or (b) the speculative contribution of information to some central agency where it can be integrated into a data pool and made available either for the interrogation of subscribers or for later amalgamation into some form of strategic overview or assessment.

Whatever the reasons for sharing information, an investigator is faced by a bewildering array of choices by which it is possible to forward a message. Figure 12.1, for example, illustrates the numerous possibilities available for a law enforcement officer to send data just within the EU.

What influences an investigator's choice to use which channel? Unless there are strict guidelines or policies in place, the decision will be idiosyncratic and chaotic. It may be based on an individual's personal knowledge or previous experience (bad or good) of that channel or the organisation behind it. It may be that one system is available at that moment, whereas another is not. However, there is also an unfortunate, if understandable, tendency for investigators to try to use as many channels as possible in a scattergun-type chance to luck or in order to show that he or she has covered all the angles. Some countries have a central clearing process for international requests which limits this tendency and allows the request to be directed to the most appropriate agency on the basis of objective criteria (this will be discussed further below). The fact is, any request for a specific piece of information or assistance sent through multiple channels will eventually end up in the in-tray of the one officer (or unit) who

1 This chapter looks at the practical aspects of information exchange between law enforcement agencies and does not review the formal exchange of judicial letters of request which is usually conducted between national central authorities. For information on letters of request please refer to Chapter 10 and Appendix 3.

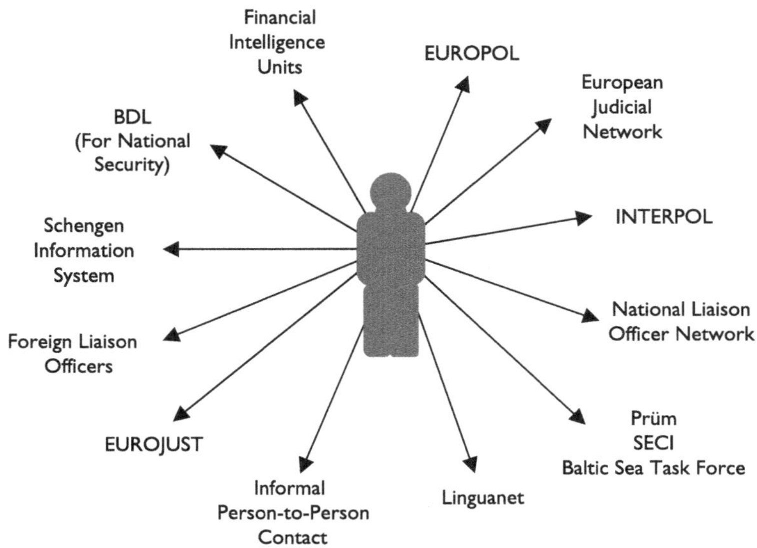

Figure 12.1 EU investigator options

has access to the required information. Six or seven requests arriving in different formats and often in a foreign language, all for the same information and all entailing the same reply, are an unwelcome distraction and a source of annoyance.

For the investigator making the request, on the other hand, the priority is to get an answer as soon as possible and whilst, in theory, different channels have the same or similar opportunities for retrieving the desired information the reality is that they are not all equally as successful or as timely in their response all of the time. By way of illustration, the author once forwarded an urgent message on behalf of a colleague in a non-EU country to one of the most developed and structured EU Member States requesting the exact whereabouts of a fugitive who, according to a newspaper report, had been arrested there on another matter. A holding reply from the EU Member State was received immediately (thus complying with agreed time response standards) explaining that the details requested were not readily available, but further enquiries would be made. So far, so good. A few weeks later a final reply was received to the effect that, with regret, the requested information was not held in the country concerned and the presence of the suspect could not be verified. However, on communicating this to the requesting officer in the non-EU country, the author was informed that not only had the information been held, but that it had been received almost immediately via another channel based in the same EU State! In this regard it has to be accepted that the enthusiasm, knowledge and ingenuity of the officer fielding the request at the national level can play a significant part in the success of a request and this, to some extent, is a matter of luck. However, any element of chance can be reduced through good management and the application of minimum standards.

There are four basic models for routing the formal transfer of information:

- the Interpol-type National Central Bureau to National Central Bureau (NCB) link;
- the direct bilateral national liaison officer approach;
- the use of an international organisation as a hub or central focal point for information exchange (such as the Schengen Information System, Europol, or, the SECI Regional Crime Center in Bucharest and, soon, the CARICC Centre in Kazakhstan); or,
- more recently, the Prüm direct search facility.

In addition, informal and unregulated contacts also exist on an officer-to-officer basis where someone will telephone, fax or email a known associate and share or request data directly. For reasons to be discussed later, this personal method is fraught with risk, even if it often appears to be the fastest and least bureaucratic way to get the message across. In some countries it will also be illegal.

INTERPOL NCB TO NCB

The International Criminal Police Office (Interpol) is the oldest and arguably the most respected of international law enforcement agencies. It has come a long way from being the small bureaucratic office in Paris it once was: based around a series of card index files and only open during office hours. An in-depth review of Interpol is given in Chapter 3, but it is also appropriate here to consider the way in which different parts of the Interpol network are linked together (Figure 12.2). Each Interpol NCB acts as a gateway receiving and dispatching messages to and from its national authorities. It has a secure electronic link to the NCBs in all other Interpol member states and can send messages to them directly.[2] Each NCB is an extension of national law enforcement staffed by local officers working under national laws and rules, but to Interpol standards and procedures. At the heart of Interpol lies the General Secretariat (now based in Lyon) which, amongst other things, also receives and dispatches information received from Interpol member states and provides a number of key databases which, again, may be accessed by any NCB. Member states are also able to notify the General Secretariat of any information of general interest which will then be disseminated as appropriate from Lyon. The

2 In some countries Interpol has also been able to establish terminals within national agencies as well.

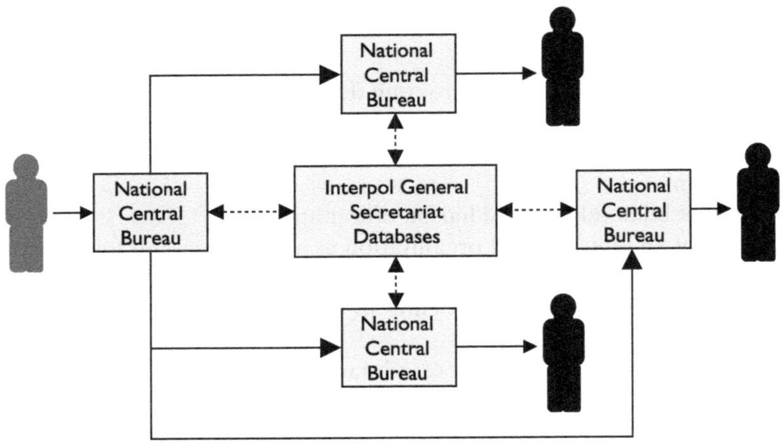

Figure 12.2 Interpol information flows

Interpol notice system is a prime example of the value of this process for identifying, locating and detaining international suspects.

An NCB can send a request to any other NCB in the world securely and at the speed of the internet. Unfortunately, the real difficulties with this model lie outside of that international connection and tend to occur once the information has been forwarded by the NCB for action to an agency within the national system over which there is no control. Any response is dependent on the effectiveness and efficiency of the national agency concerned. On the other hand, for the investigator the procedure is extremely user-friendly, merely requiring the sending of the request or data to the NCB that then takes care of the rest.

INTERNATIONAL ORGANISATIONS AS A HUB

A modification of the Interpol approach was developed at Europol, adopted by the SECI Regional Crime Center,[3] adapted by Eurojust, and is being used as the basis for CARICC.[4] Whereas the national representatives in the Interpol model are based in their home countries, this second model collocates them at the centre or hub of the network (shown within the circle in Figure 12.3). This does not mean that the information is automatically copied to any central database or unit (far from it), but it does mean that the liaison officers are able to establish and cultivate personal relationships both with each other (personal networking) and with the staff of the central body. In terms of mechanics, the information exchange mechanism for the investigator is exactly the same as

3 Southeastern European Cooperative Initiative Regional Center for Combating Trans-Border Crime in Bucharest.

4 Central Asian Regional Information and Coordination Center in Kazakhstan.

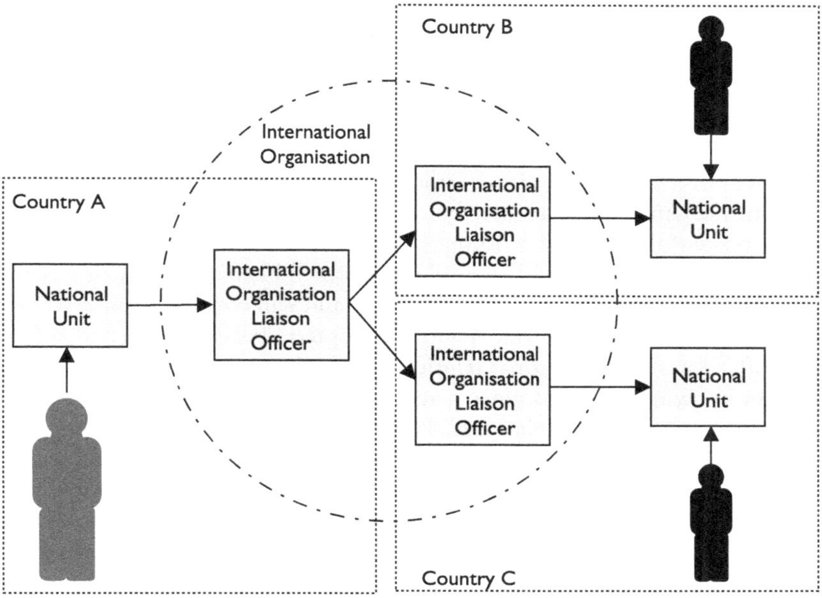

Figure 12.3 International organisation information flows

with Interpol, including the existence of some kind of national support unit, but in this model the message arrives in one central forum where liaison officers control its further processing. They have the added advantage of being able to approach colleagues with a face-to-face explanation or query and to obtain advice about local procedures. They are also available as a ready point of reference or assistance for any activity undertaken by the central secretariat or administration. Again the liaison officers work under the line management and laws of their home jurisdictions, but their profile is that much higher in respect of the additional representative role. Their presence together in the same building also facilitates the setting up of meetings or consultation at short notice. However, this process is labour intensive and adds significantly to the cost.

So, in this model, an investigator first sends his or her request to the national unit (as in the Interpol model), which transmits it to the liaison officer based at the centre or hub. The liaison officer then forwards it to the appropriate colleague representing the country concerned in the same building who then sends it back to his own national unit for action and the chain is complete. Where felt necessary the liaison officer can even follow up the message with a personal visit. This model also provides the additional opportunity for the liaison officer to consider whether the information received could be of value to any central database. This could also be done by the NCB in the Interpol model, but the liaison officer's interaction with the central organisation is that much closer and, although is entails an additional level of handling and expense, it does have its advantages.

NATIONAL LIAISON OFFICER APPROACH

National or overseas liaison officers (they have many names) do not work under any neutral organisational banner but are direct representatives of their home country posted abroad and working as a point of contact for the local law enforcement agencies. Usually, their placement will be in a country or territory chosen because of its strategic impact at home and will concern themselves with specific enquiries related to that region. As noted above, the strength of any liaison officer lies in the personal relationships and experience developed by the officer, in knowing where to place a request and in how to encourage a swift response. As can be seen in Figure 12.4 national investigators wanting to send a request through an overseas liaison officer will normally, but not always, have to submit the details first to some kind of national clearing unit. The unit will, after checking the legality and content of the request, forward it to the liaison officer (often working out of the local embassy) and that officer will place the request where s/he can. Any reply will then be sent back along the same chain, but, where the host country is dragging its feet or not providing sufficient information, the liaison officer is on hand to follow this up with the agency concerned. Thus,

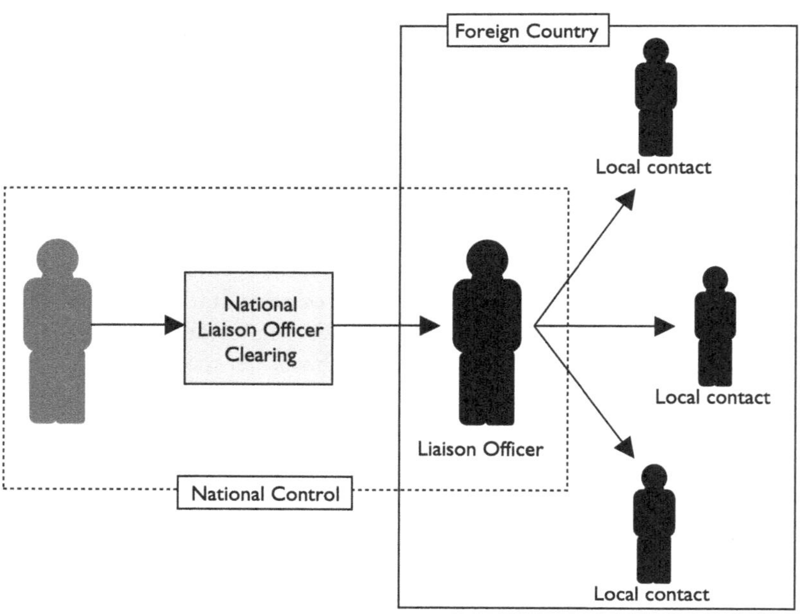

Figure 12.4 National liaison officer information flows

whereas a liaison officer in the second model is dealing with national representatives at a third location, in this model the liaison officer is in situ with a personal presence.

There is a slight modification of this model where the responsibility of the liaison officer is to represent a single agency rather than his or her country. Such a variation may not have a national clearing system for messages. For instance, FBI Legal Attachés receive from and respond to enquiries forwarded directly by the FBI field divisions within the USA, although the overall management and supervision for these 'Legats' is provided by a department at FBI headquarters in Washington DC.[5]

PRÜM DIRECT SEARCH FACILITY

The advent of the Prüm Convention[6] has amended these models in an interesting way and replaces the human interface with a technical one. Officers based in a national contact point will have direct access to the national index database of

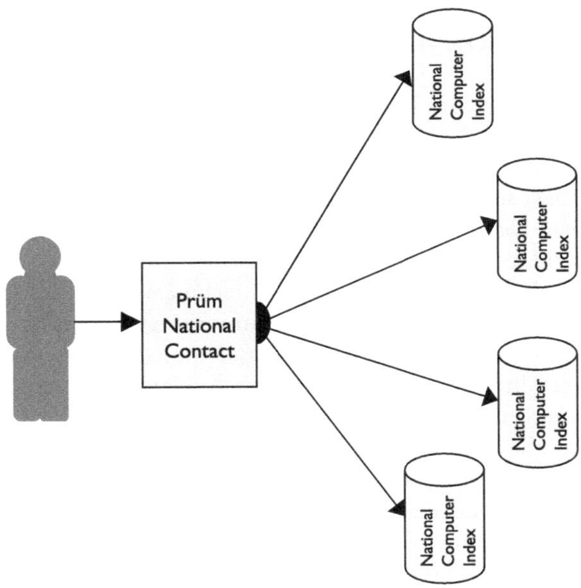

Figure 12.5 Prüm Convention information flows

5 See Chapter 9

6 The wording of the Prüm Convention actually provides for considerable latitude in how this is to be accomplished, www.register.consilium.europa.eu/pdf/en/06/st11/st11130.en06.pdf, accessed 5 April 2007.

another country in order to search for information about DNA, fingerprints and vehicle registration (Figure 12.5). The speed, efficiency and cost savings are likely to be substantial, but the outcome of any enquiry is limited to the extent that it can only search the main key data (metadata) stored and made available by the co-operation partner. Therefore, for such a solution to work, the partner must have a well-populated and well-structured database and manage the key data in a way that it remains accurate, up to date and comprehensive. This is easier said than done and expensive but, if this is not achieved, there is a real danger that an investigator will receive a false negative reply and, since he or she will not benefit from the personal relationships enjoyed by liaison officers or developed through NCBs, he or she is unlikely to have the understanding of the workings of the co-operation partner's law enforcement to challenge the automated answer.

In reality, Prüm-like networks are likely to be restricted to the select few nations with the resources available to develop and maintain such a system and who are able to accept and satisfy the legal conditions. Where national commitment to building a reference database is limited, the effectiveness of that network for partner countries will be rather one-sided.

BABEL, BABBLE OR BABBAGE?

Whilst computer languages have a certain degree of international standardisation, the same cannot be said of their human equivalents and the design of multilingual interfaces for joint information exchange is challenging. It has been relatively easy to build secure email systems such as the linguanet network[7] in Europe, where common templates are used with common fields, but where each user sees these fields on the screen labelled in his or her own language. However, in a truly multilingual system, the technical sophistication also needs to translate the content of the field. Different writing conventions or alphabets (Roman, Greek, Cyrillic, Arabic, Chinese, Japanese, etc.) as well as different traditions of transliteration need to be accommodated. For instance, in translating Russian into different western European languages there can be many ways of spelling the same word or name depending on how it is pronounced. Even simple culturally different traditions for writing dates (dd/mm/yyyy rather than mm/dd/yyyy) or placing the family name before the given name can lead to ambiguity and inaccuracy and the wrong person being targeted.[8] One way around such issues has been to create standard lexicons which can be compared with a table of equivalent terms in the target language, but, as any linguist

7 www.prolingua.co.uk/Linguanet/index, accessed 30 April 2007.

8 It is worth mentioning that substantial staff hours in international organisations are normally spent keying in data which arrive in multiple different formats which increases the risk of keying in error as well as requiring the commitment of expensive human resources to a rather mundane and unproductive function.

knows, translation involves more than consulting a dictionary. Another solution is to specify the use of one common working language for all co-operation partners, but doing so, apart from being politically sensitive, potentially excludes the services of many competent and capable officers who lack the linguistic skills (perhaps inadvertently encouraging the recruitment of those less able, but who speak the language). However, this remains the easiest and most effective of the options available to date and is used in many international organisations.

OFF THE DEEP END: POOLING INFORMATION

As noted above, the second main category of information exchange involves a reservoir or central pool of information created under the auspices of an international organisation and made available for communal use. This is something more than a data warehouse in that the information is not just stored, but may also be used to develop new information products. Opening such a pool for speculative searches can allow a suspect to be identified or located where s/he is known in another jurisdiction. It also has the potential advantage, at least in theory, of establishing trends, patterns and associations that would be impossible to discern by using purely national databases. After all, a clear understanding of the cause and effect of international crime is artificially fragmented by political borders which criminals ignore, but which law enforcement officers are obliged to obey. A central information pool can be used to provide strategic thinkers with an overview.

However, unfortunately, the response and enthusiasm with which information is provided in this way varies not just from state to state, but also between agencies within those states. Strategic analyses, and by extension any decisions based upon them, depend on the quality of the research material (information) available and any limitations will be reflected in the analysis produced.[9] Because information provided to a central body is sourced at a distance it is often unclear to what extent the value and nature of the data have been vetted for suitability before submission. Indeed, it is possible for policy directives to endorse the quantity of submissions over their quality because perceptions of success of a database are often measured by the number of entries it contains.

When it comes to data for strategic analysis, international organisations often seek to supplement unsolicited submissions by circulating questionnaires to their national partners asking a series of specific questions. The extent to which such questionnaires penetrate the national environment and reflect the

9 For example, at the national level, the failure to achieve quality of content was cited as the reason for cancelling the US Department of Defense's Talon database in August 2007: 'Pentagon to Close Disputed Database', New York Times, 22 August 2007.

experience and views of all relevant national authorities is unknown. There are perhaps also other shortcomings in this approach. Some countries may simply not have a culture of gathering statistics or collecting data (so may revert to anecdote or guesswork in order to provide a response), or may do so using extremely different methodologies of inconsistent reliability and some may not even respond at all, but what other choice does an international organisation have than to work with such variables? Some information is better than no information and whatever the quality or substance of information received, it comes with the label of national contribution, endorsed by the national member and must be formally relied upon as such. Unfortunately, although the submission of poor information results in unreliable analysis (what computer-speak calls 'Garbage In, Garbage Out' or GIGO), the value of an international organisation will often be predicated on its ability to provide supranational perspectives despite it having little influence over the inward flow of data. Thus a vicious circle can be easily established: poor analysis equals poor value; poor value means the organisation lacks credibility; no credibility discourages the sending of information; poor information results in poor analysis . . . and so on.

In the EU context, concerns about the low volume of information sharing prompted, at least in part, the proposal for a so-called 'principle of availability'. The intention is that officers in one EU state should be able to access any police information held in a second EU state as easily as any national officer. The EU Council Decision giving effect to this principle also proposed that any such information exchanged should be made available centrally to Europol.[10] It is too early to tell whether these intentions will have any real effect.

CHINESE WHISPERS

The technical procedures by which information is actually input or retrieved from an information pool need not concern the investigator. The user of a system really only wants to know whether the desired information is available and, if it is, whether she or he can obtain it. There are almost no technical limits to the promise of e-law enforcement, but barriers are raised on the one hand by the demands of political, administrative and judicial traditions or, on the other, by the lack of funding for IT infrastructure development. Connecting the users by secure, technical means is, by now, quite a routine process. Interpol's I-24/7 network, for example, is truly worldwide having enabled police to police communication across the globe. However, the extent to which governments would support a total automation of the exchange process is more problematic.

The most efficient information pool would entail the automatic and continual

10 M. Valsamis, 'Police Co-operation: What are the Main Obstacles to Police Co-operation in the EU?', www.libertysecurity.org/article1379, accessed 30 April 2007.

upload of relevant data from national databases to a central point and to permit authorised users to browse that data in a structured way. However, no country could allow any degree of automation that would place unfettered control (and sovereignty) over its national records in the hands of a separate and independent entity. This means that any data being pooled has to be pre-selected at the national level either by human intervention (which is labour intensive and costly) or by creating strong electronic filters on the basis of acceptable criteria. This is quite feasible with modern technology, but even this is a little too drastic for some. The preferred alternative to date has been to create reference databases where only key words or short abstracts of a record are disclosed to users together with a reference number and contact details. Someone searching for and retrieving such a limited record is then able to make further bilateral enquiries directly with the named contact. However, mindless reliance on the accuracy of the content of such systems can have uncomfortable results. For instance, in July 2007, a BBC reporter on holiday in Slovenia found himself spending two days of incarceration after his name had been matched against a German police computer entry concerning a fraudster with the same name[11] and, in 2003, a British pensioner was subjected to three weeks' imprisonment in South Africa when his name was checked against a database and matched that of a fraudster wanted in the USA.[12]

PROTECTING PERSONAL DATA

Data protection is one of the political, administrative and judicial barriers to co-operation mentioned above. Since the 1980s there has been an increasing emphasis on the need to protect personal data (particularly in Europe).[13] In countries that have not adopted or do not recognise the concept of personal data ownership, the motivation for keeping data confidential has more to do with protecting the integrity of the information than with safeguarding the rights of the data subject.[14] There is also the practical requirement to protect a sensitive source so that she or he will continue to deliver information safely (to encourage other informants to come forward with confidence).

11 K. Sekyere, 'ID Theft left me in Slovenian Prison', www.news.bbc.co.uk/go/pr/fr/-/1/hi/magazine/6902922.stm, accessed 19 July 2007.

12 S. Todd, 'Yes, his name is Bond . . . but he is no fraudster', www.news.scotsman.com/topics.cfm?tid=779&id=241292003, 26 February 2003, accessed 19 July 2007

13 Defined as: '. . . any information relating to an identified or identifiable individual. An individual shall not be regarded as "identifiable" if identification requires an unreasonable amount of time, cost and manpower.': Recommendation of the Committee of Ministers to Member States Regulating the Use of Personal Data in the Police Sector, Council of Europe Recommendation R(87)15 1987, the preamble.

14 I.e. the person about whom the information is held.

Often, the two approaches have a similar impact in terms of information security procedures and two countries that share the same approach will find few legal difficulties in sharing information. However, data protection rules can become an obstacle when a country that protects personal data needs to co-operate with a country that does not.[15] In theory, at least, according to international conventions, a country with a data protection regime should not exchange personal data with any authority unless it guarantees an 'adequate' system of protection for those data.[16] In practical terms, the strict implementation of that rule would create an embargo on working with a great many countries, but, of course, it does not quite happen that way. Individually, countries can normally agree on a form of words in national legislation which allows them to avoid such an obstacle – even if only for exceptional circumstances. In Schedule 4 to the UK's Data Protection Act 1998, for instance, a number of exemptions are provided which, 'collectively . . . seem to cover the vast majority of instances where the police are likely to transfer personal data beyond the European Economic Area.'[17] On the other hand, the UK's Information Commissioner is quoted in the same document as offering a note of caution in that although these exemptions:

> . . . reflect the fact that there are instances where it will be justifiable to transfer data even though there will be a lower level of protection given to those data. As such, in interpreting these provisions, the derogations should be narrowly construed.[18]

The 'adequacy' standards for processing personal data place limits not only on the dissemination of information, but also on what can be done with it once it has been received.[19] Data provided should normally only be used for the purposes for which they have been provided (all of which purposes having been authorised by law), only those data 'essential' to achieving these stated purposes should be retained, and they should be deleted as soon as such purposes have been achieved. Nor should the data be forwarded to any third party without the agreement of whoever provided the data in the first place. Where

15 An interesting point here is that the USA passed a Privacy Act as early as 1974, but only recognises the rights of data subjects who are US nationals and permanent residents. Information shared concerning citizens form elsewhere does not, therefore, enjoy protection.

16 Op. cit., Council Recommendation R (87)15, fn 13.

17 Association of Chief Police Officers 'Data Protection Manual of Guidance: Part 1 Standards', (2006) ACPO London, www.acpo.police.uk/asp/policies/Data/ACPODPMoGV1.06, accessed 30 April 2007.

18 Ibid.

19 This was written before the security fiasco in November 2007 when the UK's revenue and customs authority (HMRC) mishandled and exposed the personal data of 25 million people to the risk of fraud by sending unencrypted data disks to the National Audit Office using unregistered normal post.

these rules are in force, law enforcement bodies are held to account by independent oversight and by the right of the data subject to take the matter to court. They also mean that managing and exchanging police information is not as easy or as flexible as it once was and, with all due respect to the rights of the individual, there will be times when the rights of those other than the data subject will be adversely affected because of it.

There is a further data protection issue in respect of international organisations. By definition, an international organisation is not subject to the national law. Any data protection rules, therefore, as well as any arrangements for independent oversight have to be created specifically for that institution. As discussed in Chapter 4, EU agencies such as Eurojust, Europol and the Schengen Information System, are covered by EU data protection legislation and special bodies have been created to undertake its supervision. However, these arrangements function within a context where all national members are committed to the data protection ethos. Finding a common solution is less easy when part of the membership has a different view on the issue. Interpol has gone to great lengths to establish an 'adequate' and highly credible data protection regime,[20] but has had difficulty in convincing some of its members that the rules will be fully respected by those states that do not recognise the doctrine in national law. As a result there has, apparently, been a disappointing brake on the provision of information from some countries.[21] An interesting aside is that, although US law does not generally protect the personal data of non-US citizens or residents, the USA has signed up to Interpol's regulations on the protection of such information.

In addition to data protection considerations, national attitudes towards human rights can also impact on the exchange of data. It is a sad fact that some countries obtain information through torture or through other methods condemned elsewhere as unacceptable, but how should such information be treated when received by an agency in a liberal democracy? This can create a real dilemma. The political and easy response would be to reject the information on the basis that to accept it would be to condone the methods used in its acquisition. However, any country submitting such information is unlikely to disclose how it was obtained and, in any case, the subject matter may be so compelling that it demands action irrespective. Under such circumstances, were the information to be ignored and were the serious crime or major outrage threatened in it come to pass, then the agencies concerned would soon be chastised for their failure to protect the innocent. On the other hand, if the information were to be actioned, it is likely to be challenged in any resulting court case or enquiry as

20 www.interpol.int/public/ICPO/LegalMaterials/constitution/info/default.asp, accessed 5 May 2007.

21 S. El Zein, 'Reconciling Data Protection Regulations with the Requirements of Judicial and Police Co-operation', www.pcpd.org.hk/english/infocentre/files/elzein-paper.doc, p. 5, accessed 15 January 2007.

inadmissible and could, with the benefit of hindsight, easily prove to be the false product of a victim's attempt to avert further torture.

Accepting such information not only gives a tacit approval and encouragement to those breaches of human rights used, but also establishes a reciprocal debt which the provider will expect to be honoured with information in return. Unfortunately, information exchanged with such a partner could well then be used to initiate further breaches of human rights. Dealing with information when the source is tainted by suspicions of mistreatment is an uncomfortable responsibility that is better managed by experts well versed in the concomitant risks and who are able to refer to clear policy guidelines.

NATIONAL POINTS OF CONTACT

No regular investigator can be expected to know all the international ropes in sending messages abroad – the procedures have become too complex – but any such uncertainty can be easily addressed by establishing a single unit at the national level incorporating the expertise to deal with the dispatch and receipt of all international requests. This is not a novel concept. In fact, the use of some kind of national point of contact is a common feature in most of the communication models described above and is mentioned by many of the contributors to this book. An international co-operation unit can act as gatekeeper and conduit, offering advice and guiding information to the most appropriate quarter. It can also enforce commonly agreed standards for the international transmission of data and help to promote best practice and build confidence in sharing information. Although logic dictates that all channels of international co-operation should be commonly managed, implementation of the single national unit concept has been somewhat slow (some suggestions as to how such a unit could look are given in Appendix 4).

CONCLUSION

It may seem paradoxical that in the 'information age' the sharing of information should be so prescribed by procedures and protocols, but the sort of information involved in criminal justice has value in terms of reducing harm to the public, in terms of organisational performance, as well as in terms of hard operational results, and should be handled responsibly. There are a number of different models for sharing information from direct bilateral exchanges to the use of a central international hub for multilateral communication. As these possibilities become more and more complex, rationalisation of information management can be made more secure and effective if a single national unit is created. Even so, special consideration needs to be given to procedures that manage risk when dealing with countries that have a less rigorous attitude to the collection and manipulation of data. No one would question the precautions taken to protect a bank vault or a great work of art. Indeed one would not only expect the latest security to be installed to guarantee their safety, but would also expect properly authenticated documentation as a precondition for any transfer of ownership. The worth of criminal information may be less tangible but, in terms of an investigation, it can be invaluable. As such its handling should be treated with no less respect and similarly strict precautions should be introduced to guarantee that the message arrives, intact, in time and with integrity.

Chapter 13

Keeping in context

Meaning what you say

Kevin O'Connell

The increase in the number of people travelling globally has ensured that within hours of the commission of a serious crime its perpetrators can distance themselves by thousands of miles. Although the majority of criminal offences is still committed by local criminals, resourceful criminals – local or otherwise – know that operating in a different country, perhaps under a different identity, can defeat attempts to trace them. There are notorious cases of individuals who have evaded capture by crossing national boundaries (including, for instance, the celebrated industrialist, Asil Nadir, who skipped bail in London and fled to northern Cyprus in 1993 whilst under investigation by the Serious Fraud Office[1]), but exploiting national boundaries for personal protection should not be perceived as being the act of a particularly sophisticated criminal. In Europe in particular, the removal of internal border controls to facilitate trade and travel within the EU has not removed the advantages to the criminal of administrative and linguistic boundaries. The main advantage of cross-border flight for prolific criminals is that they can begin again with a clean sheet in a new country where their details and biometric data (such as fingerprints) are not held on file, and where, even if they are convicted, they will not attract the heavier sentences associated with recidivism. This has prompted the EU, with its commitment to open borders, to consider introducing a community criminal record.[2]

Any international exchange of information is heavily dependent on the accuracy of data handling, communication and interpretation, and investigators naturally expect to be able to rely on established mechanisms to allow them to communicate across political, administrative and linguistic boundaries. The necessary accuracy can be achieved in part by assiduous use of those limited mechanisms that already exist. However, if they are to avoid some

1 P. Clarke, 'Man who helped Polly Peck boss escape felt he "deserved a break"', London: The Independent, 23 July 1998, London.

2 The debate about whether to have a computerised database for criminal records across the EU is well advanced, www.eu2007.de/en/News/Press_Releases/June/0613BMJStrafregister.html, accessed 15 June 2007.

uncomfortable consequences, investigators need to remain vigilant in order to avoid misunderstanding and to double-check even the most basic assumptions.

From directly observed accounts of faulty communication in the European context it is possible to draw some broad conclusions as to how investigators can reduce the likelihood of data accuracy being corrupted by error during cross border information exchanges. Other areas of international co-operation have been confronted with similar problems and the solutions applied there can also provide clues for law enforcement on how to enhance investigative dialogues.

GENERIC PROBLEMS

Communication can be impeded at many different levels: by incompatible or inconsistent rules; linguistic confusion; complex decision-making processes; or, mismatched technology. However, as already stated, law enforcement agencies are not alone in facing such problems. In the wider security context, for instance, the effective networking and unification of different command and control structures has long been a challenge. In 1999, Brigadier General Michael H. Clemmesen, provided a clear overview of problems of interoperability facing small countries that, as newcomers, wished to integrate with established NATO forces on an operational level. In particular, he highlighted the advantages that poor interoperability can give to an adversary:

> Without a common language, military forces cannot co-operate effectively. Two units with a common mission, but without common language will have to divide the tasks between them in a way that makes interaction unnecessary. They must then hope that nothing and nobody will interfere with the line of division. However, no military operation can be safely built on such a premise. Any competent military opponent will seek these divisions of responsibility and exploit them.[3]

Although there is some reason to believe that issues of communication become more difficult in the generalist culture of criminal justice, the same challenges faced by NATO are those now confronting international law enforcement. The solutions for NATO were rooted in standardisation of language,[4] procedures, formats, communications and encryption. A failure to adopt a common approach would have otherwise divided its multinational forces and prevented unity of command during operational emergencies. In a parallel context, Brigadier General Clemmesen pointed out that:

3 www.bdcol.ee/fileadmin/docs/bdreview/13bdr199.pdf (1999), accessed 15 June 2007.

4 NATO Standardisation Agreements (2007), www.nato.int/docu/stanag/aap006/aap6.htm, accessed 15 June 2007.

> Armies are very much social organisms and even if they are sometimes influenced by . . . 'role model' armies, they remain very different. These differences are much less pronounced in navies and air forces that are much more dominated by the medium in which they work and the technology they have to use to be effective.[5]

National law enforcement agencies are also social organisms and are rooted in their own criminal justice systems and cultures. They, too, remain very different but face the same imperatives in terms of co-operation and common understanding. In this regard, standardisation can be a useful way forward.

Edward Johnson, an expert on the operational use of structured language in police and emergency services, has emphasised how an operational environment can affect an understanding of meaning in a communication exchange:

> Projects in operational communications are not just words and phrases, they are completely context dependent . . . 'PoliceSpeak' was no exception. It involved close examination of the Channel Tunnel as an operational environment as set out in the engineering drawings and other planning documents. It required a review of the anticipated technical communications provisions, and a study of the contrasting British and French police organisations and the legal and administrative framework being put in place to enable both sides to work together.[6]

CO-OPERATING IN COMMUNICATION

Official structures for international data exchange require requests to be channelled from the investigator up through administrative hierarchies to a central national message clearing facility where they can be passed across to a similar office or contact point in another country. From there they are passed down along the chain of communication, usually to another investigator.[7]

International investigations are becoming more extensive not only because of the increased need to access a source of information in another country, but also because of the need to secure evidence that proves a case beyond a reasonable doubt (for instance by eliminating additional lines of enquiry, further clarifying the facts or reducing operational risks by undertaking more background checks). This can be the case even where a criminal act is local, but where the actors (victims, witnesses or suspects) originated or have subsequently

5 Op. cit., fn 3, p. 3.

6 Policespeak is an international police communications system operating across the English Channel, E. Johnson, 'Talking across borders', www.prolingua.co.uk/talking, accessed 15 June 2007.

7 See Chapter 12.

travelled abroad. Even where such enquiries are routine, this will increase the quantity of data being exchanged and reduce the time available to do it.

There is only one global platform for law enforcement co-operation, Interpol, and it holds communication at the heart of its strategic goals. On a practical level, it provides standardised communication tools that allow messages to be sent on a specially designed communication network, including within a system of 'notices' that is both readily understood and actionable.[8] The success of Interpol and other major information exchange agencies depends on their ability to manage contextual information. Three strategies for such management have developed over the years:

- investment in additional time in explaining the context of a request;
- elimination of the need for contextual information; or
- usage of a standardised context mechanism.

Interpol notices began as a mechanism for circulating judicial decisions where the contextual complexity had already been evaluated, filtered and transcribed by the judges. In other words, originally, an Interpol notice was the summary of a judge's assessment of a situation and this still continues to be the situation in the majority of cases. For example, statistics show that in 2005, more than 70 per cent of Interpol's notices were 'Red', that is, they were straightforward accounts of persons wanted for arrest and extradition. As such they required no contextual explanation. However, a small, but significant number, about 10 per cent, of the message traffic consisted of 'Green' notices, involving intelligence information and therefore carrying a message which is contextually demanding.

Because it is focused on the exchange and provision of intelligence information, Europol has sought to develop a powerful mechanism for exchanging contextual information across the 23 official languages of the EU.[9] In its central work, however, it has adopted English as the common working language. Europol is assisted in its work by the excellent network it hosts of liaison officers from the Member States (and other associated countries) who are able to provide more personalised help in inquiries and can reduce the likelihood of misunderstandings to a significant extent. Europol itself manages databases that may contain additional information but, because they are not a complete record of the data held in Member States of the EU, it is difficult for an investigator to evaluate the implications of a positive or negative search result.

For many years a group of law enforcement users with cross-border responsibilities in 10 European countries have been operating and developing a

8 See Chapter 3, p. 46.
9 See Chapter 4, p. 62.

straightforward application called LinguaNet.[10] This is a purpose-built e-mail system first installed, point to point, between four European nations (the UK, France, Belgium and the Netherlands) in 1993. This context-specific system (routine communication between operational police units across frontiers) uses standardised messages and combines free-text, formatted text, images and annotations. It thus allows information exchange in and between national languages using terminology already standardised by its users. The 'declared-context' methodology also provides opportunities for better directed human translation and the selective application of certain free-text translation systems.

More recently a sub-group of EU countries[11] have also set up a system of information exchange that requires no contextual information to operate. Under the Treaty of Prüm, forensic information and vehicle registration data is compared on a 'hit – no hit' basis and contextual matters are reviewed only after a match. The system is still in its infancy and is expected to be extended to all the countries of the EU.

In general, however, the current situation suggests that complex solutions are needed to resolve the problem of mutual comprehension in critical information exchange. Although liaison officers can provide a partial solution, they are a limited resource and cannot easily manage the growing volumes of traffic.

The widely different international priorities and importance afforded to the protection of personal data are also divisive and impact on attitudes in different parts of the world as to how law enforcement information should be exchanged. Most European countries have their own data-protection procedures to safeguard the rights of the citizen against the risk of the state mishandling his or her personal information. From the point of view of an individual investigator, the practical effect of data protection means that any information containing personal details must be kept confidential and, unless there are national bilateral agreements in place, may only be exchanged with those countries that can demonstrate an 'adequate' (in other words an acceptable minimum) level of protection. The data must also be kept accurate and current. Where a criminal investigation is concerned and the exchange of data happens between police authorities, the expectation is that the data will be checked for accuracy by both the sender and the recipient. Compliance with these rules will normally be double-checked by the national message clearing facilities. However, where a data subject[12] does suffer damage from an error in the information process, data-protection-compliant procedures should ensure that the cause of the error (as well as who caused it) can be readily identified and appropriate reparation made. Such rights of an individual are not actually in conflict with the need for investigators to have only data which are accurate and relevant in

10 www.prolingua.co.uk/talking.pdf, accessed 15 June 2007.

11 Austria, Germany, Luxembourg, Belgium, the Netherlands, France and Spain.

12 The individual whose personal details are contained in the information.

order to avoid false lines of enquiry and the unnecessary waste of scarce resources.

Comparative studies of different criminal justice systems can provide a comprehensive view of the breadth and variety of contextual factors.[13] Here, there is only space to provide some direct anecdotal evidence to illustrate how terminology can have alternative meanings and how understanding the context in which an international investigation is taking place has a direct bearing on meaning. In some jurisdictions, the exchange of evidential information between 'investigators' happens as a two-stage process consisting of an initial informal and exploratory message to ascertain whether information of value is held (and is available to be shared) followed by a formal request for mutual judicial co-operation.

When investigators in some systems speak of detecting a crime, they mean the process by which the existence of a crime is confirmed rather than the identification of a suspect. Indeed, in many jurisdictions, police officers do not have independent powers of investigation once a crime has been detected (in the sense of an act becoming suspected as criminal), but must act on the instructions of a prosecutor.

For many international colleagues, the English word 'intelligence' has negative connotations, associated with the work of security services. Indeed, the fact that some native speakers of English also associate the word exclusively with secretly obtained information adds to the confusion.[14] This can have cultural implications and, as a consequence, lead to the lack of a consistent method for assessing crime threats. Some national methodologies do not attempt to make assessments in operational terms but, instead, prefer environmental scanning or scenario generation techniques to help set investigative priorities. In fact, in some investigative cultures, worrying about future crimes is not even part of the investigative remit.

Misunderstandings between native speakers alone are enough to indicate the likelihood of confusion internationally. Natural language (as opposed to deliberately structured language) contains many hidden traps where wrong assumptions are made and the errors are never discovered. This is true not only when one language is translated into another, but also when the same language is used internationally. When people use their own languages it is generally easier to recognise misunderstandings, but errors of interpretation are more difficult to detect in multinational situations. In Belgium, the Netherlands (and at Europol), the word 'operational', for instance, implies data that contain personal information, as opposed to 'strategic' data that do not. But 'operational' and 'strategic' have also retained their meanings of 'using coercive powers' and

13 For example, Craig Bradley, *Criminal Procedure: A Worldwide Study* (Durham, NC: Carolina Academic Press, 1999).

14 See S. Brown, 'The Meaning of Criminal Intelligence' in International Journal of Police Science and Management, 9(4) (2007).

'long-term and logistical planning' respectively. The opportunities for confusion with such 'false friends' are endless because the speaker and listener actually recognise the word being used, but do not realise that they interpret it differently. In this situation, it is perhaps more a question of inherited or conditioned context acting on each side of the dialogue separately.

Given such potential for misunderstanding, the use of a liaison officer, where one is available to help, is currently the best way to exchange information, particularly in complex cases. Unfortunately, not all countries have the resources to support a liaison network and there have been moves within the EU to allow the mutual use of liaison officers from other Member States beyond the border of the Union.[15] Liaison officers have a distinct advantage as a method for communication. They provide local awareness, overcome the language barrier and can interpret the state of an investigation in the terms of the host state. They can also usually gain access to decision-makers at different levels and make representations in support of a particular case. However, their use often involves handing over some of the initiative of the investigation.

It is safe to assume that the volume of international communications will continue to grow and that this growth will put formal information exchange mechanisms under more pressure (not least because international mobility is on an upward trend and enquiries will be increasingly needed concerning persons from distant locations). If cross-border communication remains complex and costly, the impact on investigative decisions at all levels is likely to be negative. Budgets are already a deciding factor in whether there is sufficient cost-benefit in pursuing a line of enquiry abroad or whether to settle for a prosecution strategy based on evidence which is available locally. Delays involved in escalating and progressing inquiries at the international level can also have negative effects on an investigator's decision-making. There can be no doubt that ease of communication affects not only the access to but also the quality of justice being delivered globally, but the extent to which the international dimension limits the scope of a criminal investigation has yet to be measured. However, there is also some reason to suspect that international inquiries are not always directed along the formal exchange routes and that some information passes across semi-formal networks where determined investigators attempt to obtain a more timely response. Even though all parties concerned may be acting in good faith, investigators who manage their own international communications need also to manage the concomitant risk.

15 www.futureofeurope.parliament.gv.at/sides/getDoc.do?pubRef=-//EP//NONSGML+TA+P6-TA-2006–0126+0+DOC+WORD+V0//EN, accessed 15 June 2007.

SOME POINTERS

Experience has shown that confidence in law enforcement action is only possible where data have been delivered accurately without distortion and have then been properly interpreted. Even where formal mechanisms are used, it is wise to assume nothing. Based on this experience, there are perhaps three basic guidelines for achieving effective cross-cultural information exchange:

- obtain data from sources that are believed to be true by the provider and would appear, on objective assessment, to be so (if not, then some measure of classifying their reliability is required);
- ensure that the data remain unchanged in the process of transferring them from one person to the next;
- double-check that the person on the receiving end of the transmission understands the data in their original context.

The first guideline is still not so easy to achieve despite the introduction of modern technology and formal information exchange networks and it being given special mention by the Council of Europe 20 years ago:

> As far as possible, the different categories of data stored should be distinguished in accordance with their degree of accuracy or reliability and, in particular, data based on facts should be distinguished from data based on opinions or personal assessments.[16]

Investigators should be aware that distinguishing fact from opinion can be a time-consuming activity that is not always practised with equal enthusiasm globally. Not all data can be expected to have the same levels of precision.

The greatest danger for the second guideline lies in the quality of translation, transliteration and interpretation of a text in a foreign language. Manual (that is to say typing) errors are also a common source of mistakes, particularly where a communication chain or procedure requires the re-keying of the same data more than once. Where machine (computer) translation tools are available, they can be used to get a general appreciation of the content of a text in a foreign language, but they are far from being 100 per cent accurate and should not be used for interpreting critical information or for rendering one's own language in a foreign one.[17]

The third guideline is, as indicated above, the most important and significant

16 The Council of Europe Recommendation R (87)15, Regulating the use of personal data in the police sector (Principle 3), www.coe.int/t/e/legal_affairs/legal_co-operation/combating_economic_crime/1_standard_settings/Rec_1987_15.pdf, accessed 15 June 2007.

17 This is the policy used by the European Police Office and developed with the advice of Dr Edward Johnson, Wolfson College, Cambridge.

as a source of difficulty – 'context'. The proper understanding of any message requires the recipient to understand the motivation and reasons for sending that message. Messages, be they requests for assistance or simply supplying useful information to a colleague, should never require the recipients to make assumptions. They need to be in plain language without jargon or technical terms that would be unknown or ambiguous in the receiving state. An appreciation of the level of resources and facilities available to agencies at the other end of any inquiry is also advisable. There is little point in requesting a DNA sample, a link chart or a psychological profile if they are alien concepts locally. The use of drawings, photographs and scientific material to supplement the written word can also help to reduce the amount of 'decoding' that is needed on the recipient's side.

Although the use of a secure e-mail or fax is preferable for auditing purposes, as well as for controlling potential ambiguity before dispatch, it will not be universally available and live conversations may well be necessary when seeking to contact colleagues in other countries (across different time zones). When this is necessary native speakers should not overestimate the language ability of non-native speakers. Even where they could normally be expected to have a good linguistic understanding of the source language, it is dangerous to assume this is actually the case. In such a situation, the recipient of the message may not easily admit his or her lack of comprehension. The concept of 'face' or *bella figura* applies more often than one might think and the most natural thing for the other person to do to avoid embarrassment is to fill in the gaps themselves, unconsciously or otherwise. In the end, the main responsibility for the effectiveness of a communication lies with the investigator.

BACK TO THE FUTURE

It is not possible to conclude an account like this without wondering why more technological help against information error is absent. Modern technology is certainly bringing forward possibilities of avoiding written language altogether with the use of oral communication, video, pictures, maps and drawings sent digitally in real time. Unfortunately, in the past, far too much has been promised and never delivered and strategic planners, in law enforcement as much as in any other sector, have found themselves committed to ambitious IT projects which have quickly spiralled out of control to the embarrassment of all concerned.[18] On the other hand potentially helpful technologies do exist which are already available and affordable: Voice Over Internet Protocol (VOIP) telephony or teleconferencing can bring investigators together from across the world

18 H. Goldstein, 'Who killed the virtual case file' (2005), www.spectrum.ieee.org/sep05/1455, accessed 15 June 2007.

without the need for them to leave their office desks; powerful encryption protocols for ensuring secure data transmission can be easily obtained at low cost; analytical software can convert vast quantities of data into diagrammatic form and data mining can sift through the mountains of information churned out on a daily basis identifying and collating data which might be useful. The main drawback with such advances is the cost of infrastructure and training needed to accommodate them and the risk that the technology starts to lead the business rather than supporting it. This can happen all too easily where law enforcement professionals have to rely on the IT professional to explain even the most basic of computer processes.

There is nothing new about ambiguity or misunderstanding in communication. In the modern world however, more than ever before in history, law enforcement, law making and law breaking is implicated in a kaleidoscope of languages and cultures that have to be interpreted and understood if there is to be any kind of objective justice. The burden now sits uneasily and perhaps unfairly on the investigator who is charged with the responsibility to do what s/he can with the inadequate tools at his or her disposal. The task is not impossible, though it can sometimes appear to be so. All it really needs is a willingness to be aware that words do not always mean what they say and that there is a real need to understand 'where the other person is coming from'.

Part IV

Major tools and techniques

Chapter 14

Controlled deliveries

Steven David Brown

Imagine for a moment that you are the commander of a national counter-narcotics team and you receive information that in the next 24 hours a lorry will be loaded with 80kg of heroin, driven across a continent through several countries to arrive finally in your city where the drugs will be repackaged and distributed nationwide. You know that if the heroin is seized at the point of loading, you will net the 80kg and the driver and, perhaps, a few others. This might be a quick win for seizure statistics, but it will make little impact on the overall flow and supply of illicit drugs. A far more effective, but riskier, option would be to allow the lorry to travel to its destination as planned and to monitor the journey, identifying with whom it comes into contact and to whom it finally delivers. In that way, you will have the chance to wind up a complete network and prevent it from doing any more harm.

This, in essence, is the international controlled delivery.[1] It means allowing an illegal commodity to travel to its destination but, at all times, in a controlled manner. The UN Convention against illicit traffic in narcotic drugs and psychotropic substances 1988[2] describes it in this way:

> 'Controlled delivery' means the technique of allowing illicit or suspect consignments of narcotic drugs, psychotropic substances, substances [*listed in an annex to the Convention*], or substances substituted for them, to pass out of, through or into the territory of one or more countries, with the knowledge and under the supervision of their competent authorities, with a view to identifying persons involved in the commission of offences . . .[3]

Sometimes transit and delivery networks can be so complex that controlled deliveries will be an essential strategy for understanding the full extent of the trafficking. For example, two Colombians, brothers-in-law, arrived in the UK

1 Controlled deliveries can also happen locally or nationally.
2 www.unodc.org/pdf/convention_1988_en.pdf, accessed 4 May 2007.
3 Ibid., Art 1(g).

requesting asylum in 1990 and were given leave to remain. They had jobs, raised their families in quiet suburbia and lived respectable unassuming lives. One of them even won £100,000 in a national competition and sponsored an orphanage in his home town in Colombia. So much for appearances![4]

In fact these brothers imported up to an estimated 1.5 tonnes of cocaine annually into the UK and had been doing so for more than a decade. In fact, when this organised crime group was finally dismantled, the street price of cocaine was reputed to have doubled (no doubt causing a commensurate local increase in acquisitive crime[5]). The planning involved in this illicit enterprise was both thorough and impressive. Cocaine would be taken by ship from Colombia to off the coast of Spain or Portugal where it would be ferried ashore. The drugs would then be parcelled into small amounts (concealed in jars of jam or smeared with mustard to confuse sniffer dogs, or dissolved in a chemical solution and soaked into clothing) before being forwarded to London where it was again repackaged and distributed across the country.

The cash proceeds were returned to Colombia in the same way as the drugs were imported, in bags full of cash on the delivery lorries, or in swallowed condoms filled with rolled bank notes, or sent as electronic money transfers in amounts small enough not to attract attention. There were hundreds of such transfers and literally thousands of people involved. It was estimated that up to £20 million annually was transferred in this way.

The investigation took four years and involved close co-operation between the British and the Colombian authorities. At the time of the arrest, 645kg of cocaine were seized along with 1.5 tonnes of cannabis and £5 million in cash. Thirty-four people, including a Canadian, a Panamanian and four Spaniards, were convicted in the UK (sentenced to a total of 350 years) and 17 in Colombia. The two brothers-in-law were sentenced to 19 and 17 years and recommended for deportation on prison release.

In passing sentence, the judge summed up how difficult it can be to bring the higher echelons of organised crime to justice when he stated those who run the drugs industry are:

> very rarely caught . . . because they pay other people to carry out the dangerous work where an arrest is more likely . . . Their fingerprints are not found on the drug packaging, no telephone is shown to have made relevant calls, nothing incriminating is found in their homes. Others carry out their tasks. Meanwhile they make enormous profits from this foul trade.[6]

4 Whilst there is no public corroboration that this case involved controlled deliveries, the case did involve the use of undisclosed 'covert' measures.

5 'Acquisitive crime' is the term given to crimes committed in order to acquire funds for drugs.

6 R. Cowan, 'Smuggling in suburbia: how two men ran cartel flooding UK with £1bn of cocaine', London: The Guardian, 7 December 2006; S. Freeman, 'Colombian drug lords who ran UK cocaine trade are jailed', London: The Times, 6 January 2006.

Controlled deliveries are a mainstay of international operations and are not just for combating illicit drugs trade, they are equally applicable to cases involving trafficking in human beings and illegal immigration, firearms, counterfeit goods, protected wildlife species, nuclear material – in fact, any illegal commodity that needs to be transported from one place to another.

Three sets of circumstances can prompt a controlled delivery:

- information received from an informant (perhaps a person arrested already en route in possession of the illegal wares);
- information arising out of another law enforcement activity (for instance, from telephone interception); or
- a 'cold' find where a concealment has been discovered during a routine inspection such as a drug detection 'sniffer' dog searching through cargo.

The most important part of a controlled delivery is the 'control' element which can, again, be divided into three categories:

- direct, physical observation and surveillance;
- direct participation in the transportation by an undercover officer or participating informant; or
- electronic surveillance (such as placing a transmitter or beacon with the contraband).

At all times the option to seize and recover the commodity at a moment's notice needs to be available to those monitoring the drugs' journey and the risk of losing control of the shipment is carefully assessed, taking into account the possible danger both in terms of loss of the consignment and risk to life.

Where controlled deliveries involve the transportation of people, for instance, the humanitarian and human rights element of the cargo is of utmost concern. People traffickers have shown no qualms about throwing their human cargo overboard or locking them into airtight compartments when confronted by the risk of detection. In choosing the controlled delivery option, the officer in charge has to balance the risk to those being transported against the misery and harm the criminal organisation will undoubtedly cause in the future. Whenever possible, the bulk of the consignment will normally be removed and replaced with a harmless substitute (except for a token amount left there for evidential purposes), but such precautions, of course, are not viable where a human consignment is involved.

Because an (international) controlled delivery implies the involvement of other jurisdictions, the correct permissions must be obtained in advance to allow clearance (especially if an undercover officer or participating informant is involved or if an officer from the requesting country will join the surveillance team). As can be expected, different countries require different forms, formats and formulas. Often, but not always, an official letter of request will be required in the language of the country concerned and will need to include sufficient information to satisfy a judicial authority before it will be granted. For things to happen, and for them to happen on time, you must know the correct procedure for submitting the request and what details the country will require. These are difficult waters to navigate and once again the benefit of having an expert central point of contact cannot be overestimated. In reality, however, controlled deliveries will normally be undertaken and managed by specialist agencies or units and the procedural paths will have been well trodden.

Some countries also have certain policy thresholds that your application will need to satisfy. For instance, they may require a precise and identifiable destination address for the delivery to be named or they will stipulate a minimum quantity of contraband below which they will not allocate resources (especially, for instance, where the country regularly deals with the importation of much larger quantities). Normally, a transit country will also seek assurances that, should they need to intervene and make an arrest, the requesting country will provide all necessary assistance and information to secure a conviction.

Established procedures also safeguard the officers involved. There was a case, for instance, where an enterprising police officer arranged for his personal informant to act as a courier for drugs arriving from south Asia. Unfortunately, he did not obtain any of the necessary clearances or inter-agency permissions. The plan was to meet the courier at the airport, follow him to the delivery address and witness the handover to the dealer at which point his team would swoop and arrest all those present. However, the police officer did not reckon on the eagle eye of the customs officer who searched the courier and found the drugs. Immediately the courier explained it was all taken care of and that he was, in fact, working for the police who were waiting outside on the concourse to follow him. The customs officer went out to meet the police officer, identified him – and then arrested him on suspicion of conspiracy to import a controlled substance. The customs officer was not being mean spirited. He simply had no way of determining whether the courier was part of a genuine operation or whether it was all a ruse.

Organising a controlled delivery across a number of different countries can be a logistical nightmare. If one country fails to give its permission (or does not have a surveillance team available) the proposal will collapse. Add to this the fact that information about an illegal consignment will often be received only at the last minute, the pressure can be immense. At such times, the investigator may well feel that a bird in the hand is worth more than two in the bush.[7]

There are a number of things that can go wrong:

7 For those who are not native English speakers, this means to settle for what one already has rather than to risk losing everything by going for more.

- the more links there are in the chain, the more the likelihood that details of the operation will be leaked;
- the courier may notice that s/he is being followed;
- the consignment may be split half way along the line or travel off into a completely different direction (into a jurisdiction in which no prior permission has been obtained);
- national officers who are unaware of the operation may stop and conduct a routine check of the vehicle and find the consignment accidentally (or worse, do so and try to elicit a bribe);
- there may even be an equipment failure (something as simple as the battery on the beacon running flat or the frequencies not being compatible with receivers in one or more of the transit countries);
- where boats are used, the target vessel may meet and transfer the cargo to another unknown boat in international waters where law enforcement or the consignment may be dropped overboard before the vessel docks.

Despite all this, controlled deliveries remain an extremely effective way of making a significant impact against international organised crime. Other strategies may give more apparent success statistically, but if a consignment or single courier is lost to the crime group, that is merely another business expense; but, by dismantling a whole network, the crime group is neutralised permanently and its business associates lose their source of supply.

The technique of controlled delivery has been slow to catch on in some regions. In some countries the concept of cross-border co-operation is subordinate to other national differences. In others, performance is based on targets related to quantity of drugs seized rather than on the dismantling of the group or network used to transport them (thus encouraging high-volume low-level seizures and discouraging long-term investment in an operation which may well result in a 'success' for another agency in another country).

A controlled delivery need not involve a complicated pattern of international surveillance teams. In fact in the majority of cases controlled deliveries happen in a far less glamorous way. Drugs and other contraband are often dispatched using the normal mail or an international delivery service (particularly where the traffickers are in a small way of business). The importers rely on the volume of legitimate packages hiding their own. However, postal employees or customs can still discover the contents are not what they should be. This is often as the result of a routine inspection (no doubt in accordance with a profile of similar packages discovered in the past) or where perhaps an accident to a parcel during transit has exposed its contents. When this happens, the package is seized and the appropriate authorities are notified. The consignment can then be placed under close observation until it reaches its destination where whoever finally takes possession of it will be faced with some difficult questions.

In 2002, when US customs officials at Miami Airport took a close look at a United Parcel Service (UPS) express package from Bolivia in transit to the

Philippines, they discovered a false bottom containing 700g of high-grade cocaine. A controlled delivery was arranged with the Filipino National Bureau of Investigations (NBI) and the package was allowed to travel on to Ninoy Aquino International Airport in Manila where it was received by the Bureau of Customs and handed over to representatives of the US Drugs Enforcement Agency (DEA) and the NBI. Posing as deliverymen for UPS, undercover Filipino officers went to the address on the package where Goswill Emenike, a Nigerian, was found to be living. Mr Emenike, or 'Willy', accepted the package at which point he was promptly taken into custody. The case attracted a great deal of attention at the time and was hailed proudly by the president as the first controlled delivery under new drug laws recently passed. However, after two years in prison awaiting trial, Mr Emenike was found not guilty. The package had, indeed, been addressed to a 'George Nmadu care of Willy', but the prosecution failed on two points: (a) to prove that Mr Emenike and George Nmadu were one and the same person; and (b) because it was discovered by the court that someone calling himself George Nmadu had not only rented the premises before Mr Emenike, but had even introduced the new tenant to the landlord[8] – which only goes to show that a controlled delivery is only one part of an investigation and, even when successful, it should never be considered as conclusive.[9]

8 www.unionfc.org/Trompetazos/2004/040329-The_golden_week.htm, accessed 10 May 2007.

9 'GMA presents Nigerian man arrested for cocaine trafficking', www.gov.ph/news/printerfriendly.asp?i=1728, accessed 10 May 2007.

Chapter 15

Analyse this (and that)

A consideration of the international role of analysis

Nick Ridley

In the last 30 years, analytical techniques have become increasingly prominent in international law enforcement methodologies. Indeed, the analyst has become a new specialisation and evolved into a distinct law enforcement professional. However, the deployment, acceptance and spread of the practice of analysis is still far from universal. Even where law enforcement has recruited and trained analysts to an adequate level, issues exist over staff retention. It is all too easy to trade those same skills for a lucrative position in a commercial company.

This chapter will outline and define the main types and characteristics of analysis available for international investigation with special reference to financial crime.

ANALYSIS IN GENERAL

Much has been made of the concept of analysis and, in the context of an intelligence model, it has been widely promoted as a magic bullet for defeating transnational crime.[1] Expectations are, therefore, high but it is necessary to maintain a certain sense of proportion and, in order to avoid over-eulogising the concept of intelligence analysis, three qualifications must be made.

First, the whole process of analysing and developing intelligence is dependant on human ability and team work, supported by varying degrees and at various stages by technology (although it must be stressed that effective analysis is also possible manually on paper given time and staff resources).

Second, although distinctions have been made between different types of analysis, these cannot be placed into rigid compartments, nor be subjected to strict and artificial walls. In simple language, all such terms applied to analysis (strategic, operational, tactical) are terms of pragmatic convenience, used to

1 'Fight against organised crime: the Commission recommends common methodologies', 2 June 2005, www.europa.eu/rapid/pressReleasesAction.do?reference=IP/05/659&format=HTML&aged=0&language=EN&guiLanguage=en, accessed 13 June 2007.

describe component parts of the whole and indivisible essential function, that of criminal intelligence. The various 'techniques' are not specialist but adaptable, changing in response to criminal trends. The priority in formulating terms such as strategic intelligence or tactical intelligence or operational intelligence is not to create an analysis technique or rigid, quasi-scientific blueprint, but to utilise the information content in the most efficient and practical form of intelligence for use in support of law enforcement investigations

Third, it must be recognised that analysis is a support function. It is not a hub for law enforcement activity nor is not indispensable to an investigation but, if performed efficiently and thoroughly, it can offer invaluable support.

TYPES OF ANALYSIS

There are basically two types of analytical approach: strategic and operational.

Traditionally strategic analysis is long term, predictive and affords insight and projections into the intelligence 'bigger picture'. This type of analysis has been particularly adopted by international and regional organisations as a product through which, because of their overview, they can contribute some additional value. Its approach tends to be more wide-ranging and can potentially provide evidence for long-term planning and law enforcement policy and in doing so enhance preventative law enforcement strategies.[2]

One of the other reasons why strategic analysis has been adopted and is favoured by international organisations is that it is not totally reliant on specific operational data or on the need to negotiate the use of personal data. Even so, open source material has already been manipulated by filters and delays before it is released and, where access to operational data is concerned, such access will often be embargoed whilst operations are still 'live', where criminal proceedings are pending or where there are other security concerns. Even when the data are eventually released, they will be in a truncated, anonymised or 'sanitised' format to protect sources. All these factors compound the delay and mean that strategic analysis may often be dealing with old and previously modified news.

Just as strategic analysis is long term and relies upon data which may be, frankly, out of date, so operational analysis is dependent upon the speedy interpretation of real-time data. For such analysis to be effective, such data must not only be up to date, but also accurate and reliable.[3] The speed and intensity of ongoing inquiries demand corresponding speed and intensity in reviewing the data and drawing useful conclusions.

Similar obstacles apply to operational analysis in international investigations

2 P. Ekblom, *Getting the best out of Crime Analysis*, Crime Prevention Unit Paper no. 10, UK Home Office, 1998.

3 N. Cope, N. M. Innes and N. Fielding, 'Smart Policing – the Theory and Practice of Intelligence-led Policing', UK Home Office, 2001 (unpublished).

as they do for preparing strategic analysis. Getting information in real time is a question of trust and effective lines of communication and, as mentioned elsewhere, in many situations these are unresolved challenges. However, given that operational analysis will only be undertaken in the ambit of a live operation and, if all sides have agreed the ground rules in the first place, such data exchange and trust issues should have already been ironed out. Another issue for the analyst is how the results are to be presented (and not just in terms of language and format). Analysts who have access to advanced analytical software, for example, may produce 'link charts' which depict graphically the different associations and links between people, places, objects and events, but in countries where such techniques are unknown, investigators, prosecutors and judges may not be able to interpret them.

ANALYSIS AT WORK: FINANCIAL CRIME

Because of the international nature of the banking and financial services industry (where funds are routinely transferred, invested and re-invested globally in order to achieve the best return) financial analysis, by its very nature, has to look beyond national borders. Investigations into financial crime have made significant progress since the 1980s, with teams of law enforcement officers and specialist accountants and experts working in tandem on many types of cases, particularly those of fraud. The banking industry itself has also made great strides in developing new and innovative ways to analyse spending and investment behaviours, particularly in terms of automated systems. This has been driven not a little by international pressures to combat money laundering (and given additional impetus by the need to address the financing of terror).

The examples and types of analysis given below are non-exhaustive, but serve as illustrations of the type of support analysis can give to investigations into financial crime and money laundering.

Strategic perception

We have already considered how strategic analysis may assist with prioritisation and one of the prime concerns for law enforcement is how to spot potential trends and acquire a strategic perception of financial activity (against which illicit activity can be plotted). Sometimes a strategic product is commissioned, but the strategic managers then fail to look beyond the immediate implications of the findings reported. Sometimes this is due to the danger of becoming overly equated with short-term governmental policies to the detriment of an appreciation of potential threats in the long term.

One example is to be found in a question asked following the events of 11 September. Strategic managers wanted to know whether there had been any manipulation of global markets and stock exchanges immediately prior to

9/11 in order to raise further funds for terrorism. Despite much media speculation, subsequent inquiries by law enforcement and private financial sectors alike revealed little or no evidence to indicate any such manipulation. However, once this immediate question was resolved the possibility of future criminal collusion and manipulation of European stock markets as a potential source of terrorist financing was sidelined.

Deposit analysis

This involves looking at how money is deposited, whether there are any discernible patterns and what they reveal. The results can be either strategic and/or operational.

Deposit-centre patterns

Analysing deposit-centre patterns concerns looking at trends over a large geographic area by monitoring deposits over a period of time. The key factor is the unusual increase of cash deposits when considered against the overall background. For example:

- in 1981, Miami's city banks collectively received cash deposits of US$4.5 billion whilst, on the opposite side of the continental USA there was only a modest excess of US$343 million;
- between 1985 and 1989 banks in Los Angeles were turning over a US$3.8 billion surplus. This amounted to a noticeable 2.2 per cent increase over the previous period. At the same time the US Federal Reserve reported, on a national level, a deficit of US$1.6 million;
- in 1991 Miami's collective bank deposits showed an excess of US$5.7 billion, whilst those of Los Angeles had soared to an excess of US$5 billion.

By comparing the combined data against other corroborating information it was possible to identify a significant geographical emphasis in laundering locations that coincided with an overall increase in cocaine trafficking and large-scale cocaine dealing.

To be able to perform such analysis requires access to wide collective bank sources across a considerable time frame. However, in terms of strategic planning, and identifying large-scale laundering, the time and resources spent were well justified in this case by the trends identified.

Deposit investment patterns

This type of analysis is performed at an operational level and involves a consideration of the behaviour of depositors as well as their types of investment. A number of indicators have been identified from previous analyses and include:

- the opening of several bank accounts for no apparent reason, especially where the deposits are in cash;
- deposits into accounts using bearer instruments[4] where the source of funds is unidentified;
- deposits into accounts made using monetary instruments payable to persons other than the account holder;
- depositors obviously indifferent to unfavourable conditions such as interest rates and payment schedules, which would normally be unacceptable to a legitimate customer;
- requests to banks that certain payments should not be recorded against their own accounts, but against that bank's nostro accounts.[5]

Where behaviour matches one or more such indicators further enquiries may be necessary (but, of course, these are merely indicators and, without more, do not amount to criminal activity).

Transit customer recognition

Such indicators can be confirmed by an additional focus on the individuals actually conducting the transactions. Transit customer recognition involves a reasonably simple analysis of circumstances which suggest intermediaries are being used to carry out the transactions. Significant indicators can include:

- use of accounts for short periods of time by foreign nationals when equivalent facilities are apparently available closer to home;
- cashing in large mixed amounts of cheques, commingled with an unusual proportion of traveller's cheques;
- purchase or sale of significant amounts of precious metals by casual customers;
- purchase of amounts of precious metals, diamonds and similar high-value commodities by casual customers using individual bank cheques;
- transactions unnecessarily routed through an agent;
- the holding in trust of investments of unlisted companies that are unknown to the bank;
- cash deposits made by a large number of persons to the same account.

4 A document that states the 'bearer' or person holding the document has ownership of certain property. Common examples are shares or bond certificates.

5 A banking term referring to an account one bank may hold with another bank in a foreign jurisdiction, usually in the latter's currency.

ANTI-MONEY LAUNDERING

These last three types of financial analysis mainly concern the banking sector and its potential for criminal exploitation. Anti-money laundering, both in investigations and in proactive analysis, has been beset with problems relating to obtaining information.

Since the 1980s, international legislative measures for the banking industry have helped raise standards[6] and the importance of national regulation against money laundering have been recognised in three EU Money Laundering Directives, various UN Conventions, as well as in the establishment of the Financial Acton Task Force and the Egmont Group.[7] In many countries, responsibility (backed by a criminal liability) has transferred to those offering financial services requiring them to identify and notify suspicious activity to a national financial intelligence unit for further investigation and consequently this has led to the creation of 'Compliance' professionals. 'Know your customer' requirements have, however, greatly added to the personal information held by banks on their legitimate clients and forced criminals to find new ways of circumventing the rules. This has included wealthy crime groups buying their own banks.

Given these changes, transaction information and information from financial institutions should, in theory, be more available for analysis. However its accessibility is often still severely limited by national data-protection laws and national banking regulations. In terms of obtaining financial information on an international basis, particularly from banks, there are in effect two consecutive barriers: (a) national legislation and confidentiality and (b) the onward transmission of that information by the national law enforcement agency. The result is stultification in information-flows which prevents the preparation of any meaningful operational analysis in a viable time frame.

Further legal difficulties have also been encountered in conducting effective analysis from international organisations. Whilst the use of bilateral memoranda of understanding have been in operation for well over 30 years and have helped to facilitate the real-time exchange of data on money laundering, until 2001 the Europol Convention (the only multilateral agreement in place) only permitted money laundering analysis in respect of a restricted list of predicate offences. During this period, for example an anti-money-laundering operation involving six EU Member States could only exchange and analyse data related to the proceeds of drug trafficking and illegal immigration. Yet vital information about proceeds from arms trafficking had to be ignored, despite the fact that the monies were being moved during the same period by the same criminals

6 This series of pan-EU legislation, passed in the 1980s and early 1990s was hailed as, 'the dawn of the achievement of a single European capital market', Romanian Central Bank, 'Proceedings of the International Symposium on Monetary Systems, Past Present and Future', Bucharest, 3 May 1997.

7 See, for instance, www.imf.org/external/np/leg/amlcft/eng/aml4.htm, accessed 13 June 2007.

involved in the drug trafficking and illegal immigration, and that there was every indication that the monies from these latter offences were being partially commingled with those from the arms trafficking.[8]

Due to these and similar legal difficulties and the slowness in resolving them, analysis into money laundering on an EU-wide basis has been retarded by over a decade.

'Red flags' in money laundering

Through the experience of anti-money-laundering analysis, it has been possible to develop persuasive and reliable indicators that can identify a potential money laundering operation. Such indicators are known as 'red flags' (some examples of these have already been outlined above in the Deposit Investment Patterns and Transit Customer Recognition sections). Red flags generally fall into two broad categories:

- customer related;
- transaction related.

Customer-related 'red flags' can either refer to individual behaviour and verbal statements whilst at the bank or financial institution, or relate to background information about the individual. Red flags related to the transaction look either at the nature of the transaction (such as the amounts, their timing or frequency), or at their origin or destination locations (for example suspect jurisdictions or suspect individuals).

It is essential, however, that the lists and definitions of such indicators are continually updated, a process which is dependent upon a comprehensive and reliably sourced flow of information. Otherwise, their value will diminish in the eyes of the investigators who are supposed to apply them. As one officer remarked:

> Some red flags or indicators, by the time they are circulated and disseminated, are out of date; others are so obvious they contain little or no new value. That doesn't leave much of use on the lists with which we are bombarded.[9]

Offshore entities

In basic terms, 'offshore entity' means an outside territory or sovereign jurisdiction that is not subject to the general supervision of bank and tax disclosures

8 Europol Operation 1996–1997 led by Austria.

9 Senior FBI officer confidential briefing during Police-Banking sector co-operation discussions, October 2002.

or to international law enforcement inquiries. This combination of qualities ensures an account holder an extreme degree of secrecy, sometimes even providing anonymity. It is, therefore, highly attractive for criminals trying to hide the source of their funds.

In many cases, but not always, offshore entities are small islands which welcomed and cultivated the easy revenue and lucrative business provided by the growing international financial service industry during the 1970s and 1990s. Certain offshore entities have become synonymous with exploitation by money-laundering and according to at least one scholar, are widely used at the layering stage of money laundering.[10] The Caribbean contains many such entities. Saint Maarten, for instance, was identified by Italian law enforcement authorities in 1998 for laundering the proceeds of Italian-US heroin traffickers; Aruba was identified by the FBI in the late 1990s as being used by Colombian and Italian organised crime groups for laundering the proceeds of cocaine trafficking, and the Cayman Islands, in the late 1980s was a central laundering point for the drug money of General Noriega. During 1998–1999, 70 per cent of all criminal monies originating in the former Soviet Union either transited through, or were invested in, Caribbean jurisdictions, but this trend changed within 18 months, and Russian organised crime groups were soon found to be utilising first one, then two locations within the EU.

Terrorist financing and anti-money-laundering

The attacks of 9/11 had a cataclysmic effect on law enforcement in terms of priorities and tasks at national and international level.[11] The nature of terrorist attacks has evolved to include:

- global target reach;
- short-term planning cycles;[12]
- mass fatalities.

Thus the imperative for effective operational analysis to produce real-time results has intensified.

10 J. Sheptycki, 'Policing the Virtual Launderette, Money laundering and global governance', in J. Sheptycki (ed) *Transnational Policing* (London: Routledge, 2000) and J. Drage, 'Countering money-laundering, the response of the financial sector', in H. L. McQueen (ed) *Money Laundering*, Hume papers on Public Policy Vol. 1 No. 2 (Edinburgh: Edinburgh University Press, 1993).

11 David Veness, former Assistant Commissioner Specialist Operations New Scotland Yard and now UN Head of International Security Affairs, confidential international law enforcement briefing, late 2001.

12 Al Qaeda are known to take up to two years to plan and perfect attacks; south-east Asian Islamic terrorist groups in 2003 to 2005 took less than two months to plan, recruit, obtain finances and equipment and carry out successful attacks.

Until recently the collective international response to the financing of terrorism was based upon anti-money-laundering principles[13] and task forces or specialist units were invariably formed or supplemented with staff experienced in anti-money-laundering. It took five years for the *modus operandi* utilised by Islamic extremist groups for funding their activities to be identified and categorised as such. A similar period of time elapsed before the characteristics of terrorist fund-raising were recognised (short-term, pragmatic and changeable and involving local petty criminality). Each of these is distinct from methodologies commonly applied in money laundering. Given the ongoing threat of terrorist attacks, intelligence services and law enforcement agencies cannot afford to repeat the luxury of such a time lag in recognising the vital red flags.

ONWARD OR BACKWARD?

Notwithstanding the progress made in developing and disseminating the concept and practice of analysis internationally, the cardinal maxim for analysis still holds true:

> . . . any analytical technique, no matter how elaborate or eloquent, will not replace good data, or make up for poor or inadequate information.[14]

Despite the enormous increases in staffing levels in the analytical departments of national and international law enforcement organisations, or the considerable investment in technical aids to handle massive amounts of data, the acquisition of good data remains a fundamental challenge. In international organisations in particular, analysts are often at the mercy of the generosity of member countries and the quality and quantity of data they wish to supply (as well as under what conditions). Slowly, a recognition of the need and virtue of sharing information and intelligence is dawning. Slowly, strategic and operational managers are beginning to understand the competitive advantage that analysis can confer in the fight against serious, organised crime and terrorism. However, competing interests (such as those of banking secrecy and data protection) though important concerns, inhibit information-flows and delay the analytical insights which, for instance, could allow funding for the next terrorist outrage to be interdicted.

13 FATF Emergency Plenary Session, New York, 29–31 October 2001.

14 F. A. J. Ianni and E. Reuss Ianni, 'Network Analysis', in P. Andrews and M. Peterson (eds), *Criminal Intelligence Analysis* (Loomis, CA: Palmer Enterprises, 1990).

Chapter 16

Applying the science

Tim Wilson

This chapter explains how forensic science can add value to international investigations. Its scope is confined to the use of forensic science and medicine for investigative (sometimes termed 'operational') purposes – that is, to obtain information about a person or thing that may either initiate a line of enquiry or complement existing information, thus confirming or invalidating earlier assumptions, with the intention of detecting or preventing crime.[1]

INTRODUCTION

Globally the role of the forensic expert has changed. In the UK, for example, the Home Office (Ministry of Internal Affairs) in giving evidence to a parliamentary enquiry on this subject stated that originally 'forensic science was focused on the application of science for the provision of objective and reliable evidence to the courts. Today it may be the initial and only crime scene response by the police to certain types of offence.'[2] For those states that have invested in modern high-volume forensic science activity (in particular that based on bioinformation, such as DNA and fingerprints), enhanced international co-operation is possible without the need for significant extra resource costs.

Unfortunately, there is no evidence that international co-operation has increased in line with such national investments. A study by the University of Leiden and the Netherlands Forensic Institute found that there was little

1 For the significance of the distinction between 'operational' and later judicial/evidential co-operation in respect of forensic science see C. Joubert and H. Bevers, 'International Exchange of Police Data and Forensic Expertise', in J. F. Nijboer and W. J. J. M. Sprangers (eds), *Harmonisation in Forensic Expertise: An inquiry into the desirability of and opportunities for international standards* (Amsterdam: Thelma Thesis, 2000), pp. 485–498.

2 Home Office, 'Memorandum of Evidence', in House of Commons Science and Technology Committee, Seventh Report of Session 2004–05, *Forensic Science on Trial*, Volume II, Oral and Written Evidence, HC 96-II (London: The Stationery Office Limited, 2004).

information available on international forensic co-operation.[3] More recently a report on the sharing of DNA information by a DNA Expert Working Group of the European Network of Forensic Science Institutes (ENFSI) indicated:

> During 2004–2005, the UK received only 149 DNA search requests. These generated 21 potential matches although the majority of the profiles were unreliable; this was due to poor discriminating power. The USA had a similar experience – they received even fewer requests for assistance even though they have a larger database with over 4 million profiles.

The reasons for this, according to this group of experts, reflect inadequacies in current international law enforcement arrangements as well as different technical processes for deriving a DNA profile:

> DNA has proved to be a useful method of identifying criminals and bringing them to justice. However, there has been slow progress in exchanging DNA information routinely between countries. There are various reasons for the slow progress including the differences in Member States' domestic law and data protection arrangements together with the technical complexities around DNA analysis and exchange.
>
> Although there have been many successful developments and initiatives to help Member States co-operate to exchange DNA information, the current arrangements are inadequate in their present form. They are incapable of development on a scale that will meet future requirements and they are not always sufficiently transparent or capable of being audited.[4]

Another major obstacle may be inadequate forensic awareness among investigators and their superiors. This issue was highlighted in the UK by a well-informed and respected chief officer of police, David Coleman, when he referred to colleagues who '. . . often put pressure on forensic managers to cut spending, without really understanding what the impact of this is, or how effective that spending can be, as compared to spending on other issues.'[5] This problem is likely to be greater in those countries and international institutions where forensic science plays a far less important role in day-to-day policing. The first part of this chapter, therefore, offers a brief guide to the range of expertise

3 Op. cit., Joubert and Bevers, fn 1, p. 485.

4 ENFSI, Search Request Network Study: Final Report (2007) pp. 5 and 2, www.enfsi.org/ewg/dnawg/documents/Annex%20F%20AGIS%Final%20Report, accessed on 15 April 2007.

5 D. Coleman, 'Beyond DNA in the UK – the police perspective', in M. Townsley and G. Laycock (eds) 'Forensic Science Conference Proceedings: Beyond DNA in the UK – Integration and Harmonisation', Home Office Science Policy Unit 2004, www.homeoffice.gov.uk/documents/Forensics_Part_1.pdf?view=Binary.

available from forensic science and medicine, and some examples of how this has contributed successfully to law enforcement internationally.

Forensic science co-operation is likely to take place most frequently in response to *transnational crimes*.[6] As will be seen from case studies in this chapter, biometric traces left by criminals at the crime scene in what may not be their country of birth or residence may be critical for identifying suspects. Science may also be needed to identify victims. Within the UK it is clear that such crimes account for a small but significant proportion of recorded national crimes. The limited research and data available suggest that:

- the volume of transnational crime appears to be growing faster than overall offending in the UK;
- this increase appears to be linked variously to geographical and historic relationships with certain countries, more frequent and cheaper travel, failures positively to assimilate and integrate some migrants who may be subject to clan loyalties that link mafia-type activities across continents, and rapid economic changes that have transformed logistics and business organisation;
- at least some of the changes in the volume and nature of transnational crime may be amplifications of changes in criminal activity manifested within national borders;
- forensic science is important for both detecting and monitoring patterns of behaviour among more mobile criminals.[7]

This pattern is likely to be replicated in many other countries with developed economies. The limitations of present arrangements for dealing with offenders who operate across national frontiers are also apparent from the current low levels of co-operation and data relating to transnational crime, even in respect of organised crime.[8]

Transnational crime is only a partial and often highly imprecise indicator of the cumulative impact of global criminality on crime within individual

6 Defined for the purposes of this chapter as crimes committed in one country by the nationals of other countries as either visitors or residents. Such offending is not necessarily organised crime; it may be unclear for much of the investigation of a transnational crime whether it is organised or not.

7 T. Wilson, (a) Evidence to Nuffield Council on Bioethics 2006/07 review of the forensic use of bioinformation: ethical issues, www.nuffieldbioethics.org/fileLibrary/pdf/Tim_Wilson.pdf; and (b) 'Forensic Science and the Internationalization of Policing', in J. Fraser and R. Williams (eds), *Handbook of Forensic Science* (Cullompton: Willan Publishing, forthcoming).

8 A. Bouloukos, G. Farrel and G. Laycock, 'Transnational Organised Crime in Europe and North America: Towards a Framework for Prevention', in K. Aromma, S. Leppä, S. Nevela and N. Ollus (eds), *Crime and Criminal Justice in Europe and North America 1995–1997: Report on the Sixth United Nations survey on Crime Trends and Criminal Justice Systems* (Helsinki: HEUN, 2003), pp. 176–192.

countries. For example, a high proportion of national acquisitive crimes and trading in counterfeit goods (likely also to be a fiscal offence) may be fuelled by narcotics grown in another continent or at the end of an international supply chain that mimics or exploits those of the legitimate businesses. A sense of scale of the impact of such activities might come more appropriately from estimates of their contribution to GDP or GNP than recorded crime statistics, as the latter tend generally to be an underestimate of the level of criminal activity. The forensic disciplines relevant for international co-operation are likely to be different from those most used to counter transnational crime, for example, drug analysis, the addition of trace elements to precursor chemicals and forensic accountancy.

National awareness of the potential value of forensic science is the prerequisite for funding that results in large volumes of forensic data that may sometimes also be helpful for investigators in other countries. Other national considerations may, however, frustrate international co-operation. The cardinal issues, as for international law enforcement as a whole, will be those of trust and selectivity. A nation state will wish to control the recipients of sensitive criminal justice information of any kind (not just electronically stored data that falls within the aegis of data protection laws) and will only share it with those states where it is unlikely to be compromised (including through its unauthorised release to a third state). Hence, co-operation is likely to be hedged by internal restrictions and controls. For example, The South Limburg Aachen Agreement (1997) between the Netherlands and Germany requires Dutch police officers to obtain the approval of a public prosecutor before releasing information to German colleagues from files about potential suspects for severe, frequent and organised crimes.[9] In the case of forensic information the level of restriction or control may be increased because of the source or type of information rather than the criminal context to which the information relates. Thus, ballistics and narcotics information is likely to be less sensitive than bioinformation. For example, DNA profiles are obtained from sources that could be used to obtain a wide range of potentially intimate information and might not just be used for personal identification purposes. As a consequence nation states may have stringent safeguards – often as a combination of measures – in place to prevent the misuse of such information in response to specific criminal justice forensic database legislation (for example Canada and most EU states), or data protection laws (all EU states), or in response to current legal challenges and political debate (USA). International co-operation will only be possible if it can be managed in a way that recognises and observes such national sensitivities and imperatives.

This is particularly important for forensic science co-operation because the greatest advances in recent years that benefit day-to-day policing have been in

9 Op. cit., Joubert and Bevers, fn 1, p. 489.

the field of bioinformation. This consists of forensic science techniques (fingerprints fall within the scope of this term even if in some countries the technique is regarded as a separate discipline) based on an analysis of a range of physical characteristics of a person. These are used to identify that person (including in administrative documents such as passports, identification cards and driving licences) and either separately, or in addition, as *trace biometrics*, to detect contact with another individual, place or object. The practical advantages for law enforcement have increased, either through the introduction of new techniques such as DNA or the application of new technology to older disciplines such as fingerprints. In the UK it is now possible to search the prints of an arrestee against the six million personal profiles to confirm personal identity (where an alias may have been given) and check his or her prints against national records from undetected crimes in less than 10 minutes.[10] The extent to which bioinformation can be collected, used, retained and shared at speed and in respect of millions of citizens and residents is likely to attract a high level of legislative, judicial, media and public scrutiny aimed at balancing criminal justice needs with those of individual privacy and civil liberty. How these are resolved can vary immensely resulting in significant differences in law and procedure even between neighbouring countries that share common legal traditions and political values. Options and initiatives for enabling investigators to co-operate more efficiently with colleagues internationally are considered in the second part of this chapter.

PART ONE: FORENSIC SCIENCE AS AN INVESTIGATIVE TOOL

Forensic science is not a replacement for other forms of investigative technique. Frequently, however, it plays a decisive fact-finding role within criminal investigations. The information it provides may be used for *inceptive* purposes: that is, initiating new lines of enquiry to identify suspects, to eliminate the innocent from the investigation, as well as to identify objects such as the type of (as well as the actual) tool, weapon or vehicle used in committing an offence. Forensic science can also play a *corroborative* role: that is, in confirming the case against an already identified suspect (perhaps by corroborating other facts linking an individual to objects and locations). The value of different techniques will vary depending on the circumstances of the crime, the technological/scientific resources available and the forensic awareness of both investigators and criminals. Moreover, the effectiveness of forensic science/medicine depends on the quality assurance and overall management of the investigation or prosecution

10 M. Timmins, 'Ident 1 and Livescan Help Forensic Investigation', Norfolk Constabulary website article, www.norfolk.police.uk, accessed 15 May 2007.

procedures used. For example, a double rapist and murderer (crimes committed in 1983 and 1986) almost escaped justice due to failures in the procedures surrounding initial DNA testing in the enquiry. Local males had been asked to volunteer for intelligence-led screening (sometimes termed 'mass screening') for elimination purposes against crime scene samples. However, a friend of the offender was later overheard explaining how he had taken the rapist's place at the time the voluntary sample was taken. It is also interesting to note that, in the same case, DNA testing successfully eliminated someone from enquiries even though he had confessed to the second murder![11]

Forensic contributions to the investigative process may provide vital facts about locations, movement, the passage of time and cause of death. Sometimes the information can come from unexpected sources. For example, forensic entomology (the study of insects) can use knowledge about the distribution, variety, life cycle and, with toxicological analysis, the digestion of insects to provide important information about time and circumstances of death.

The complex interplay of seven forensic disciplines and techniques combined with more traditional police work across several countries can be illustrated from successful convictions in 2005 for the murder of an Armenian gangster, who was himself wanted for murders in Ostend and Moscow.[12]

- In January 2002 the badly burnt body of a male was found in a field in Cambridgeshire, UK. During post-mortem examination, the pathologist discovered both gunshot and stab wounds. Amongst a bag of rubbish found close to the body were some used paper towels and a charred scrap of paper which appeared to refer to a medical appointment and on which were written two names (neither of which, it transpired, belonged to anyone involved in the murder although one of the persons named was arrested and questioned as a suspect at an early stage of the investigation). A distinctive cigarette lighter and a latex gloves packet bearing a serial number were also found near the body.
- DNA and fingerprints were obtained from the deceased, but could not be matched against individuals known on UK databases. Facial reconstruction was undertaken and the distinctive jawbone and the dental work indicated that the victim was of eastern European origin. Forensic tests for pollution levels in the skin and bones suggested that the victim had been in the

11 J. Roach and K. Pease 'DNA evidence and police investigations: a health warning' Police Professional 52 (May 2006).

12 B. Deane, 'Body of evidence', Police, March 2006, www.polfed.org; and 'Mystery Victim Buried with No Name', London: The *Guardian*, 21 July 2003; BBC news reports 'Two blame each other for murder', 19 October 2005 and 'Victim has been stabbed and shot', 11 October 2005 www.news.bbc.co.uk. All three items accessed on 9 May 2007. Also the author is grateful to the editor for additional information obtained at a briefing given by the Cambridgeshire Police in 2005.

Ukraine, and were also able to indicate the areas of the UK in which he might have been living during the last three to six years of his life. As a result, the investigation team wrote to every person listed in local authority records in those areas with the two surnames found on the scrap of paper sending over 2,000 letters speculatively.

- Almost ten months after the murder a positive response to the mail shot brought the police to the medical room of a factory where a packet of latex gloves was found bearing the same batch number as the packet found at the first crime scene. Also found were paper towels similar in size and texture to those found in the rubbish bag. The room was forensically searched and traces of the victim's blood were found behind a filing cabinet and in the creases of a medical couch even though the room had been cleaned immediately after the murder and regularly over the intervening months. Tests also managed to find gunshot residue.
- An Armenian security guard at the factory who had not reported for work since the night before the body was discovered was arrested on suspicion of murder. The deceased was believed to be an individual who frequently accompanied the suspect to work and who had been introduced to workmates as his 'brother'. The suspect's partner was also interviewed. She knew the 'brother' only by the name 'Sako'.
- The police circulated the victim's description and nickname through Interpol and the Belgian police responded with a possible identity of a known criminal wanted for a murder in Ostend who had gone missing. Matching a DNA sample from a close living relative and a partial thumb print to records held by Belgian police, positively identified the victim.
- A further lead was provided from a separate witness in Belgium who claimed the father-in-law had admitted to killing Sako. As a result of co-operation with the Dutch police his DNA was matched to that on the cigarette lighter found with the body. This was enough to secure the father-in-law's arrest in the Netherlands and extradition to the UK. Although he claimed never to have been to Britain and to have an alibi for the time of the murder, his fingerprint was found on a document in a hotel in the same British seaside town in which his son-in-law lived. Documents showed he had arrived in the UK the day before the murder and left the day after.
- The victim was part of an Armenian organised crime group involved in narcotics, facilitating illegal immigration and prostitution and, it was believed, had come to the UK to lie low. The rubbish bag had been dumped with the body after the suspects had tried to clean the scene of crime. Following a trial at which both suspects pleaded not guilty, one was sentenced to life in prison for murder, whilst the other was found not guilty of murder, but sentenced to three years as an accessory.

The success of this complex investigation was attributable to old-fashioned detective work complemented by the imaginative application of forensic techniques as investigative tools including DNA and fingerprint identification, firearm and blood residue analysis, facial reconstruction, ondontology (dental records) and analysis of radiation and lead pollution levels in skin and bone. Investigators are not always so fortunate, so dedicated nor able to continue so long without the identification of the victim or suspects. The cost of the investigation and the time required would probably have been reduced significantly, however, had the victim's fingerprints and DNA, as a known criminal, been immediately accessible from criminal justice databases anywhere in the world. In some investigations this is not just an issue of being able to use investigative resources more efficiently, but also the only prospect for making progress. This has been realised at both the national and international levels with the exchange of DNA and fingerprint data becoming a priority issue.

The reasons for this are clearly illustrated by the following case studies:

Identification of suspects

Francesco Arce Montes, a Spanish citizen, raped and murdered an English schoolgirl whilst she was on a school trip to France in 1996. Montes was also responsible for a large number of other sexual offences in many different countries over a period of more than 20 years. Following the murder in France, Montes travelled through Spain where he was arrested for an attempted rape at knife-point, but he had not at this point been linked to the murder and after his release on bail disappeared. He was finally located, after having been arrested in Miami, when an immigration officer in Detroit read about Caroline's murder in a UK newspaper discarded at his airport. This reported that Montes had been named as a suspect by the French investigating magistrate. He checked if the name was on any US databases to which he had access. Fortunately he located Montes but this was solely by chance, as a result of an initiative taken by a single individual, not through international law enforcement co-operation. After initial problems in matching DNA records due to the different DNA marker systems used in the USA and France, Montes was finally positively identified as the suspect by a fresh DNA profile using the French marker system. This new sample was also consistent with trace biometrics previously found on material that he had left at the crime scene for use in suffocating his victim (additional evidence which helped to prove his intent).[13]

Detecting and disrupting transnational offending

An anonymous DNA profile linked to a series of burglaries in Austria was matched via the Interpol database with the DNA profile of a known

13 J. Dickinson and A. Pierce, 'Why the international exchange of DNA information is important', in *Maximising the Opportunities for Sharing DNA Information across Europe* (London: Home Office, 2006).

individual submitted by Croatia two years earlier. This information was then linked, also via Interpol, with fingerprints recovered from burglaries in Germany.[14]

Corroborative evidence for the purpose of mounting a prosecution

A Dutch lorry driver was arrested in the UK after a container lorry he was driving was found to contain the bodies of 58 Chinese migrants. He claimed that he thought that he was conveying tomatoes, however, DNA and fingerprints helped to show that the driver had been in contact with the migrants before they had been locked into the container. Forensic information in the Netherlands also made it possible to identify four further suspects linking them both to the driver as well as to other trace biometrics belonging to the victims.[15]

Forensic science can also have a humanitarian dimension in helping to identify the victims of natural disasters and crimes involving catastrophic and mass loss of life (for instance, terrorist attacks or genocide).

Following the 2004 tsunami in the Indian Ocean, a team of law enforcement personnel from 31 countries worked in Thailand under a unified international operational command identifying victims from 36 countries. Rapid decomposition meant that three forensic disciplines were used to obtain primary identifications – fingerprints, ondontology and DNA – with secondary identification arising from any reliable visual features and articles associated with the bodies. One of the officers responsible for managing this victim identification work, Derek Forrest, identified the first lesson learned as the need for all to agree to work to a common business process.[16] This is an important insight for overcoming barriers to efficient and effective international forensic co-operation between law enforcement agencies more generally.

It has long been an Interpol role to provide support to incident response teams sent to the scene of disasters resulting in mass fatalities. Following the tsunami Interpol has also created a Crisis Management Support Group. One of its tasks is to identify good practice for collaborative procedures in multinational teams assembled at the scene of future disasters and incidents. This work culminated in the publication of Interpol's Disaster Victim Identification Guide that offers guidance on the organisational structure, business processes

14 'Interpol records 100th international DNA match. More countries urged to use unique global database', Interpol media release, 29 November 2006, Lyon.

15 A. Kloosterman, 'International case study: investigation and identification – the Dover case', in *Maximising the Opportunities for Sharing DNA Information across Europe* (London: Home Office, 2006).

16 M. Free and D. Forrest, 'Disaster Victim Identification (DVI); lessons learned from the 2004 tsunami', in *Maximising the Opportunities for Sharing DNA Information across Europe* (London: Home Office, 2006).

and scientific approaches most likely to provide optimal links to national DVI (disaster victim identification) capabilities.[17]

The need for common, mutually understood and acceptable processes is equally applicable where investigators from different nation states are linked by electronic communications rather than by physical proximity. Hence, this part of the chapter concludes with a review[18] of those branches of forensic science that are particularly amenable to storage and retrieval in electronic systems. This very fact means that they are the types of forensic expertise most likely to feature regularly in international law enforcement.

DNA

In many ways, the introduction of DNA has become almost the tool of choice in developed countries for identifying offenders and for linking them to a crime scene. Within international groups, such as the G8 Lyon/Roma Group, in international law enforcement organisations, especially Interpol and ENFSI, and in new multilateral initiatives, such as the Prüm Convention 2005,[19] the exchange of DNA and fingerprint data has been the focus of high levels of interest among countries with national forensic databases. Figure 16.1 shows the extent of current development in European DNA databases in August 2007. The UK database is excluded by reason of scale as it is approximately equivalent to 5 per cent of the resident population. The largest DNA database outside Europe is that of the USA (approximately equivalent to 1.5 per cent of the resident population).

Fingerprints

Before the advent of DNA as an investigative tool, fingerprint analysis was the only forensic methodology for identifying suspects and victims from databases with a large number of subjects. Although the collection of prints from a crime scene and their comparison with those on record is a skilled job, it is essentially

17 J. Garton, 'Interpol Perspective', in *Maximising the Opportunities for Sharing DNA Information across Europe* (London: Home Office, 2006) and 'Interpol Crisis Support Group (CSG) overview for NCBs, 01.04.2005', www.interpol.com/Public/asiandisaster/CMSG/NCBOverview.asp. The Disaster Victim Identification Guide was published in May 2007 at www.interpol.int/Public/DisasterVictim/Guide.

18 The author gratefully acknowledges additional contributions from the editor based on his operational experience and comments from Lyn Fereday, lately of the National Policing Improvement Agency, whose work as manager of the DNA Expansion Programme ensured its success.

19 A German initiative with Belgium, Spain, France, Luxembourg, the Netherlands and Austria as the other initial signatories, intended to facilitate the sharing of DNA profiles, fingerprints, vehicle registration data and other information and joint cross-border operations. See K. Hager, 'The Prüm Treaty', in *Maximising the Opportunities for Sharing DNA Information across Europe* (London: Home Office, 2006).

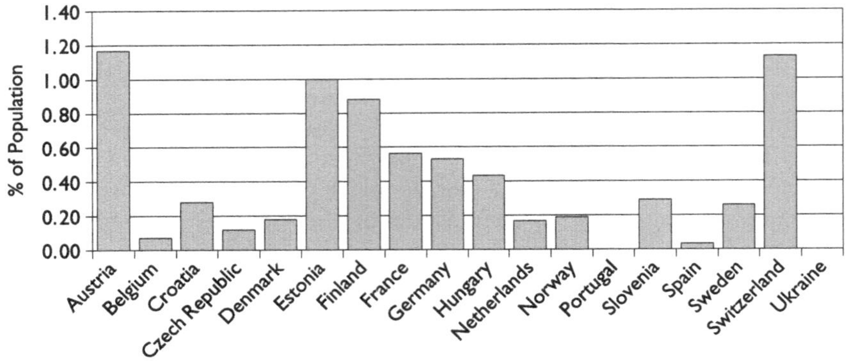

Figure 16.1 DNA databases in Europe (excluding the UK) August 2007

Note: 0 per cent indicates less than 0.01 per cent of the population (i.e. will not show up on the chart; Portugal only keeps crime scene stains)

Source: ENFSI

a low-tech solution which still has considerable application in practical investigation. The use of Automatic Fingerprint Identification Systems (AFIS) has now become widespread[20] and Interpol has made great strides in providing international access to national records. However, the spread of automatic systems is limited in the same way as those for DNA, by lack of infrastructure and investment. Where countries do not have the scientific or computer infrastructure, fingerprint impressions still have primacy. After all, a paper-based filing and classification scheme can produce the same results as an automated system, but will take much longer and with greater risk of error due to the human factor. Paper systems will also have the advantage that impressions of fingerprints received in any paper format from another country can be compared by any fingerprint expert against national records. The differences in techniques refer more to scoring the comparison rather than the way that fingerprints are taken.

Ondontology

This area of forensics can refer to the condition and arrangement of the teeth, in terms of dental work, bridges, dentures and the composition of cavity filling materials or to the pollutants to be found in the teeth themselves (see the Sako case above).

Bite marks (especially in the investigation of sexual offences) and other

20 The EU has had a system in place for a number of years for recording the fingerprints of asylum seekers in different Member States. This may in the future also be employed as a criminal justice database.

impressions made by teeth are also useful indicators of identity. They do not require significant levels of investment and samples can be collected with a minimum of training.

Firearms

The smuggling of firearms has also become the focus of international concern in recent years. Analysis of firearm residue, cartridge cases, and the ballistic characteristics of bullets and weapons can be digitised and reduced to a computer record. Many countries have ballistic databases, but international standards for making comparisons are still awaited.

Explosives

With the heightened risk of terrorist attacks, analysis of the causes of explosions (for example bomb or fractured gas main), and the composition and design of explosive devices can help to identify the source of the attack as well as assist with the safe defusing of live bombs. Europol, for instance, has a bomb database project.

Drugs

International co-operation can assist in the identification and analysis (for example strength and purity) of narcotic substances and of traces found on clothing, etc. They can also assist with the analysis of trace elements added to precursor materials in order to identify supply and distribution chains.

The US Drugs Enforcement Agency (DEA) has a number of forensic laboratories that analyse drug purity and the solvents used in their processing. It also has a computer forensics program related to the analysis of computer and digital media seized during investigations (including the identification of each suspect's contacts and suppliers with details of how they process the narcotics).[21]

Europol maintains a database on the distinct and individual 'manufacturers marks' found on ecstasy tablets as well as a database on the packaging and logos found on other drug shipments.

The difficulty with chemical comparison of drugs samples is the potential variance in results that can result from different environmental conditions (such as temperature and humidity) in the testing laboratory. Legal problems can also arise where drugs have to cross national borders even when this is so that they can be tested for law enforcement purposes.

A good deal of international assistance and advice is provided by the

21 www.dea.gov/programs/compforensics.htm, accessed 20 May 2007.

UNODC Laboratory Services Section. This is normally targeted at those regions and countries where the most need is apparent. Apart from assessing and assisting with equipment needs, the UNODC provides literally thousands of small, simple-to-use test kits that allow the presumptive testing of narcotics and precursor chemicals by officers in the field. Such compact and portable kits can be used in remote and hard to reach locations.[22]

Forged or counterfeit documents

Those who counterfeit or forge documents employ a variety of techniques and raw materials that can be classified and input onto a database. The nature and quality of paper and inks, for instance, enable certain conclusions to be drawn about the source and preparation of the document. The European Central Bank introduced the Counterfeit Monitoring System to store information on the technical aspects of counterfeit euro currency – the world's only multinational currency. The Europol Information System also holds data about forged euros, but is more related to the circumstances of detection.

Forgeries may, in addition, be based on the amendment of real or genuine documentation. These are often altered through chemical techniques which can be easily detected by the appropriate test. Whilst not strictly speaking related to forensic techniques, it might be useful to know that both Interpol and Europol have databases of stolen blank vehicle documents whilst Interpol and the Schengen Information System have a similar system for stolen passports.

Image analysis

Image analysis is a growing area, but one that has been in use for some time. The use of the internet for the transmission of child porn is one of the saddest and most sinister of developments of recent times. However, law enforcement systems exist that can classify aspects of the image and then search against those aspects in order to identify the victim and, sometimes, characteristics of the scene. Given the anonymous and international exchange of such images, this sort of information can be invaluable. Interpol has such a database.

Similar technology is also available for use in the identification of stolen works of art or antiques in which comparison is made with digital images held on a database. However, another way of automating such a search facility is to use a hierarchy of classification which allows possible identical items held on file to be matched against the specimen. This is essentially an automated filing system and can be duplicated by manual procedures.

In the next generation of these techniques, automated video searching is

22 www.unodc.org/unodc/laboratory_services.html, accessed 20 May 2007.

being developed to identify images of individuals and objects by using (for example witness) defined features/characteristics.

Voiceprints

The searching of voice prints across international boundaries is an area fraught with legal challenges. The legal acceptability of electronic eavesdropping on a national level also differs considerably. There is reputed to be an intelligence database in operation which scans the airways and computer highways for key words or certain voices. In law enforcement circles, where any information provided has to conform to evidential standards, indiscriminate scanning of public networks is likely to be viewed as breaching human rights. On a practical level, the interference and background-noise contamination of voice samples are challenges that need to be addressed in order to increase the reliability of the comparisons to standards acceptable to the court process. Voiceprints recorded operationally will rarely be done under controlled circumstances and will obviously be affected by the quality of the telecommunications network over which the voice is recorded.

PART TWO: UNLOCKING THE POTENTIAL OF FORENSIC SCIENCE AS A TOOL FOR INTERNATIONAL LAW ENFORCEMENT

Unlocking the potential of forensic science to assist international law enforcement is not just a matter of forensic awareness. There are three immediate strategic issues:

- the ability to fund forensic science on a sufficient scale (that is to say whether a country can realistically afford to fund a sufficient level of forensic science expenditure);
- capacity and speed of service by forensic providers; and
- business processes.

These issues pose major challenges because their resolution depends not only on the political willingness and the availability of financial investment, but also on the resilience and open-mindedness of investigators and scientists in each country to embrace new ways of working.

There is, however, an equally important role for international institutions; for example, some of the Interpol, Europol and ENFSI initiatives relating specifically to sharing forensic science information have already been mentioned. Much will depend on the willingness of the small leadership teams of such organisations to co-operate effectively together and explain to politicians, legislators, jurists and civil rights organisations why improved models of co-operation and substantially more funding are needed. Since his appointment as Secretary General of Interpol, Ron Noble has tirelessly promoted an agenda that includes 24/7 support 365 days a year to national police forces, the introduction of a DNA database and has lobbied governments for resources to enhance DVI support capabilities.[23] More recently Interpol's engagement with ENFSI, G8 Lyon-Roma Group and Europol in the DNA search engine study and the successful pilot testing of this concept in June 2007 between Canada, the USA and the UK using Interpol's I-24/7 as a communication platform, has demonstrated further determination to encourage a greater sharing of information from national databases in a way that complements its earlier DNA Gateway initiative.[24] There is an important role for Europol in influencing policy formation and, in co-operation with Eurojust and national agencies, engaging in consultations about law-making in Brussels and Member States (for example the proposed framework for criminal justice data protection and its implementation in the laws of Member States). Also existing EU financial support for forensic science (a good example is the excellent new forensic science laboratory in Vilnius) needs to be increased as investment in transport within the EU promoted by the European Commission makes transnational crimes, as a *technological externality*, easier to organise and execute.[25]

Even where greater resources are provided, progress cannot be guaranteed. For instance, problems can arise over the ownership of information and from potential conflicts of jurisdiction both locally and internationally. Fingerprints may be a matter for the police and ministry of interior while DNA may come within the domain of magistrates and the ministry of justice; there may be more than one national police database for the same forensic discipline; and the minimum dactyloscopic points used for a fingerprint identification may even vary within a country between different police forces, or between forensic laboratories and police forces.[26] Sometimes bilateral requests for forensic co-operation fail or are very much delayed because the magistrates who control the data are unable to deal with them when they are sent directly or on behalf of a

23 M. Naím, *Illicit: How Smugglers, Traffickers and Copycats are Hijacking the Global Economy* (London: William Heinemann, 2005), p. 191; 'Interpol DNA Database Online', in *The Police Chief*, April 2007 and 'Interpol Head to seek EU support in tsunami operation', Interpol media release, 27 January 2005, Lyon: Interpol.

24 Op. cit., ENFSI, fn 4, and 'Interpol network links forensic laboratories in G8 countries', Interpol media release, 6 July 2007, Lyon: Interpol.

25 Op. cit., Wilson, (b), fn 7.

26 L. van der Weston, 'Legal Regulations Governing forensic Scientific Methods', in J. F. Nijboer and W. J. J. M. Sprangers (eds), *Harmonisation in Forensic Expertise: An inquiry into the desirability of and opportunities for international standards* (Amsterdam: Thelma Thesis, 2000).

police organisation and not a prosecutor or magistrate.[27] Such factors can act as a severe impediment to any investigation that needs to access forensic information from abroad in which the investigators can have confidence if the enquiry is to have any chance of progress.

At the beginning of this chapter the point was made that for those states that have invested for national motives in modern high-volume forensic science activity, enhanced international co-operation is possible without significant extra resource costs. It is necessary to qualify this with the observation that transnational crime is not obliged to confine itself to operating exclusively in regions that are wealthier and better prepared to meet its challenge.

The uneven distribution of wealth between different states is likely to be the ultimate obstacle to international co-operation when this can only take place if all the countries involved have access to global 'state of the art' equipment and can afford analytical processes for which the intellectual property right (IPR) is held by international biotech companies. The situation in many countries with a medium or low GNP will be that:

- even after making adjustments for the notional purchasing power parity of different national budgets, the value of law enforcement spending is likely to be lower (in absolute terms) than richer states;[28]
- yet, possibly because, frequently, governments give a higher priority to maintaining law and order than more discretionary social expenditure, criminal justice is already likely to consume (in relative terms) a much higher proportion of national wealth than in richer countries.[29]

The research on which this analysis is based comes from comparing Western Europe with Central and Eastern Europe, but if it is applicable globally the level of forensic investment in recent years in North America and parts of Western Europe is unlikely to be repeated in most developing and transitional economies. If the greater use of forensic science has to be funded solely or mainly from the existing criminal justice and investigative budgets or other national resources of such countries it will not happen. In such states the information that might be available both for detecting crimes nationally and improving international co-operation will simply not exist, thus failing to

27 Noted by the author from discussion at a conference held by the Institute National de Criminalistique et de Criminologie Justice, 9 October 2006 at the Free University of Brussels (unpublished).

28 CEPEJ European Judicial Systems 2002 (Strasbourg: Council of Europe, 2002), p. 59.

29 Ibid, p. 60; this part accounted for by more police officers (a mean of 424 per 100,000 population in CEE compared with 320 in WE) see P. Mayhew, 'The Operation of Criminal Justice Systems', in K. Aromma, S. Leppä, S. Nevela and N. Ollus (eds), *Crime and Criminal Justice in Europe and North America 1995–1997: Report on the Sixth United Nations survey on Crime Trends and Criminal Justice Systems* (Helsinki: HEUNI, 2003), p. 87.

optimise the efficiency of an expensive national resource (the criminal justice system).[30]

The availability of funding by itself cannot guarantee effective and timely forensic science services to support investigators. UK experience has demonstrated that channelling additional funding into those forensic science techniques offering opportunities for automatic processing can reduce both the time required to deliver results and the unit cost of each analysis.[31] In support of this approach, the UK has found considerable benefit in a business model based on outsourcing forensic services to private companies and by encouraging competition between laboratories.[32] External independent quality assurance of both laboratory processes and management is, of course, required for all laboratories, including those still owned by the state.[33]

On a practical level, technical incompatibility, the risk of failing to link information due to differences in analytical processes, reliability, and the speed of response are important for both national and international investigations. The potential impact of such challenges may be reduced through a process of international harmonisation that combines those aspects of forensic work normally undertaken by investigators (such as the recovery and integrity of physical evidence from crime scene, victims and suspects) and those issues dealt with by scientists (such as the quality of testing, laboratory conditions and appropriate storage procedures). Work that would make this possible is taking place under the auspices of scientific bodies such as ENFSI, within academia and private companies, as well as with expert groups sponsored by stakeholder organisations such as Interpol and UNODC. In the longer-term it would be highly desirable for international standards and formats to be agreed that will be recognised and admissible in national courts.

In the meantime, the risk of delays, missing critical information and mistakes, etc. can be minimised by agreeing upon and implementing a common business process. Such a process should reflect a series of principles that can satisfy different legal systems, but which also recognise the primacy of national sovereignty. A model process developed for exchanging information about DNA profiles, but applicable to other electronically stored and retrievable information, was published in 2007 by ENFSI.[34]

The premise of this chapter is that more efficient and effective co-operation

30 Op. cit., Wilson, (b), fn 7, for an explanation of how this economic issue should be regarded and dealt with as a weakest link public good.

31 Op. cit., Coleman, fn 5.

32 Op. cit., Wilson, (b), fn 7.

33 House of Commons Science and Technology Committee, Seventh Report of Session 2004–05, 'Forensic Science on Trial', HC 96-I (London: The Stationery Office Limited, 2005), p. 35.

34 Op. cit., ENFSI, fn 4, pp. 5, 2.

through the use of forensic science and medicine is possible in a way that will add value to many investigations. It must conclude, however, with a caveat. Without the political will to find the international funding and capacity building needed to ensure that such co-operation can take place globally, the participants will be confined to a club for rich nations.

Chapter 17

The cyber side of crime

Steven David Brown

Any discussion about international law enforcement would be incomplete without some reference to the way in which advances in technology have been exploited for criminal purposes. Although adopted here for convenience, the term 'cybercrime', despite being a popular catch-phrase, is not entirely appropriate, but other labels such as 'e-crime', 'computer crime', 'netcrime' or 'hi-tech crime' are equally problematic. Indeed, a recent European Commission communication 'questioned whether there is any need for the term at all' suggesting that 'cyberspace is just a new specific instrument used to commit crimes which are not new at all'.[1] The same EU document goes on to propose three general types of crime involving information technology:

1 traditional forms of crime in a cybercrime context;
2 the publication of illegal content over electronic media; and
3 crimes unique to electronic networks.[2]

On the other hand, wider ranging international negotiations within the Council of Europe resulted in a Convention on Cybercrime (2001) that uses a slightly different way of categorising cybercriminal activity:

1 offences against the confidentiality, integrity and availability of computer data and systems;
2 computer-related offences (for example forgery and fraud);
3 content-related offences (for example child pornography); and
4 offences related to infringements of copyright and related rights.[3]

The Cybercrime Convention which entered into force on 1 July 2004 is a major vehicle for developing international co-operation in this area and is open for

1 European Commission 'Towards a general policy on the fight against cybercrime', 22 May 2007, Memo/07/199 Brussels.
2 Ibid.
3 www.conventions.coe.int/treaty/en/Treaties/Html/185.htm, accessed 20 May 2007.

signature to all countries in the world, not just to European states. So far, it has been ratified by 22 countries, including the USA but, strangely, not by the majority of EU Member States.[4]

The Convention, however, is not the first international initiative to review the subject. As early as 1986, the OECD produced a discussion document entitled, 'Computer-Related Crime: Analysis of Legal Policy' and in 1994, the UN published its 'Manual on the Prevention and Control of Computer-related Crime'.[5] Prior to this, in 1990, Interpol had already established its European Working Group on Information Technology Crime (since followed by others in Africa, the Asian-South Pacific region and Latin America) and has also produced a manual of best practice for investigators in computer crime.

Long distance

One of the unique characteristics of cybercrime is the potential separation and distance of the criminal from the deed.[6] This attribute has eliminated the traditional nexus between offender and crime scene which has long been the customary starting point for reactive investigations and has shifted the nature of the chain of evidence from the physical to the digital realm. A computer connection can easily be routed 'virtually' across continents so that investigating a single transaction may potentially involve enquiries in multiple jurisdictions in different time zones even when the culprit lives just around the corner. Indeed, who has jurisdiction in an enquiry (and who bears the costs) will not always be easy to ascertain – a business concern, such as an Internet Service Provider (ISP) for example, can be physically based and conduct its business in one country, but it may well have its servers located in another with its transactions processed in yet a third.

An additional difficulty is that not all countries through which a connection is channelled will necessarily recognise mutual legal assistance measures. Indeed, some jurisdictions may not yet even have outlawed the relevant activity and the creation of so-called 'data havens' makes this more likely.[7]

The nature of the evidence itself also needs special attention in cybercrime investigations. The conventional court process relies on physical evidence, but the digital evidence and forensic skills necessitated by a cybercrime investigation require additional precautions. Digital evidence is highly volatile and the

4 As at 1 June 2007, including Austria, Belgium, Czech Republic, Germany, Greece, Ireland, Italy, Luxembourg, Malta, Poland, Portugal, Slovakia, Spain, Sweden, or the UK.

5 www.unodc.org/pdf/Manual_ComputerRelatedCrime.PDF, accessed 7 June 2007.

6 The differences are nicely summarised in M. D. Goodman and S. W. Brenner, 'The emerging consensus on criminal conduct in cyberspace', UCLA Journal of Law and Technology, 6(1) (2002), pp. 7–8.

7 www.american.edu/ted/havens.htm, accessed 10 June 2007. www.spamhouse.org is also a source of interesting information in this regard.

interaction of the investigator with the data files carries a very high risk of altering it (even if it does not a defence advocate is likely to say it did!). In 2003, in seeking a solution to this problem, the European Commission funded a project to devise 'Cyber Tools for On-Line Search for Evidence (CTOSE): a set of standardised procedures aimed at securing evidence with sufficient safeguards to be admissible in court proceedings',[8] but this is still a developing area.

Unless a suspect is caught red-handed (either seated at the terminal or in possession of something physical), a much higher degree of circumstantial assumption has to be made in terms of suspect identification than is normally desirable. For example, a line of rational thought might suggest the following:

- the crime was committed by a computer at the identified location connected to the identified port;
- the suspect had access to that computer;
- the suspect had the requisite IT skills;
- therefore the suspect was probably responsible.

Such a train of thought can help to identify a possible suspect but, without more, it is less than conclusive in establishing a case in court beyond reasonable doubt. Establishing exclusivity of access through policies and procedures requiring user authentication (such as with passwords) can help, but are often circumvented by familiarity and informal practice (such as by the sharing of passwords between colleagues).

TRACKING THEM DOWN

Of course the computer criminal, like his or her physical counterpart, always leaves behind a digital footprint that, with special forensic skills, equipment and care may be recovered and recorded (sometimes even where it has been deleted at the first level). Unfortunately, a technologically aware criminal can just as easily completely erase that footprint at the press of a button. Since mutual legal assistance permissions are rarely achievable in real time, this leaves the investigator with a dilemma.

Such a dilemma was confronted in 2002 by FBI Special Agents pursuing a pair of extortionists from Russia (one of many countries that does not extradite its own nationals). Using a known vulnerability in the Windows NT operating system, the suspects had, from their base in Russia, hacked into 40 US companies, stolen customer credit card details which were then used to buy goods fraudulently, and threatened to destroy computerised company records

8 'On-line Detectives', www.ec.europa.eu/information_society/activities/policy_link/documents/factsheets/jus_ctose.pdf, accessed 7 June 2007.

unless a ransom was paid. In fact, the software weakness they were exploiting had already been addressed by Microsoft with the issue of a security 'patch' two years earlier, but apparently the companies targeted had failed to install it.

Once they had managed to identify the suspects, the FBI Agents covertly tempted them to travel from Russia (where they did not have jurisdiction) to the USA (where they did) on the false promise of an IT job. On their arrival at the fake offices of an FBI 'front' company, the suspects were asked to demonstrate their skills in an 'interview test' for which they had to access their own computers via the internet. Of course, they obliged, but, unbeknownst to them, the FBI had installed key-logging software on the terminal. Thus, once the 'test' was over, the agents were now able to gain access to the suspects' computers at home in Russia. Fearing that vital evidence would be deleted as soon as the suspects were arrested, the Agents decided to download the Russians' files before applying for a warrant from the court.

This was viewed somewhat negatively by the Russian authorities who considered the act a breach of sovereignty and who instigated criminal charges against the FBI Agents in Russia for hacking. Meanwhile, in their defence before the US courts, the Russian suspects sought to claim that the Agents had exceeded their powers in violating Russian law as well as infringing their individual right to privacy. Both of these arguments were adjudged without merit.[9]

EVIDENCE

Tracing suspects and evidence can also carry with it other unusual challenges. For instance, information crucial to tracing illegal activity across the internet is held by ISPs who store traffic data for billing purposes, but the data are normally stored only for as long as they are required for the billing after which they will be deleted. This would seem commercially reasonable given the fact that storing data has a cost implication. The deletion of such data has also been a legal requirement in the EU where personal data (information from which an individual may be identified) have to be deleted once the purpose for their retention has been achieved. However, this requirement is unhelpful for investigative purposes.[10] Attempts to force ISPs to retain their data in case they are needed for future investigations have been strongly resisted, but under a new EU Directive, EU Member States were required to introduce legislation by

9 'FBI Agent Charged with Hacking', www.msnbc.com/news/563379.asp?0na=x22034Q2p, accessed 7 June 2007.

10 It is rather telling that, in June 2007, the EU consented to the USA holding all flight passenger data for 15 years that might in the future have some security interest when such a time period is illegal within the EU itself.

15 September 2007[11] requiring data retention periods of between six months and two years.[12]

Even where copies of traffic data can be obtained, identifying a suspect is not always so easy. Skilled cybercriminals can take over the computers of unsuspecting users through the implantation of a virus, not only obtaining confidential information held on that computer (such as credit card numbers, PINs and passwords), but also using it as a 'zombie' to attack computers elsewhere. Some enterprising criminals have used viruses to create a slave network of machines (called 'bot-nets' derived from 'Robot-Networks') which they can then use to launch 'denial of service' attacks (a kind of computer onslaught where a target system is flooded by low grade electronic messages until it is brought to a standstill) or hire out to others.[13] The legitimate owner often remains in complete ignorance and unaware of this proxy use of his or her equipment until a police officer knocks at the door. For the investigator this complicates matters. Not only is it difficult to be sure whether the owner (or person in possession) of the machine has used it in the way the audit trail suggests but, if he or she has not, how does an investigator then proceed to trace the true culprit? In fact, a major British hi-tech investigation against on-line paedophiles has been strongly criticised for failures to address this deficiency.[14] When added to the inherent delays in obtaining multi-jurisdictional warrants, the chain of evidence may soon become frustrating and unwieldy, but cannot be neglected.

SETTING UP THE RESPONSE

Because of the specialist nature of cybercrime, investigations in which a computer plays anything more than an ancillary role are dependent on the level of technical understanding of the investigators and on the availability of advanced forensic tools. But there are many countries where private facilities and access to a computer network are not matched by equivalent public investment in cyber-policing facilities.[15]

11 EU Directive 2006/24/EC of 15 March 2006, Official Journal, L105/54, 14 April 2006, Brussels.

12 Ibid., Art 6.

13 From $200–$300 an hour according to the 'McAfee Virtual Criminology Report' (July 2005), www.mcafee.com, p. 13, accessed 1 June 2007.

14 D. Leppard, 'Child porn suspects set to be cleared in evidence shambles', London: The Times, 3 July 2005, www.timesonline.co.uk/tol/news/uk/article539974; D. Campbell, 'Operation Ore Flawed By Fraud', www.guardian.co.uk/crime/article/0,,2059880,00.html, both accessed 10 June 2007.

15 A detailed account of issues involved in developing a hi-tech crime response in Korea can be found in J. S. Park, 'Establishing a High-Tech Cyber Crime Response System', undated, but post-2005, www.innovation.go.kr/include/file_down.php?id=2190, accessed 1 June 2007.

One of the first organisational considerations in developing a response is the required type and background of the personnel. The question needs to be asked: is it better to train technical experts to be investigators or to train investigators to be technicians? To some extent, it depends on the category of crime and the degree to which technology is involved. 'Whilst experts must be developed to handle sophisticated computer crimes, traditional crimes that are merely facilitated by technology generally should remain the investigative responsibility of the units that traditionally investigate those crimes'.[16] These 'traditional' types of crime can be adequately dealt with by investigators who have a basic appreciation of the technical issues involved, but who can call on a central resource for the supply of forensic support on a case by case basis (in the same way, for instance, that a detective calls on the services of any forensics expert).

Regrettably, recruiting technical people with the requisite skills for cyber-sophisticated crime means either offering salaries that are competitive with industrial levels or tolerating a significantly lower skills profile than that available to criminal organisations. However, training investigators to be computer experts also requires significant investment in time and money. Whatever human resources policy is pursued, technical skills and equipment will inevitably require regular and expensive updating and upgrading which restrictive law enforcement budgets are unlikely to find easy to accommodate. The risk and likelihood that trained personnel will be tempted to offer their new-found skills to industry is also high and can lead to staff retention issues. This has led for some to call for a partnership between police and commercial industry to share expertise.[17] However, the use of technical experts from private industry on a temporary basis, although not without precedent, does require assurances in respect of the good character of the persons concerned and the protection of commercial confidentiality (after all, they would be given the legal power to search within the technical infrastructures of competitors). The value to a commercial company of such an arrangement is also hard to assess unless there is an agreement that seconded experts would work only on cases of interest to the parent company. However, such concerns do not preclude the gift of equipment or technical training which are equally at a premium. The danger in this latter regard is that any equipment or software donated will eventually require updating, maintenance or repair, the cost of which may be beyond the financial resources of the recipient even though operational commitments, procedures and investigations have become dependant on the new technology. It could also tie a law enforcement agency indefinitely to a particular IT product line which

16 D. Koenig, 'Investigation of Cybercrime and Technology-Related Crime' (2002), www.neiassociates.org/cybercrime.htm, accessed 1 June 2007.

17 S. W. Brenner, 'Private-Public Sector Co-operation in Combating Cybercrime: In Search of a Model', Journal of International Commercial Law and Technology, 2(2) (2007).

may be more expensive than other solutions. This is a very real concern for law enforcement in developing countries.

LEGAL POWERS

Life can be made easier for the cyber-investigator, as it can for any investigator, when the right laws are in place. A number of recommendations for establishing an effective legal framework for fighting cybercrime were written into the Convention on Cybercrime and can be said to represent the accumulated wisdom of the countries involved in its negotiation. These include the powers:

- to obtain traffic data (including subscriber information) and the content of computer systems expeditiously;
- to order any records to be preserved or supplied in real time;
- for law enforcement agencies to search, access and seize computers or storage media and to compel a service provider to support the collection and recording of such data.

In an attempt to extend the coverage of these laws and to inhibit the development of data havens, the agreement also calls for national powers to be extended to include aeroplanes or shipping registered in parties to the Convention (so that even international waters and airspace will be covered by the laws). However, as mentioned above, many key players have yet to ratify the treaty.

To facilitate international co-operation further, the Convention calls for a 24-hour contact point and a national central bureau to be established for dealing with computer-crime requests. It also provides legal grounds for forwarding information proactively and as an offence-specific instrument for extradition where a extradition treaty between the parties is lacking. As documented elsewhere in this book, such provisions are the mainstay of international law enforcement strategy generally.

Dual criminality (where co-operation depends on an activity being an offence in both requesting and requested country) is discussed in Chapter 10;[18] however, it can be a very real concern in the field of cybercrime. For instance, investigators who in 2000 believed they had tracked the author of the 'love bug' virus to the Philippines were frustrated to discover that, locally, computer offences did not exist. The virus had caused millions of dollars worth of damage and had closed down large sections of industry across the world, but prosecutors had to resort to credit card legislation just to effect an arrest for fraud.[19]

18 See also Chapter 10, p. 136.

19 www.archives.cnn.com/2000/TECH/computing/06/29/philippines.lovebug.02/index.html, accessed 3 June 2007.

Unfortunately the fraud charges had to be dropped through lack of evidence and, although new laws were subsequently enacted, the suspect was never brought to court for the damage caused by the virus. Indeed, he was last reported considering a number of job offers from software companies.[20]

And yet there is more than one way to skin a cat. In 2003, Oleg Zezev, an IT expert from Almaty in Kazakhstan, was convicted in the USA of illegally accessing Bloomberg Inc.'s computers in New York. He had bypassed the company's system security (using internet software that Bloomberg had innocently supplied to Zezev's employers in the course of a business relationship) and then sent an email threatening to 'destroy' Bloomberg's system unless he was paid $200,000. Zezev was encouraged to travel to London to receive the cash and was met by Bloomberg's head of IT and a British undercover officer. After making some incriminating statements in the presence of these gentlemen, Zezev was arrested and extradited to the USA to face prosecution. He was convicted and sentenced to 51 months' imprisonment.[21] It is interesting to note how both this and the previous case (involving the Russians) involved a 'sting' operation by law enforcement in order to bring the suspects into a controlled environment where further direct evidence could be obtained.

A novel situation lacking a clear legal framework and with which investigators are likely to have to concern themselves increasingly in the future is the matter of jurisdiction in 3D virtual worlds. In November 2007 a news report announced that a Dutch youth had been arrested and a number of others questioned concerning the alleged misappropriation of virtual furniture in a social networking site called 'Habbo Hotel'.[22] This 'furniture' had been purchased by other users and was said to have a real life value of €4,000, but what is the substance of the property allegedly stolen and where did the theft actually take place? According to the owners of the site, the Sulake Corporation, Habbo Hotel has 80 million registered avatars and the Habbo 'community' is 'localised' in 31 countries across five continents, so where is the so-called community actually physically located and whose laws apply?[23] A spokesman for the Amsterdam police is quoted as saying, 'We are trying to bring charges of theft. It is a little difficult and new.'[24] That would seem to be a masterpiece of understatement.

20 www.findarticles.com/p/articles/mi_m0NEW/is_2000_August_22/ai_64464020, accessed 3 June 2007.

21 www.usdoj.gov/criminal/cybercrime/zezevSent.htm, accessed 3 June 2007.

22 'Virtual theft leads to arrest', www.news.bbc.co.uk/1/hi/technology/7094764.stm, accessed 14 November 2007.

23 Sulake itself has its headquarters in Finland with 14 other offices around the world. www.sulake.com, press report 25 October 2007, accessed 14 November 2007.

24 'World's First Arrests for Virtual Theft', London: Daily Telegraph, 14 November 2007.

CONCLUSION

Offences involving computer networks are uniquely easy to commit internationally and any investigation has to at least consider the possibility that such an offence may have an international component. Cyberspace is borderless and investigations must reduce digital material into evidence useable in the appropriate court system; they must link criminal with crime scene where the only connection between the two may be transient electronic impulses transmitted across the worldwide web. However, not only the impulses are transient. Whereas conventional investigative techniques, such as fingerprinting, are characterised by longevity '. . . cyber crime investigation methods are unique in that technology accumulation is tricky [sic].'[25] Technology is expensive, has built-in obsolescence and carries with it the risk of 'tech-lag'.[26] Cybercrime may, therefore, be described not only in terms of criminal innovation, but also in respect of a rapid depreciation in value of law enforcement skills, technical resources and the legislative framework.

Further and substantial practical difficulties may also be confronted:

- the relevant computer-related offences may not have been criminalised in one or more of the countries involved;
- electronic evidence is 'highly perishable and can be easily deleted or modified from half-a-world away';
- any encryption employed and user anonymity have to be addressed;
- transaction records need to be obtained in a timely manner;
- data protection rules may have resulted in the deletion of traffic data.[27]

After a slow start, cybercrime legislation and the creation of centres of law enforcement expertise are beginning to provide international coverage, albeit far from universal. Unfortunately, the threat is prodigious. Cybercrime is a global threat[28] with a higher financial turnover than drug trafficking,[29] yet only 5 per cent of cybercriminals are ever caught or convicted.[30] Today, even the computer security industry has admitted failure in being able to tackle cybercrime alone and sees international police co-operation as an imperative.[31]

25 Op. cit., Park, fn 15.

26 B. Etter, 'Critical Issues in Hi-tech Crime', paper at *Embracing the Future Together Conference 2002*, p. 13, www.acpr.gov.au/pdf/Presentations/cpacongNov02.pdf, accessed 7 June 2007.

27 See K. DiGregory, 'Fighting Cybercrime – What are the Challenges facing Europe', 19 September 2000, www.usdoj.gov/criminal/cybercrime/EUremarks.htm, accessed 1 June 2007.

28 Op. cit., Goodman and Brenner, fn 6, p. 9.

29 J. Leyden, 'Cybercrime more lucrative than drugs' (2005), www.channelregister.co.uk/2005/11/29/cybercrime/, accessed 25 June 2007.

30 Op. cit., McAfee, fn 13, p. 6.

31 T. Green, 'Kaspersky seeks help from international police to fight cybercrime' (2007), www.networkworld.com/news/2007/013107-kaspersky-cybercrime.html, accessed 30 June 2007.

Part V

In practice

Chapter 18

Across two continents

A case study

Phil Tucker

I am off-duty at home and settle down to watch a World Cup football match between Serbia and Montenegro and the Netherlands. I am not on call today, so I can relax a little for once. It is early summer and the temperature on this Sunday afternoon is unseasonably high; I have my windows wide open to let in the breeze and I am drinking a much-needed cold beer. The whole of Europe is suffering from a heat wave and the match commentators repeatedly refer to the ordeal that the players are going through out there on the pitch, grateful for the relaxed FIFA rules allowing them to drink as much liquid as is necessary to get them through to half-time.

About the same time, under that same sweltering sun, a refrigerated meat lorry makes its way to the international ferry port of Hoek van Holland, its cargo of chilled pork carcasses destined for England. It has been driven from Denmark and its enterprising Lithuanian driver has just made a lucrative diversion in order to take onboard some extra cargo. It will take him another hour or so to get to the port. He will wait for boarding for an hour, the sea crossing will take about 12 hours, then he has another hour's drive before he can stop again. He makes sure he has plenty to drink and will eat two full meals during the crossing. He will enjoy watching the football game and probably drink a beer or two. Underneath the chilled compartment, in a toolbox designed for meat hooks measuring 2.4m × 90cm × 61cm, he has locked five men. They cannot be heard from the outside, although they are soon screaming and clawing desperately at the unyielding metal door. They have no water, no food and no means of escape and are dying from heat exhaustion and dehydration. The lorry will be carrying an extra carcass by the time it makes its stop in the UK.

It is late on Sunday evening by the time the lorry eventually stops at a lay-by on a major trunk road in the South-East of England; the smuggled men have suffered severe bouts of diarrhoea, two are either dead or close to death and one is desperately ill. The driver drags them from the box, dumps them at the side of the road and leaves. He does not offer them water. He does not call for medical assistance.

As the evening cools slightly, two of the men recover sufficiently to think about getting themselves to safety. One of them realises he cannot go anywhere in his faeces-stained underpants and trousers and so he discards them, replacing them with those he removes from a dying companion. These fortunate survivors make their way into a nearby town where they seek water and are eventually able to make contact with those who sponsored their journey. They are collected and disappear into one of England's many Asian districts, never to be seen or identified by the police.

The next morning I am asked with a colleague to attend the scene of a suspicious death. A man of Asian appearance is lying in the undergrowth, a second lies unconscious at his side and is taken to hospital where he dies a few days later, never having regained consciousness. A third who had been deliriously wandering around, naked from the waist downwards, is also hospitalised. I call for a helicopter to photograph the scene and to search for any further survivors or bodies, but I cannot help but think that the only picture will be of a clueless detective standing by the side of the road wondering where to go from here.

The scenario described is based on real events[1] and poses many questions. Where do I start? How will I identify the victims? Where are they from? Who is responsible for their deaths? What offences am I investigating and where have these been committed? How will I ever get to the bottom of this? Any investigator arriving at that scene could well have concluded that these young men of Asian appearance, lying as they were beside the main route from the coast to London, had been smuggled into the UK, but was that the only possible hypothesis? Every incident is different and an investigative law enforcement officer is unlikely to be faced with these exact same circumstances. Nevertheless, the challenges posed and, perhaps, more importantly, their solutions are common to most international investigations and a close examination of the various options for international co-operation may be helpful to those faced with similar situations in the future.

We will first examine the initial approach, including the setting of parameters in a plan. We will then discuss the impact that such an investigation is likely to have on the responsible law enforcement agency and the concept of a Strategic Command Group. Finally we will look in detail at the tactical options available for the investigator, examining each international line of enquiry in turn and observing the parts played by each of the bodies involved. The above scenario also involved many lines of enquiry which were carried out in the UK – witnesses were interviewed, close-circuit television video recordings were seized and viewed, records of movements at ports were examined and forensic scientists were called in to assist. However, I will not go into these aspects of the investigation except where they overlap with the international lines of enquiry with which the reader is concerned.

A modern senior investigating officer will normally record all of the main

1 Some facts and events have been altered for operational reasons.

investigative strategies to be used in an investigation and will formulate a plan to focus the work of his or her team of detectives. Such planning is even more important in an international investigation where enquiries are likely to take longer, be more expensive and often be carried out by foreign officers. The detective in charge should decide upon the extent and boundaries of international activity and write these into an 'international investigation plan'. This plan should include the aims and objectives for the investigation, state where in the world those aims and objectives need to be achieved and identify who is going to achieve them. The plan is simply a guide for the investigator, a consideration of what the investigation needs to discover and the practical factors which impact on success. Whilst writing the plan is one of the very first things that the investigator should be doing, it is very unlikely that a full plan can be completed at these early stages due to a lack of information. Paradoxically, this is its strength: by attempting to set out what offences are being investigated in which country and by whom, the investigator will quickly be able to see where the knowledge gaps are. Filling these gaps is what drives the investigation, keeping it on track. The plan needs to be flexible and regularly updated as information is received. Eventually it will form the basis for an international prosecution plan that will set out which offences are to be prosecuted in which country and by whom. The international investigation plan will encompass strands from several of the generic investigative strategies such as those dealing with forensic matters, search parameters and interview plans and should be recorded alongside them. For example, in our scenario, the forensic strategy is likely to make reference to the need to collect DNA from the bodies of the men for identification purposes. Comparison of these profiles against a national DNA database (where one exists) is unlikely to yield results if the men have only just entered the country, presumably for the first time. Therefore, these profiles would need to be checked abroad and decisions about where they are to be checked should be written into the international investigation plan. In our scenario, I have assumed that the investigator knows little or nothing about how human smuggling works; one key strand of the international investigation plan will be to ascertain who has this information and to obtain a briefing as soon as possible, because this strategic overview (or criminal business analysis) will inform the direction that the investigation takes. I will return to this in more detail later. During the investigation I am about to describe, I referred back to my original plan many times, reminding myself of what my objectives were, as it is so easy to become side tracked and start to focus on issues which are intensely interesting, but unlikely to lead to the solving of the case.

The scenario described throws up two broad investigative aims: first, the identification of the dead men and the hospitalised survivor and, second, the investigation of the circumstances. Whilst information gleaned in the pursuit of one of these aims will clearly inform the other, achieving those aims will require very different responses. For example, identification of the men is likely to require enquiries in South Asia, whilst investigation of the circumstances is likely to focus initially on Europe. These enquiries will be time consuming, resource intensive and expensive. Furthermore, where will the investigation stop? If a European people-smuggling gang is identified, who will investigate its ongoing activities? And, will we then try to identify the criminals based in the Indian subcontinent who fed the smuggled men into the Europe-based gang? All of these considerations should be included in the plan to provide clarity to investigators.

Whilst the international investigation plan should set out to acknowledge and decide upon these difficult issues, the investigator is likely to have very limited control over the resources required to carry out the plan. It is vital to the success of the investigation that senior management provides sufficient support in terms of resources and strategic direction to enable the investigator to work in the confidence that his or her team will not be diverted to deal with pressing local priorities. The most efficient way to achieve this is to establish an investigation-specific Strategic Command Group (SCG) to provide the necessary oversight and to exercise command and control at the strategic level. The task of this group is not to make tactical decisions about how to deal with specific lines of enquiry, but to set the parameters and provide sufficient resources to ensure that the investigation can achieve its aims. Members of the SCG should be drawn from representatives of the highest level of the organisation who have the authority to make necessary decisions: operational command, criminal investigation, media, finance and personnel should all be represented and the senior investigating officer in the investigation should always be present at meetings in order to update the group as to progress. It may also be appropriate, depending on the circumstances, to invite partner agencies (such as border control agencies) or at least to allocate the function of partner agency liaison to a member of the group. Needless to say, the SCG will pay close attention to the international investigation plan. The investigator should see the establishment of the group as a positive tool and should be proactive in calling meetings if he or she feels that a lack of resources is affecting delivery against the plan. The SCG can also be an opportunity to achieve structural change within the organisation or to obtain extra equipment specifically needed for the investigation and of overall benefit to the organisation in the future.

THE ROLE OF NATIONAL ORGANISATIONS IN AN INTERNATIONAL INVESTIGATION

Whilst the investigator will obviously look abroad for solutions to problems in an international investigation, it pays to check whether there are relevant domestic specialist centres that will already have built significant international links. In this case the advice of the UK's National Human Trafficking Centre (NHTC) was very useful. I met with the NHTC's specialist lawyer who was able to advise on my international investigation plan and to give sound advice on the most practical way of co-operating with prosecutors abroad.

Many countries have central national databases used to store details of previous unusual investigations and any specialist experts used to assist. In the case of the UK there is a national expert database available within the National Policing Improvement Agency (NPIA). In the scenario, the NPIA was able to put me in touch with the senior investigating officer of a previous similar case. This first step allowed me to benefit from the experience gained in the earlier investigation: the simple but valuable advice I received was to focus on the accounts provided by survivors. With more and more domestic major investigations having an international element, national expert database administrators will increasingly have access to and be able to share the methodology applied in other international investigations.

The way in which forensic science support is delivered varies widely throughout the world; at one end of the scale is the UK, where the service is provided to law enforcement agencies by private commercial companies, whereas in most countries the scientists are directly employed by the Ministry of Interior. In the scenario a specialist adviser was appointed to oversee and co-ordinate the various forensic methods deployed, including etymologists (insects), palynologists (plant spores and pollen) and DNA experts. DNA profiles were obtained from the bodies of the dead men and from the known survivor for identification purposes. Interestingly, a fourth DNA profile was obtained from the faeces in a pair of discarded underpants at the scene. I had wondered why the survivor was naked from the waist downwards – the discovery of the fourth profile led me to conclude that one of the survivors who had left the scene must have removed his own soiled underpants and taken those of his sickly travelling companion.

Forensic scientists also carried out isotopic analysis of the bones of the dead men but could come only to the conclusion that they originated from the Indian sub-continent. Unexpectedly, the forensic science company was also able to carry out research, mainly internet open-source based, on the origin of the clothing retrieved from the dead men. This is work that could arguably have been carried out by a police officer but I found that, because the scientists involved were so experienced in carrying out such work and were dedicated to the task, they worked much faster than police officers would have done and the results were very useful and cost-effective. Their report told me that the underpants of the victims were only manufactured and distributed to outlets in India. I used this information in deciding to focus a subsequent media campaign on India rather than on the whole of South Asia. The specialist forensic adviser was able to give an objective overview of my forensic strategy and, in the international context, provide advice on carrying out forensic examinations and obtaining samples abroad.

Domestically based services such as expert and investigation databases, forensic scientists and specialist crime centres all play a vital role in the investigation of international crime and should be the investigator's first port of call. The next step was to establish contact with the national department responsible for international liaison.

NATIONAL GATEWAYS TO INTERNATIONAL LIAISON

Many countries have a central department that acts as the national gateway to international investigations. In the UK, international services are accessed via the Serious Organised Crime Agency (SOCA), which, as well as being the gateway to Interpol and Europol, is the employer of the vast majority of UK Law Enforcement Liaison Officers based abroad, including the UK's Europol Liaison Officers. Building a good relationship with such a department will be fundamental to any international investigation and an investigator should advise them of the circumstances of the case and share the broad details of the international investigation plan. You may have sensitive information which you do not feel needs to be shared in order to achieve your aims, but my advice is to set a policy of sharing as much as is possible rather than the other way around. Where there is some information that you are not able to share, you should explain why. This will demonstrate your commitment to openness and will help this all-important relationship get off to a sound start. This international liaison unit or gateway, if there is one, will advise on the most appropriate international channel or combination of channels for your case. Whether such an international liaison unit or gateway exists or not, you will have to put all of your requests for services abroad in writing.

Wherever information is to be requested from abroad, the request should be clear, concise and, above all, justified. In my experience of international liaison, the biggest failing of officers requesting assistance is a failure to explain and justify their requests properly. The opposite is also true: those requests which are clear, concise and are justified are the most successful. Being asked to write something down certainly focuses the mind on the fact that at the end of all this liaison there may be a court hearing in which your activity will be scrutinised by lawyers and judges.

It is worth noting that in almost all cases where you want to use information received from abroad in a criminal trial you will need to reinforce your request with an International Letter of Request, sometimes referred to as a Commission Rogatoire or letter rogatory, signed by a prosecuting lawyer or judge. In practice this means that you will often receive an intelligence-only response quickly, but that receiving this information in a form in which it can be used in evidence will take longer. There are various ways to fast-track Letters of Request, but the principle remains the same.

INTERPOL

One of the two main strands of our investigation was the identification of the two dead men (and confirmation of the stated identification of the survivor), a task which is routinely carried out via Interpol. Disaster Victim Identification (DVI) forms, used extensively to identify victims in cases such as the tsunami of 26 December 2004, were completed for our unknown victims and circulated by Interpol. However, the victims had not been reported missing by their families, as, due to the clandestine nature of the men's journey, their families did not know when to expect them to surface in the UK and did not yet consider them to be missing. In the event, it was liaison through Europol that led to the first clue as to who the men might be.

ENQUIRIES IN EUROPE

Whilst I had hypothesised that the men were victims of a human smuggling enterprise gone wrong, I had no idea how the business of human smuggling worked. Europol has an Offences Against the Person Unit that was able to provide key strategic intelligence over the telephone out of hours, shedding light on the probable country of origin and transit countries and the most likely modus operandi. This was crucial in informing my decisions about what to do in those all important first few hours – as a result of talking to the Europol expert, I now knew that I was probably looking for a van or a lorry as opposed to a car and that there would have been more than just three smuggled men. Soon afterwards I received the most recent Europol strategic reports on human smuggling routes and methodologies.

By this time we had started to debrief the hospitalised survivor and now had a vague picture of his journey. Using all these sources of information (and some open-source intelligence), I was able to task an analyst to prepare a criminal business analysis report. In effect this report compared the circumstances of our case with the current trends, identified what we needed to be looking for and made recommendations as to where we might find it. Simply put, during the early interviews with the survivor, he was unable to tell us the details of each and every leg of his journey.[2] However, using the information from Europol and an analyst, I was able to reconstruct his most likely journey from start to finish and to identify the points along the way where he would have probably come into contact with criminals. This was very valuable indeed and the analytical report in effect became the international investigation plan, allowing me to focus in on three groups of people: the lorry driver, the organised criminals based in Europe and people in the UK who may have funded the journey.

2 He was later to tell the court that he had paid €5,000 to be transported to the UK.

All of the information and intelligence arising from our investigation was contributed via the Europol officials to the Europol Analytical Workfile on Human Smuggling. This helped to inform the European strategic picture on human smuggling and enabled Europol to fine-tune their analytical products. This then allowed for direct comparison of data from our investigation with that of other current European human smuggling investigations. The surviving victim was gradually becoming a more lucid witness and information that he provided us led us to identify money transfers between the UK and Belgium; Europol's Financial Crimes Unit was able to make use of good liaison with the financial sector to provide us with useful intelligence in relation to these transactions.

Early on in the investigation, it became clear that, whilst the victims themselves originated in South Asia, the criminality involved in transporting them to the UK was based in Europe. Information from the surviving victim led us to believe that his arrival point in Europe was Italy and a piece of paper found on one of the dead men contained a Portuguese telephone number. The survivor knew he had been carried to the UK locked in the toolbox of a lorry, but he neither knew where this final leg of the journey had started nor how long it had taken. However, the etymologist was able to give an approximate time of their arrival in the UK and this was then confirmed by sightings of ill-looking young Asian men in a nearby small town, where they had tried to buy water and make contact with family. Working backwards from this time and estimating the driving time from the most likely ports, I was able to identify those ferries which were the most likely to have been the crossing used by the smugglers. Extensive enquiries with UK ports, working on the description provided by the survivor, led us to believe that the most likely lorry involved belonged to a Danish company operating between Holland and England driven by a Lithuanian. Other leads (not least those in relation to the money transfer) suggested that the criminals responsible for arranging the transport were in Belgium.

As there were several European countries involved and since Europol officials were supporting the investigation, it was decided, in consultation with the international department at SOCA, that Europol Liaison Officers (ELOs) would be the principal channel for information exchange with European colleagues. The UK Liaison Office at Europol was organised in such a way that specific officers were responsible for different areas of organised crime; in particular there was a liaison officer responsible for immigration crime. Bearing in mind that I had little experience in investigating this type of offence and my team had even less, we arranged for the ELO to come to the UK to be briefed about the specifics of the case, to advise on information exchange and to give the whole team a lesson on people smuggling routes and methodology. This meant that officers despatched to carry out enquiries were able to put them into context.

Following this, a further meeting was arranged at Europol involving operational officers and ELOs from UK, Denmark, Belgium and Holland plus ELOs from Lithuania, Italy and Portugal and officials from Europol's Offences

Against the Person, Financial and Analytical Units. During this meeting I delivered a briefing on the operation and described the aims of my international investigation plan. Agreement was reached that direct police-to-police contact would be established between the UK and Denmark (principally in order to retrieve forensic evidence from the lorry that we suspected was involved) and between the UK and Belgium (principally to assist the Belgians in instigating their own investigation into the Belgian crime group). This direct contact was backed up by written requests exchanged via Europol, so that the ELOs were always kept in the loop and were able to copy intelligence to Europol specialists as appropriate.

This connection proved to be successful in that Italy confirmed, by checking records of asylum seekers, that the surviving victim had been in their country previously. This corroboration of the survivor's account would be essential if his version of events was to be called into question during any subsequent trial. Portuguese officers visited the subscriber of the telephone number found on one of the victims and the details provided eventually led to the identification of one of the dead men. Lithuania carried out intelligence checks on the suspect driver, confirming that a man of his details, whilst not having a criminal record, did indeed live in Lithuania.

Denmark, assisted by the UK Police Crime Scene Manager and in co-operation with the Danish haulage company (that had been unaware of the driver's activities) carried out a forensic examination of the toolbox on the lorry and provided copies of the relevant tachograph[3] disc. By this time several months had passed so we were not surprised to find little more than a crumpled cigarette packet inside the toolbox. However, meticulous scientific techniques revealed that there were two or three hair fragments stuck to the carton and it was with some celebration that we received the news from the British forensic scientists that one of these hair fragments had come from the head of our survivor, proving that he was linked to that lorry. Furthermore, examination of the tachograph disc by British police experts suggested that the lorry had stopped at the exact spot on the roadside where the bodies had been discovered on the evening before they were found.

In consultation with Lithuanian ELOs, I was preparing an arrest plan for the lorry driver when we had a stroke of luck – he was stopped at the French border with the UK at the entrance to the Channel Tunnel in Coquelles, France, having been circulated in the UK as wanted. We had not yet reached the stage of circulating his details worldwide but assumed that as an international lorry driver he might well present himself at a UK frontier – this transpired to be the case. The border controls for the Channel Tunnel are juxtaposed, with French officials and British officials working side by side at both ends of the tunnel with joint jurisdiction, so a British arrest was easily effected.

3 This is a device which records the travel, speed and distance on commercial haulage vehicles.

Having already briefed Lithuania, a simple telephone call (backed up by a written request, of course) was all that was required to achieve a premises search in Lithuania whilst the driver was in custody in the UK. This is difficult enough to achieve within the UK at times, so was a wonderful example of how international liaison at its best can work.

Many Letters of Request were required for this investigation and, in order to help both us and the British Crown Prosecution Service to keep abreast of them, we created a management spreadsheet, indicating where in the process each letter was. Good liaison with the prosecutor (in our case a senior Crown Prosecution Service lawyer) is essential if the whole investigation is not to grind to a halt. A point of interest is that some countries require a Letter of Request to carry out a check of a DNA profile against their National DNA Database, even if the result is only to be used as intelligence in the first instance.

Having consulted with British prosecutors, the international investigation plan was updated to take into account the prosecution of any offenders. We intended that the lorry driver would be prosecuted for manslaughter and any UK-based sponsors would be prosecuted for facilitation of illegal immigration and that both of these prosecutions would take place in the UK. The Belgian-based organised people smugglers, when and if they were identified, would be prosecuted in Belgium, provided that Belgian prosecutors were in agreement with this. Being in close proximity within The Hague, the ELOs at Europol have a very close working relationship with their counterparts, the national representatives at Eurojust, and it was through this route that Eurojust were approached. The UK ELO handling our case discussed our prosecution preferences with the UK Eurojust representative who, in his turn, discussed this with the Belgian Eurojust representative and the plan, simple as it was, received approval.

However, it was a separate Belgian-initiated investigation that led to the identification of the people smuggling gang. Belgian officers carried out a raid on a 'safe house' in Brussels used to shelter illegal immigrants and our Lithuanian lorry driver was found inside. This took place after the deaths of the men in the UK, but before the lorry driver had been arrested in France, implying that he had continued to involve himself in the business of people smuggling even after having discarded the dying men at the side of the road. Had we not previously briefed the Belgian officers, the connection between the arrest of the lorry driver in Belgium and the deaths in the UK would never have been made. A Letter of Request was sent to Belgium to secure the use of this information in court, but, unfortunately, the formal documentation arrived too late to allow it to be used in evidence during the driver's trial.

The inquiry in the UK did not lead to the identification of any criminal fundraisers so that, in the event, the Lithuanian lorry driver was the only man left to prosecute. Nevertheless, the involvement of Eurojust had enabled us to plan the investigation with our options open, knowing which groups of offenders would be prosecuted in which country and for which offences.

ENQUIRIES IN INDIA

The clue provided by the piece of paper with the Portuguese telephone number led us to identify a man in England who believed he knew that one of the dead men was from a remote village in Northern India. This necessitated enquiries in India and liaison there was carried out through a local Indian police liaison officer attached to the British High Commission in New Delhi. Our first contact with him was in relation to our media strategy. Following up on the clue that the forensic scientists had uncovered that the men were wearing underpants manufactured and sold in India, I wanted to launch a media campaign with the aim of appealing for relatives of men who were missing after travelling to the UK. The Indian liaison officer provided advice on the wording of a newspaper advertisement, helped us select appropriate mortuary photographs to circulate (based on his knowledge of what local newspapers would be comfortable with), prepared translations and led negotiations with the newspapers on our behalf. However, the Portuguese line of enquiry led to us identifying a possible next of kin for one of the dead men and it was clear that we would have to visit these people before publishing photographs in a newspaper. The liaison officer then travelled to Northern India to show the photographs to possible family members and, at last, one of our victims was provisionally identified. Letters of Request were required in order to allow UK officers to travel to India to take statements and obtain familial DNA samples to allow formal identification to take place.

DIRECT INFORMAL CONTACT

Direct police to police informal contact is often viewed by those in the international liaison field as unwelcome and even dangerous. This is not just a case of people protecting their empires, but is an opinion informed by bitter experience; I have personal experience of well-intentioned officers working in direct informal contact with colleagues abroad discovering far too late that what their contact had been doing for them was illegal and not admissible in court, being asked to leave the host country and then being banned from international travel by their own organisation. Such cases have also been known to trigger diplomatic incidents in countries with whom the requesting country has a sensitive political relationship. On the other hand, officers engaged in an international investigation often set out with the firmly held belief that nothing less than direct contact with their counterpart in the appropriate country will do, seeing liaison officers as unnecessary links in an already over-long chain. As usual, the best approach is a compromise; direct contact in this case with my Danish counterpart enabled me to discuss in detail what my forensic strategy requirements were before putting pen to paper and this undoubtedly contributed significantly to the successful outcome. However, there were no language barriers

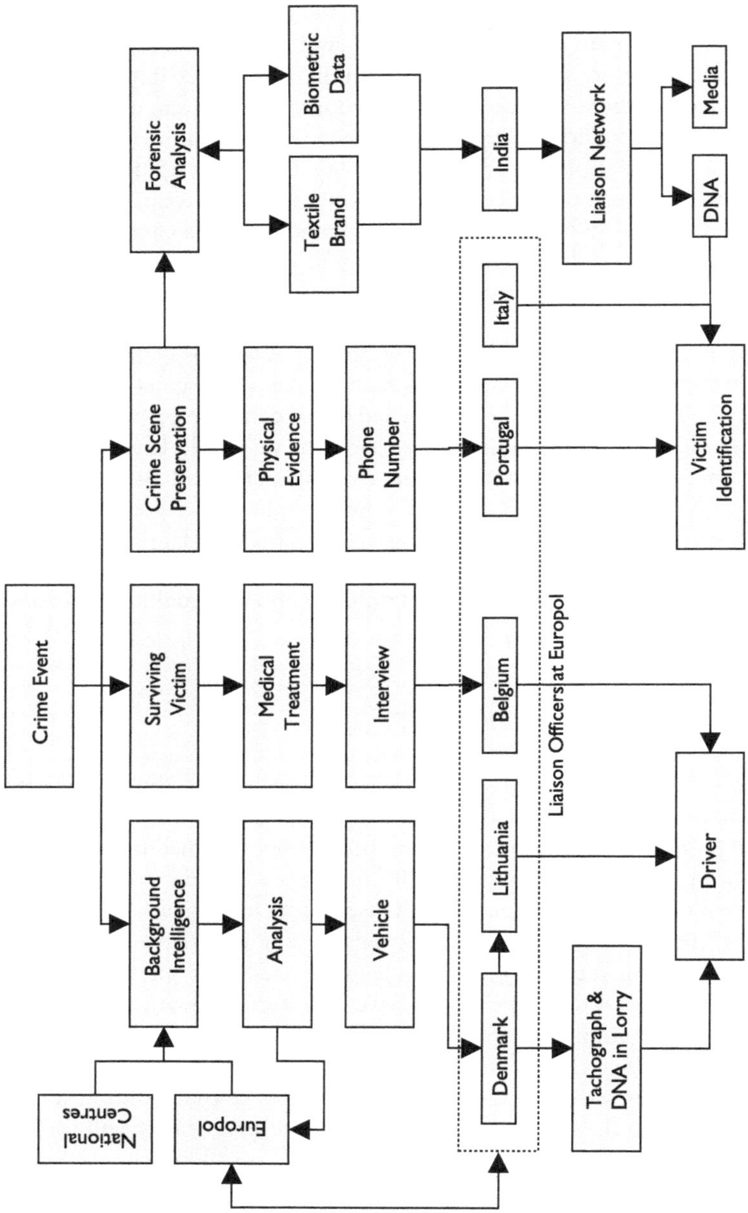

Figure 18.1 Across Two Continents Investigation.

and the contact had been facilitated through the UK Liaison Bureau at Europol, who were kept informed of my every move. The information I received was always provided on the basis that it was for intelligence purposes only and that a Letter of Request would be supplied for everything we needed to use in court.

An alternative to direct police-to-police informal contact is direct prosecutor-to-prosecutor informal contact. In most countries investigations are authorised or directly controlled by prosecutors and not police officers. Therefore, when a request for assistance amounts to the need for the receiving country to commence an investigation (often referred to as a parallel investigation), a prosecutor will be very closely involved. In this case, when the Belgian Eurojust representative contacted his prosecutor colleagues in Belgium about the case, the prosecutor sought direct contact with a UK counterpart in order to reassure himself about the parameters of the Belgian investigation – the British NHTC specialist lawyer was able to provide this.

CONCLUSION

It had been a daunting feeling standing at the side of that trunk road in the hot sun looking at the two victims, already aware of the immense challenges of the international investigation that lay ahead of us. However, the task became manageable once I had set myself clear objectives in an international investigation plan, had secured the support of my organisation through the establishment of a Strategic Command Group and had built a sound working relationship with those people responsible for providing access to international assistance. A combination of services provided by a mixture of national and international organisations and individuals helped to achieve the objectives of the plan.

As the helicopter hovered above, I could feel the heat of the tarmac burning through the soles of my shoes. We had called in extra supplies of water for the investigation, forensic and search teams at the scene to sustain us for the few hours we had to endure the temperature. As the investigation unfolded, I wondered what drove young men to such extraordinary lengths as to place themselves at the mercy of unscrupulous criminals who could leave them locked up in a metal toolbox without water and without means of escape in such extreme conditions. Much later, my colleague in India would enlighten me: 'In the village the roads are bad and extremely narrow. The village is all mud houses with a sprinkling of palatial bungalows belonging to those who went to foreign shores. These inspire the have-nots to try their luck.'

After a journey of co-operation that stretched across two continents, involving the collaboration of law enforcement agencies in so many different countries and employing a wide range of investigative methods, the case was over, but the tragedy would never be over for the families of the victims. The best they could hope for was that those responsible would be brought to justice and in November 2007 the lorry driver stood trial. Evidence lasted more than three weeks and there was an anxious moment when the judge directed an acquittal in respect of the first victim because, under English law, a manslaughter charge requires death to occur on British soil and it had not been possible to prove beyond a reasonable doubt that the victim had not died sometime during the journey before the ferry docked in the UK. However, in the end, the driver was found guilty of the manslaughter of the second victim by unanimous verdict of the jury and sentenced to eight years' imprisonment.

Afterword

Steven David Brown

Law enforcement professionals make a challenging audience. Their entire working lives are spent wading through conflicting accounts, contradictory indications and clues that simply do not add up. The facts are often elusive, but the investigator does his or her best to make sense of it all in order to build a credible case. And so an Afterword rather than a Conclusion is provided here. The authors have presented a number of perspectives and perceptions for your consideration, but as for the conclusions . . . these you will undoubtedly draw for yourselves.

Concerns over the preservation of national sovereignty when negotiating international co-operation are not restricted to criminal justice or internal security. However, the fact has slowly dawned that the liberalisation of political and economic frontiers and the mobility of populations, whilst offering many social benefits, impact on crime at all levels. As a result, governments are increasingly prepared to modify and adapt their crime strategies accordingly. The international factor now operates on very local and quite routine crime not only in terms of the offender and the circumstances of the offence, but also in terms of victimology. However, national and international differentials in law enforcement ability, capacity and resourcing mean that best practice and performance far from being universal are not even practical in every region. Consequently, the help and assistance in law enforcement development offered to less affluent parts of the world (particularly involving the latest scientific and forensic techniques) is a crucial driver for improving both local and upstream disruption against international crime networks.

The impact of wider political and diplomatic policy on the criminal industry has also been discussed. For instance, the merits of the present war in Afghanistan will exercise the minds of commentators for many years to come, but the implications for law enforcement are far from localised with the increase in the production of opium resulting in a consequent increase in the availability of heroin to the rest of the world. Economically, 'more money is provided to Afghanistan by western drug addicts than by western governments'[1] and

1 Robert Hunter, Former US Ambassador to NATO speaking in an interview on 'The World Today', BBC World Service, 24 October 2007.

this will undoubtedly affect drug-related mortality[2] and domestic patterns of acquisitive crime in far continents.

In recent years there has been a burgeoning of international instruments, organisations and networks dedicated to combating crime and new databases seem to be launched with astounding regularity. They emphasise the benefits of partnership, but, although co-operation has improved considerably, there is still a long way to go. Interpol, in particular, has risen to the challenge and made the possibility of global law enforcement co-operation a reality. Building on its system of alerts and notices, Interpol has proactively identified gaps in international coverage and worked to fill them. However, there is still a tendency for groups of countries bound together by history, language, culture and economics for the establishment and ownership of their own especial arrangements. Such a movement may sometimes be seen as divisive, duplicative and diluting the available national resources and funding, but there will also be situations in which the resulting arrangements complement the work of existing initiatives. Some have argued that regional organisations can be more specific and offer a service better tailored to local needs, but no region can afford to be isolationist in the face of the modern realities of international criminality. Unfortunately, the objective business case for and a comparative cost-benefit analysis of international networks and regional alliances are missing, as is a co-ordinated international policy on how the jigsaw should fit together.

On a practical level, there is an unresolved debate over whether international crime requires international responses, or whether it can be adequately addressed by national based investigative strategies. Both views have been represented here and both have emphasised the enhanced role of information in modern law enforcement. Although there are a variety of mechanisms and channels for transmitting or managing data, a consensus has emerged that one well-functioning central bureau or unit handling the import and export of information at the national level is the most efficient solution. The sensitivity and risk in data exchange has also been highlighted, and the use of a single gateway improves data-handling standards. However, all parties have stressed the need to develop and maintain working relationships with international partners based on trust. Often, measures of trust are made against direct personal experience, reinforced by personal networks or diminished by real or imagined risks of corruption. Corruption has received a good deal of international attention and investment, but continues to operate on the willingness to share information. Regrettably there are no quick-fix solutions and no country is immune.

2 The EMCDDA gives a conservative estimate of 113,000 drug-related deaths in the EU between 1990 and 2003, the majority of which are thought to have involved opioids (www.ar2006.emcdda.europa.eu/en/page011-en.html, accessed 19 November 2007), but this figure relates to a period before the increased cultivation reported in recent years.

The dangers of imprecise or inadequate language have also been mentioned not only in the context of operational messages or requests for assistance, but also in the wording of international agreements that, whilst permitting the parties to accept the text at the diplomatic level, may reduce certainty in the legal process and obscure both meaning and intention.

Despite the challenges and the advantages for international crime in comparison with a law enforcement corralled within political boundaries, it is still possible to view the future with some optimism. Notwithstanding the lack of a co-ordinated international approach and the complex bureaucracies encountered, the arm of the law is stretching further than ever before. Technology has enhanced the speed of communications and provided new ways of identifying criminals and linking them to their crimes. Traditional boltholes for fugitives are gradually being blocked or, better still, opened up to the possibility of extradition. The zeal with which new initiatives are proposed and pursued demonstrates how both governments and NGOs have identified and are receptive to the need for action, but it is also possible to be overzealous and perhaps it would be more effective sometimes to rationalise existing efforts and to reinforce them rather than to build anew. Where structures and organisations are perceived as deficient, would it not be better to address those deficiencies rather than duplicate them in yet another new structure?

In the long run, performance in combating international crime will depend on the priority it is given and on the strength of the law enforcement alliances marshalled in its support. However, the greatest redeeming factor for all such faults and failures should not be underestimated: ordinary law enforcement professionals throughout the world share a desire to bring the criminal to justice and, given half a chance, will readily work together to do so.

Appendices

These appendices have been compiled in order to provide readers with useful reference material. While every effort has been taken to ensure accuracy, no responsibility is accepted or assumed for any errors or for the activities of any of the organisations featured here or for the content of any of the websites.

Appendix I

International co-operation networks

Compiled by Stuart Cameron-Waller

This appendix contains brief descriptions of the major international networks and groupings involved in international law enforcement.

GLOBAL

Interpol

The international criminal police organisation is the oldest and best established international law enforcement organisation. It has a membership of 186 countries (each with its own National Central Bureaux) and a General Secretariat in Lyon, France. As well as allowing the possibility of multilateral contacts between national law enforcement authorities, it offers a number of central services, such as the Notice system of alerts and specialist databases, as well as developing standards and guidance in a number of important areas. Its three core functions are (i) secure police communications; (ii) operational data services and databases for police (including nominal, DNA, fingerprints, administrative documents, stolen vehicles or works of art, or images of paedophile abuse); (iii) operational police support services including a 24/7 command and co-ordination centre.

www.interpol.int

World Customs Organization

In 2003, the World Customs Organization (WCO) agreed a common structure and basic principles for the global network of Regional Intelligence Liaison Officers (RILOs). The tripartite structure includes: the WCO Secretariat situated in Brussels, Belgium; the RILOs[1] themselves; and, National Contact Points (NCPs). The emphasis is on information-sharing, analysis and mutual

1 The RILOs are based in Cameroon, Chile, China, Germany, Kenya, Morocco, Poland, Russia, Saudi Arabia, Senegal and St Lucia.

assistance. The programme is supported by the Customs Enforcement Network which comprises a communications network, an information and analysis database and a website for Customs services.

www.wcoomd.org

Egmont Group

In the 1980s increased efforts began to be devoted to pursuing the proceeds of organised crime. It was recognised that chasing the (financial) paper trail was likely to be more effective in damaging criminal enterprise than simply trying to build a case against individual gang members. Anti-money-laundering activities and legislation became essential elements of law enforcement promoted on a global scale by the UN, Interpol and a newly-formed group, the Financial Action Task Force on Money Laundering (FATF). One outcome of this was the creation of national Financial Intelligence Units (FIUs) whose responsibilities include the initial handling of disclosures of information, including suspicious transactions, from financial institutions. Their central role at the national level, and the need to move information quickly to keep pace with the speed at which money can be moved internationally, also made them an obvious point of reference for international collaboration in anti-money-laundering enquiries. In June 1995 representatives of a number of FIUs met at the Egmont-Arenberg Palace in Brussels and an informal organisation known as the Egmont Group was founded. The exchange of financial intelligence information between FIUs is now central to the work of the Egmont Group[2] which meets annually in plenary session. By 2005 the membership of this group had grown to 101 national FIUs.

www.egmontgroup.org

United Nations

The UN has developed a number of conventions of great significance to international law enforcement collaboration including:

- Single Convention on Narcotic Drugs (1961)
- Convention on Psychotropic Substances (1971)
- Convention against the Illicit Traffic in Narcotic Drugs and Psychotropic Substances (1988)
- Convention against Transnational Crime (2000)
- Convention against Corruption (2003)

The UN, therefore, acts as an important forum for the collection and aggregation

2 www.egmontgroup.org/files/library_egmont_docs/info_paper_final_oct_2004.pdf.

of national experience and for accumulating proposals for action in a multilateral agreement. Once agreed, the agreements provide the legal justification and authority to take certain action. The weakness of the 'Convention approach' to international law enforcement is that it creates expectations which often go unfulfilled in a practical sense. A Convention needs to be ratified and implemented in the national jurisdiction and in those countries where the rule of law is weak, a Convention may be seen simply as an expression of diplomacy rather than of an earnest intent.

Perhaps the most important of the UN's crime-fighting roles has concerned terrorism. Pursuant to resolution 1267, in 1999 the Security Council established the 1267 Committee, otherwise known as the 'Al-Qaida and Taliban Sanctions Committee'. This committee maintains a consolidated list[3] of individuals and entities belonging to or associated with the Taliban and Al Qaida and in respect of whom all states are required to take specific measures. These can involve the freezing of assets, preventing entry into or travel through their territories by designated individuals, and the imposition of an arms embargo. In July 2005 the UN established the Counter Terrorism Implementation Task Force (CTITF) which includes representation from both Interpol and the World Customs Organization as well as the 1267 Committee. The entities featured on the consolidated list provide the material for the Interpol United Nations Special Notice which is referred to above.

The United Nations Office on Drugs and Crime (UNODC) based in Vienna, Austria, also carries out a range of anti-crime activities and is an important source of analytical and statistical information for law enforcement. Its laboratory services section assists with practical advice and equipment for forensic science issues (including the provision of reference samples for calibrating instruments and drug test kits for presumptive testing of suspicious materials in the field).

www.unodc.org

Regional

In recent years, police agencies have sought mechanisms established on a regional basis to improve the effectiveness of international collaboration. The rate of growth of regional law enforcement entities combined with their varying status, roles and responsibilities renders any attempt to list them a hazardous affair. The intention is to demonstrate the breadth of global coverage by the mass of regional organisations and structures while recognising that not all such entities will be mentioned here.

3 www.un.org/sc/committees/1267/consolist.shtml.

Europe

Europol

Europol is the largest permanent *regional* law enforcement organisation. The decision to establish Europol was incorporated in the Treaty of the European Union (the Maastricht Treaty) in 1992. Based in The Hague, the Netherlands, the Europol Drugs Unit – the forerunner of Europol – started limited operations in 1994. The Europol Convention was subsequently ratified by the EU Member States and came into force on 1 October 1998. Europol commenced its full activities in July 1999. Its mandate currently extends to dealing with all forms of serious international crime as listed in the annex to the Convention. However, this mandate and the legal basis for the organisation is presently under review. Europol aims at 'improving the effectiveness and co-operation of the competent authorities in the Member States in preventing and combating terrorism, unlawful drug trafficking and other serious forms of international organised crime.'[4]

www.europol.europol.eu

Eurojust

Whereas there are now several different networks comprising police and other law enforcement agencies, Eurojust, established by the EU in 2002 and also based in The Hague, the Netherlands, claims to be the first network of judicial authorities to have been created anywhere. The College of Eurojust[5] comprises 27 prosecutors or judges, one from each EU Member State. Its purpose is to improve the co-ordination between the competent authorities of the EU Member States in the investigation and prosecution of serious cross-border and organised crime. There is particular emphasis on facilitating the execution of international mutual legal assistance and the implementation of extradition requests.[6]

www.eurojust.europol.eu

European Judicial Network

To some extent Eurojust grew out of the European Judicial Network, which is an informal association of European judicial figures formed in 1998[7] who

4 www.europol.europa.eu.

5 The judicial officials of Eurojust collectively form the College and are supported by the Eurojust Administration.

6 www.eurojust.europa.eu.

7 www.ejn-crimjust.europa.eu/publications/general/JA_EJN_0698_en.

co-operate in order to improve the proper management of requests for mutual legal assistance.

www.ejn-crimjust.europa.eu

Southeast European Prosecutors Advisory Group

Mention should also be made of the Southeast European Prosecutors Advisory Group[8] which is developing along the same lines as Eurojust in South-Eastern Europe and the Balkans.

www.seepag.org

Schengen Information System

Twenty-two Member States of the EU (Austria, Belgium, Czech Republic, Denmark, Estonia, Finland, France, Germany, Greece, Hungary, Italy, Latvia, Lithuania, Luxembourg, Malta, the Netherlands, Poland, Portugal, Slovakia, Slovenia, Spain and Sweden) plus Iceland and Norway comprise the 'Schengen area' that is effectively a territory without internal borders. The establishment of this area was initially agreed by France, Germany and the Benelux countries in the 1980s but was gradually expanded to include the 22 countries listed. The Treaty of Amsterdam (1997) incorporated previous decisions of the Schengen members into EU law. A set of 'compensatory measures' was introduced to balance the freedom of movement established by Schengen against perceived security needs. These measures, which are not dealt with in detail here, were designed to improve co-operation between those responsible for law enforcement in the countries concerned. Of particular importance, however, was the introduction of the Schengen Information System (SIS). Through SIS, those national authorities authorised to conduct border surveillance and identity checks in the 22 countries (plus Iceland and Norway which have a special arrangement)[9] may share and, to the extent that it is made available on SIS, consult each others' information relating to people (those wanted for extradition, subject of a European Arrest Warrant, third-country nationals to be refused entry, missing persons or those whose movements should be monitored) and property (lost or stolen vehicles, firearms, identification papers, banknotes, boats and aircraft, containers, residence permits, vehicle registration papers and means of payment). The national office in each country responsible for handling SIS data is known as the SIRENE Office (Supplementary Information Request at the National Entry).

8 www.seepag.org.

9 Access by Ireland and the UK is also foreseen in the near future.

Prüm Convention

The Prüm Convention envisages the designation of a network of national contact points for certain forms of international law enforcement co-operation. On 27 May 2005 Austria, Belgium, France, Germany, Luxembourg, the Netherlands and Spain signed this Convention on the stepping up of cross-border co-operation particularly in combating terrorism, cross-border crime and illegal migration. The Convention introduces new measures that are to be co-ordinated through designated national contact points. These measures include granting national contact points the power to make individual automated searches of any other Contracting Party's DNA analysis files (by comparing DNA profiles), automated fingerprint identification systems and national vehicle registration data. It creates a duty to supply personal data in specified circumstances for the prevention of criminal offences and maintaining public order and security for major events with a cross-border dimension. The Convention also provides for the supply of information to prevent terrorist offences, the deployment of air marshals carrying arms, ammunition and equipment on aircraft, measures to combat illegal migration (including training and advice to detect false or falsified documents), joint operations and cross-border actions to avert imminent danger to individuals. Under Article 1, co-operation under the Convention is open to any Member State of the EU wishing to join. At the time of writing, proposals have been made that the Prüm Convention should be incorporated into the EU acquis in much the same way as the Schengen Convention was adopted under the Treaty of Amsterdam.

Frontex

The European Agency for the Management of Operational Co-operation at External Borders (Frontex) is tasked with co-ordinating operational co-operation between Member States of the EU in the field of border security. An EU agency established in 2004,[10] Frontex is based in Warsaw, Poland, and became fully operational in October 2005. Its activities are intelligence-driven. Frontex has established a network of national Focal Point Offices (FPOs) in the EU Member States. It is also directly involved in running maritime patrols and operations against illegal immigration.

www.frontex.europa.eu

SECI Regional Crime Center

The Southeast European Cooperative Initiative (SECI) Regional Center for Combating Trans-Border Crime is situated in Bucharest, Romania, and is based

10 Council Regulation (EC) 2007/2004 of 26 October 2004, Official Journal L349/1, 25 November 2004.

on the Agreement on Co-operation to Prevent and Combat Trans-Border Crime signed in 1999 by Albania, Bosnia and Herzegovina, Bulgaria, Greece, Hungary, Former Yugoslav Republic of Macedonia, Moldova, Romania and Turkey and Croatia. The Agreement, to which Slovenia also acceded in the same year, came into force in 2000. The mission of the SECI Center is 'to support common trans-border crime fighting efforts of SECI participating countries in order to improve the business environment in Southeast Europe and make it more attractive for investments, with the declared aim of reaching economic and political stability in the region.'[11] Sixteen countries (Austria, Azerbaijan, Belgium, Canada, France, Georgia, Germany, Italy, Japan, the Netherlands, Portugal, Slovakia, Spain, Ukraine, the UK and the USA) have Permanent Observer status and Interpol and the World Customs Organization have Permanent Adviser status. Its working methods are described as information exchange (via its liaison officers) and task forces (focused on joint operations).[12] The legal basis and organisational structure are currently under revision.

www.secicenter.org

Baltic Sea Task Force

The Baltic Sea Task Force on Organised Crime was established at the Baltic Sea States Summit in 1996. As its name suggests, the mandate of the Task Force is to promote, direct and concerted action to combat organised crime in the region. The original mandate until 1998 was subsequently extended to 2008.[13] The member countries[14] are represented at meetings of the Task Force by representatives of the Heads of Government. Meetings of the operations committee, which handles the practical arrangements for information sharing and operational activity, are attended by law enforcement officials involved in combating the fields of crime concerned. The European Commission, Europol, Interpol and the World Customs Organization have observer status. The Task Force meets twice a year, but has no permanent structure. The operations committee meets five times a year and reports to the Task Force. The Task Force has been chaired in successive four year terms by Sweden, Denmark and (until 2008) Finland.

www.cbss.st/summits/dbaFile671

11 www.secicenter.org/p128/Mission_and_objectives.

12 www.secicenter.org/p222/Activity_Report_on_2005.

13 www.balticseataskforce.fi/intermin/hankkeet/balticseataskforce/home.nsf/pages/DA55ADE24A66649BC2256F79002DC0BA/$file/TF_Public_Report_12–06_FINAL_DISTR.doc.

14 Denmark, Estonia, Finland, Germany, Iceland, Latvia, Lithuania, Norway, Poland, Russia and Sweden.

European Chiefs of Police

The EU Police Chiefs Task Force (PCTF) was created following the EU Tampere Summit in 1999. Originally called the European Police Chiefs Operational Task Force, the PCTF has both a strategic and an operational planning role. Although not officially an EU body its activities are clearly recognised by organs of the EU.[15] Its secretariat is collocated with Europol in The Hague, the Netherlands.

Southeast Europe Police Chiefs' Association

The Southeast Europe Police Chiefs' Association (SEPCA) was formed in Pula, Croatia, in 2002. The current membership of SEPCA includes officials or agencies from Albania, Bosnia and Herzegovina, Republic of Srpska, Bulgaria, Croatia, Macedonia, Montenegro, Serbia and Canada (who assisted with setting up the association). The objectives of SEPCA are to improve police co-operation between members, develop professionalism and facilitate reforms in the police services.

www.sepca-bg.org

BCOC and CIS Anti-terrorist Centre

The creation of the Commonwealth of Independent States (CIS)[16] in 1991, following the break-up of the Soviet Union, led to the adoption of numerous agreements between CIS countries and also between ministries of internal affairs or other government departments of CIS countries on co-operation in fighting crime. Subsequent co-operation between the respective law enforcement agencies has developed on both a bilateral and multilateral basis. Two creations resulting from this process are the Bureau for the Co-ordination of Combating Organised Crime (BCOC) and the Anti-terrorist Centre both based in Moscow (Russia).

Asia Pacific

ASEAN Chiefs of National Police

The ASEAN Chiefs of National Police (ASEANAPOL)[17] have met on an annual basis since 1980 and focus on the preventive, enforcement and operational aspects of co-operation against transnational crime.[18] The 26th ASEANAPOL

15 www.ec.europa.eu/justice_home/fsj/police/chief/fsj_police_task_force_en.htm.

16 The members of the CIS are Armenia, Azerbaijan, Belarus, Georgia, Kazakhstan, Kyrgyzstan, Moldova, Russia, Tajikistan, Turkmenistan, Ukraine, and Uzbekistan.

17 The Member States of ASEAN are Brunei, Darussalam, Cambodia, Indonesia, Laos, Malaysia, Myanmar, Philippines, Singapore, Thailand and Vietnam.

18 www.aseansec.org/2832.htm.

conference held in Kuala Lumpur, Malaysia in May 2006 announced the launch of a new regional law enforcement system for sharing criminal information (e-ADS) and linked this with a proposal to set up a permanent ASEANAPOL secretariat which will manage the system.

www.spf.gov.sg/aseanapol2007/about_aseanapol

Central Asian Regional Information and Coordination Center

The Central Asian Regional Information and Coordination Center (CARICC) is a new international agency to be established in Almaty, Kazakhstan on the basis of a UN-led project. Its membership will include Kazakhstan, Azerbaijan, Kyrgyzstan, Russia, Tajikistan, Turkmenistan and Uzbekistan. Primarily the organisation will deal with the co-ordination of anti-drug activities, strategic analysis and information exchange between its member states.

www.caricc.org

Pacific Islands Chiefs of Police

The Pacific Islands Chiefs of Police (PICP)[19] (until April 2005 known as the South Pacific Chiefs of Police Conference[20]), meets annually to share information, discuss issues and devise and promote strategies on policing in the Pacific Islands. It also conducts a range of activities through its permanent secretariat, executive groups and project teams throughout the year.[21]

www.picp.org

South Asian Association for Regional Cooperation

The South Asian Association for Regional Cooperation (SAARC)[22] was established in 1985, but it is only relatively recently that the Chiefs of Police of the region have met on a regular basis. The 5th SAARC Conference on Co-operation on Police Matters was held in Dhaka, Bangladesh on 9 May 2006. This was followed by the 1st conference of SAARC home ministers who discussed a proposal[23] emanating from the police chiefs 'to establish a regional police

19 American Samoa, Australia, Cook Islands, Micronesia, Fiji, French Polynesia, Guam, Kiribati, Marshall Islands, Nauru, New Caledonia, New Zealand, Niue, Northern Mariana Islands, Papua New Guinea, Palau, Samoa, Solomon Islands, Tonga, Tuvalu and Vanuatu.

20 Originally founded in Fiji in 1970 by seven countries.

21 www.picp.org/index.html.

22 The member states are Afghanistan, Bangladesh, Bhutan, India, Maldives, Nepal, Pakistan and Sri Lanka.

23 www.financialexpress-bd.com/index3.asp?cnd=5/12/2006&section_id=2&newsid=24273&spcl=no.

agency in the style of Interpol'. This matter was still under discussion in March 2007.

El Paso Intelligence Center

The role of the El Paso Intelligence Center (EPIC) should also be mentioned, it is a part of the Drug Enforcement Agency (DEA) serving the USA, other associated territories (such as Puerto Rico and Guam) and Canada as well as the DEA's international network of Special Agents. EPIC is a multi-agency institution that collects and disseminates information related to drugs, illegal immigration and weapon smuggling a well as some other crime areas (including terrorism). It hosts liaison officers from other national law enforcement agencies and has co-operation agreements with Canada, Australia, and the Netherlands.

www.dea.gov/programs/epic

Middle East

Arab Interior Ministers' Council

The Arab Interior Ministers' Council (AIMC)[24] has met annually in plenary session since 1983 to discuss matters that include drug trafficking, terrorism and other forms of serious crime. The AIMC Secretariat-General is situated in Tunis, Tunisia.

A co-operation and co-ordination centre along the same lines as CARICC (see above) is also planned for the Arab states and will be based in Dubai.

Caribbean

Association of Caribbean Commissioners of Police

The Association of Caribbean Commissioners of Police (ACCP)[25] was established at a meeting of a number of English-speaking Commissioners in St Lucia in 1987 and meets twice yearly to discuss matters of interest to policing in the region. It maintains a focus on the development and implementation of policing strategies, systems and procedures, professional and technical skills

24 AIMC comprises the Ministers of Interior of Algeria, Bahrain, Comoros, Djibouti, Egypt, Iraq, Jordan, Kuwait, Lebanon, Libya, Mauritania, Morocco, Oman, Palestine, Qatar, Saudi Arabia, Somalia, Sudan, Syria, Tunisia, United Arab Emirates and Yemen.

25 ACCP comprises the Chiefs of Police of Anguilla, Antigua & Barbuda, Aruba, Bahamas, Barbados, Belize, Bermuda, British Virgin Islands, Cayman Islands, Curacao, Dominica, French Guyana/Guadeloupe/Martinique, Grenada, Guyana, Jamaica, Montserrat, St Kitts & Nevis, St Lucia, St Martin, St Vincent & Grenadines, Surinam, Trinidad & Tobago, Turks & Caicos and US Virgin Islands.

development, and proactive measures to prevent crime and improve police-community relations.[26] The ACCP established a permanent secretariat in Barbados in 1999.

www.accpolice.org

Regional Security System

The Regional Security System (RSS) was initially established through a Memorandum of Understanding signed in 1982[27] with the intention to provide for mutual assistance any threats to security in the Eastern Caribbean region. The role of the RSS was later enshrined in a treaty signed by the seven member states in Grenada in 1996. The express function of the RSS is to ensure the stability and well-being of the Eastern Caribbean region through mutual co-operation, in order to achieve social and economic development and to maintain the principles of democracy, liberty of the individual and the rule of law.[28] The operational headquarters of the RSS is the Central Liaison Office (CLO) in Barbados. The CLO is staffed by regional officers from the police and defence forces of the member states and a number of civilian staff. Whereas the initial focus of RSS was on defence of the region against external threats, its role is now seen primarily as a response to the prevailing threat of terrorism, drug trafficking and other crime.

www.rss.org.bb

Caribbean Customs Law Enforcement Council

Customs services have also embraced the regional approach, as exemplified by the Caribbean Customs Law Enforcement Council (CCLEC) whose secretariat is based in Castries, St Lucia.

www.cclec.net

Latin America

Andean Community of Nations

In South America, the Andean Community of Nations countries comprise Bolivia, Colombia, Ecuador and Peru; Chile is an associate member of the Andean Community; Argentina, Brazil, Paraguay and Uruguay, as members of

26 www.accpolice.org/cms/default.asp?V_DOC_ID=1056.

27 Signatories were Antigua and Barbuda, Barbados, Dominica, St Lucia and St Vincent and the Grenadines – and subsequently acceded to by St Kitts & Nevis and Grenada.

28 www.rss.org.bb/rss1.htm#PURPOSES%20AND%20FUNCTIONS.

Mercosur,[29] are also associate members. Venezuela was a full member of the Andean Community but announced its withdrawal in 2006. It has recently joined Mercosur. Their approach to regional co-operation on crime matters is perhaps best demonstrated in the Andean Co-operation Plan for the Control of Illegal Drugs and Related Offences which was approved by the presidents of the Andean countries at a meeting held on 17 April 2001 in Cartagena, Colombia. The plan outlined a community strategy focusing on:

> . . . stepping up the exchange of intelligence among the competent authorities of the Andean countries, among others, making more use of existing communication mechanisms, such as the Regional Liaison Offices of the World Customs Organization (RILO) and the Inter-American Telecommunications Network for Drug Control (RETCOD), in order to back regional efforts to control drugs, related offences, and the arms traffic.[30]

www.comunidadandina.org

Red Iberoamericana de Cooperación Judicial

The Red Iberoamericana de Cooperación Judicial (IberRed) is a formal grouping of 23 Ibero-American countries with the objective of enhancing judicial co-operation. It was formed at a conference in Cartagena, Colombia, in 2004.

www.iberred.org

29 Mercosur stands for 'Mercado Común del Sur' and is a free trade group of countries in Latin America.

30 www.comunidadandina.org/ingles/normativa/D505e.htm.

Appendix 2

Model information sharing protocol

Steven David Brown

The following model text proposes possible wording for an agreement authorising the exchange of information between countries or agencies. It is not intended to be exhaustive or to be universally applicable to every set of national circumstances or legislation.

....

[Agency]

and

[Agency]

Hereinafter 'the Parties'

hereby intend and agree to share information and intelligence related to the prevention, detection, suppression and prosecution of crime.

Article 1

Each Party to this protocol agrees and undertakes to amend any standing regulations and any institutional guidelines which conflict with the presumption that information, intelligence and data (hereinafter, 'information') can and will be shared or exchanged with the other Parties to this protocol and will enact appropriate implementing regulations to permit the same.

Article 2

In order to facilitate the sharing and exchange of information under this agreement, the Parties will appoint a single point of contact which will be responsible for receiving, forwarding and managing the said information. This information may include data by which an individual is identified or identifiable (hereinafter, 'personal data'). The Parties may, as appropriate, append a further protocol governing the collection, retention and handling of such data. However, nothing therein shall prejudice the opportunity to use those data without restriction once they have been rendered anonymous.

Article 3

All information shared or exchanged under this protocol shall be assessed according to the reliability of its source. This assessment shall be conducted according to a scheme agreed between the Parties prior to the entering into force of this protocol. Each separate part of any information exchanged shall be marked by the sending Party with the appropriate code. Where information is received without such a code, the receiving Party will request the same from the sending Party, but will attach the most restrictive coding until a reply has been received.

Article 4

The sending Party will also stipulate handling codes governing further dissemination and/or use of the information supplied under this protocol. The said handling codes shall be decided according to a scheme agreed between the Parties prior to the entering into force of this protocol. Where information has been received without a handling code, it will be assumed by the receiving Party that the sending Party does not set any further conditions to the use or further dissemination of the information beyond those applied herein.

Article 5

Information shall be marked with the lowest protective marking that is strictly necessary to safeguard adequately the said information.

Article 6

Each Party will apply the presumption that all information known to one Party and relevant to the work of another Party shall be shared or exchanged where the said information is known or believed, on reasonable grounds:

- to be serious of itself or related to the commission or alleged commission of a serious offence, the definition of 'serious' being agreed by the Parties in advance of this protocol entering into force;
- to relate to any person, legal or natural, or to any other circumstances relevant to or implicated in the commission of offences covered by the foregoing subparagraph;
- to relate to any person, legal or natural, suspected of involvement or otherwise implicated in the planning, preparation or attempt of such offences;
- to relate to any suspected or actual membership of, or association with, a criminal organisation, the definition of such an organisation being in accordance with national law or as agreed in advance of this protocol entering into force;
- to be otherwise relevant to enquiries relevant to or investigations concerning any of the types of offences to which this Article applies.

Article 7

Except as provided for below, the information described under the preceding Article shall be provided to the other Party as soon as practicable and in any case within 24 hours of the information becoming known to the national point of contact of the relevant Party.

Article 8

Information shall be shared or exchanged in all cases unless exceptional circumstances apply. Such circumstances apply where:

- there is a substantial risk to national security;
- there are substantial grounds for believing that sharing or exchanging the information will seriously prejudice an ongoing investigation or prosecution, incur a serious risk to substantial property, real, virtual, intangible or personal; or cause significant risk to life or limb.

Article 9

Information which has not been shared or exchanged because of exceptional circumstances, as defined above, shall be shared or exchanged as soon as those circumstances cease to apply.

Article 10

Notwithstanding additional restrictions or stipulations, all information shared or exchanged under this protocol is provided only for the prevention, detection, suppression and prosecution of criminal activity.

Article 11

For the avoidance of doubt, the Party receiving any information containing personal data guarantees:

- to update any entries of the said data in any systems or records as soon as notified of any material inaccuracy;
- to delete the data provided as soon as they cease to be relevant to the purposes for which they are kept or to anonymise them so that the data subject cannot be identified or is no longer readily identifiable;
- to keep under constant review the necessity of retaining the said data and, in any case, to conduct such a review within a time limit not exceeding a period defined by national legislation or agreed between the Parties in advance of this protocol coming into force, beginning with the date on which the data were provided;
- to use the data only for the reasons provided for by this protocol or for any additional reasons as stipulated by the sender of the information;
- to comply with any handling codes stipulated by the sending Party;
- to introduce appropriate systems for the safe deletion, destruction and secure disposal of all sensitive or confidential information.

Article 12

All Parties will ensure any information provided is accurate and up to date and will indemnify any Party receiving the information against any financial claim arising from the inaccuracy or wrongful supply of the information so provided.

Article 13

This protocol can be terminated by any Party by that Party giving 3 months notice in writing to any other Party. However, all Parties will make all due efforts to resolve any difficulties and to continue to pursue the principles and ideals established herein.

Article 14

Any amendment to this protocol can be proposed by any Party to any other Party in writing. However, all Parties must agree on any such amendment in writing before it becomes applicable.

Article 15

This protocol will enter into force on the day following one calendar month from the date of the signature of the second Party, but shall only bind the signatories thereto.

Signed	Signed
Dated	Dated
On behalf of	On behalf of
[AGENCY]	[AGENCY]

Appendix 3

Letter of Request briefing[1]

Steven David Brown

A Letter of Request is an official request for assistance from criminal justice agencies in another jurisdiction. It has to be completed according to national law and normally signed by a judge or a nominated prosecuting authority. The type of assistance available in response to such a request is also governed by national law. This appendix cannot replace the advice of local lawyers nor does it explain how to write a Letter of Request (this is a task for experts), but offers some suggestions on what sort of information an investigator will need to provide to a prosecutor to help them to prepare such a letter. Further information on the legal requirements of a Letter of Request is contained in Chapter 10.

In general, you should provide the following background information:

- a concise summary of the facts of all and any offences to which the Letter relates and the current status of the investigation (Has the offence been substantiated? Has a suspect been arrested?);
- the personal details of everyone under investigation including the names, aliases, addresses, dates and places of birth, nationalities and numbers of any personal administrative documents (such as passport, driving licence or identification cards);
- what kind of assistance is requested and why?;
- what use will be made of the information provided?;
- the name of and full contact details for the investigator involved;
- whether officers wish to travel to conduct the necessary enquiries themselves (and if so, their names), or whether the requested state is asked to undertake the enquiries.
- full details of anyone in the requested state from whom help has already been requested and with what result.

1 It may also be called a Letter Rogatory, Rogatory Letter or Commission Rogatoire.

Appendix 4

An international liaison unit

Steven David Brown

Comparing best practice and existing implementation of single national points of contact for managing international information exchange, it is possible to suggest a blueprint of minimum requirements:

- There must be a very clear, objective and strictly applied decision-making process for deciding which international channel(s) should be used (involving a risk assessment of issues such as data protection and sharing information where there may be implications for human rights).
- International exchanges (as well as national communications) should be conducted using standard formats with the supply of all information being fully auditable (including a record of who has accessed information, to whom it has been sent and why).
- All information exchanged should be quality assured. Outgoing information should have (a) the source of the information marked against a scale for reliability and (b) be given a classification or code setting any limitations on the further use and dissemination of that information.
- Even if there are no national rules on the protection of personal data, the co-operation unit should apply best practice and data protection compliant procedures. This will enable other co-operation partners to have confidence in sharing data.
- Memoranda of Understanding or Service Level Agreements should be in place with all national law enforcement agencies (including prosecutors). These should document the formal basis for co-operation and the expected response standards.[1] These memoranda should permit staff in the international co-operation unit to approach individual officers and internal police departments directly with enquiries and the unit should be accessible to all national law enforcement personnel on a non-stop 24/7 basis.
- The supply of the requested information to the co-operation unit should be

1 It is assumed that such agreements already exist for international co-operation otherwise the unit would not exist in the first place.

compulsory (except for good reasons, such as where supplying the information would undermine an ongoing investigation, prejudice a prosecution or involve risk to life or limb). National agencies should also be obliged to furnish the co-operation unit with any operational information or intelligence that has an international dimension (again, unless it would undermine an investigation, etc.) and the co-operation unit should be permitted to exercise its discretion in forwarding the data to relevant agencies abroad.

- The co-operation unit must have secure and real-time means of communication with relevant national and international agencies and have direct access to all national law enforcement databases. It should also be the focal point for foreign liaison officers based in their country as well as for national liaison officers posted abroad.
- All staff should be security approved (vetted), represent all the main national law enforcement services and be recruited under a transparent process involving open competition. Serving law enforcement officers should serve a maximum time in a role dealing with international issues before being rotated back to national duties. A posting in international law enforcement should be recognised as being beneficial to a career profile and the unit should not be permitted to become a dumping ground or haven for unpopular staff.
- The work of the unit (and of the international co-operation network as a whole) should be marketed on a regular basis within national law enforcement and included as a module in basic recruit training curricula.

Appendix 5

An international organisation

Steven David Brown

The following characteristics are ideal components for an international organisation involved in law enforcement. In many respects they are the same or similar to those suggested for an international liaison unit (see Appendix 4).

To function at an optimum level an international organisation needs to be independent from the influence of any particular interest group, to receive adequate and guaranteed resources to achieve what is asked of it, and to be sufficiently resilient to withstand the vagaries of operational activity. For countries with limited resources, membership of such an organisation can maximise the opportunities for international liaison with other countries by giving access to a number of partners in a 'one stop shop' arrangement.

Legal basis

First and foremost, any international organisation, and especially one dedicated to criminal justice, requires a clear and comprehensive legal framework consisting of one or more legal documents agreed and ratified by its member countries. These documents should:

- ensure that the member countries explicitly recognise the international status of the organisation and provide it with a legal personality;
- define, clearly and unambiguously, the organisational scope and objectives (consideration needs to be given, for instance, as to whether activity should be exclusive to international organised crime or to serious crime or to a mixture of these);
- describe what the organisation is expected to do within this business remit (for instance, does it support prevention and suppression of the relevant crimes? Does it have a role in supporting or conducting prosecutions?);
- be clear as to how the organisation will complement (rather than compete with) the work of existing organisations;
- allow for the legal framework to be amended without undue delay (and especially without the need to be ratified by the parliaments of the member states) so that it can be flexible and respond to new demands or threats.

Tasks

Ideally, an international organisation should be allowed, as a minimum, to:

- exchange information related to serious and organised crime (including personal data);
- collect, store, analyse and disseminate such information without the requirement to refer back to the provider of the information in order to do so;
- produce and publish (on a restricted basis) the results of any analysis or assessment;
- collect, store, evaluate and disseminate best practice;
- provide a forum for training in any areas relevant to the core business of the organisation;
- co-ordinate cross-border operational activity (including active investigations);
- recommend operational activity in member countries (and to receive a written justification if this recommendation is rejected);
- act as a common depository for specialist equipment (such as tracking devices) and/or expertise (such as forensic computer analysis) which can then be used by or deployed within the member countries as appropriate and in accordance with national law.

Co-operation and partnership

Clear guidelines are required on the extent to which the organisation may access law enforcement networks at national level. However, in support of co-operation there should be:

- one contact point or liaison platform at national level the staff of which represent all relevant investigative and prosecutorial interests;
- 24-hour availability (either in the form of a 24-hour duty roster or on-call response schedule);
- the power to establish co-operation with third parties, organisations and countries that are not members (this may require the formality of a memorandum of understanding, but informal co-operation should be permitted under special circumstances).

Information management

In terms of managing information there should be:

- secure means for transmitting to and receiving information from national agencies;

- ideally, a direct or indirect means for interrogating national databases (relevant national agencies should be required to share proactively any relevant information either concerning international criminality or other member countries);
- the power to maintain central databases containing information provided by the member countries (but only where they complement or provide additional benefit to those that already exist).
- fully protected and auditable access (namely a system for identifying who accessed what information, when and why);
- access should be on a 'need to know' basis and restricted to authorised personnel who have been positively vetted (security cleared) to the same objective standards in each country.

Protecting personal data

Although not all countries subscribe to the doctrine of data protection, the incorporation of compatible rules on manipulating personal data will enable those countries which do have data protection legislation to share personal information when necessary. These rules should include:

- Personal data may only be transmitted, stored or processed as permitted by the legal framework.
- Personal data will be accurate and kept up to date, stored securely and only contain those details necessary for the purpose of their storage.
- Such data will be retained only for as long as that purpose continues to apply or as subsequently agreed (after which they will be deleted).
- These data may not be transmitted to third parties unless that third party itself provides adequate protection.
- Where there is an urgent and immediate need for the transmission of personal data in the interests of saving life or limb, the transmission of the said personal data to a third party may be specially authorised on a case by case basis.
- Personal data may be anonymised to remove any references by which the data subject may be identified. Once this has been done, the data will no longer be subject to data protection rules.
- An independent authority will have responsibility for monitoring and overseeing organisational performance in the handling of personal data.
- All information, intelligence or data managed by the organisation should be subject to a protective marking scheme[1] and any person in receipt of such information obliged to apply an equivalent level of protection.

1 All countries will have a way of categorising documents according to their level of confidentiality and secrecy, but these are not always structured or defined in the same way.

Staffing

In such an organisation the quality, reputation and reliability of the human resources are paramount. As a result:

- Staff should be recruited in open competition by means of a fair, equal and objective procedure and appointed on merit for a fixed term, but renewable, contract.
- Where liaison officers are involved, they should be governed by the rules of the organisation and their presence subject to the agreement of the chief officer of the organisation.
- Liaison officers should be financed by their home countries.

Oversight

In terms of accountability, the organisation should have:

- an executive board that oversees its performance, sets and agrees organisational objectives and approves the budget (normally this executive board will represent the member countries);
- a decision-making process based on majority voting (experience has shown that unanimity or consensus voting has been impractical);
- oversight of strategic decisions, but the chief officer should have operational independence.

Appendix 6

Key international legal instruments

ORGANISATIONAL LEGAL FRAMEWORKS

Interpol Agreement

www.interpol.int/Public/ICPO/LegalMaterials/constitution/constitutionGenReg/constitution.asp

Europol Convention

www.europol.europa.eu/index.asp?page=legalconv

Europol Council Decision Proposal 2006

www.eu-oplysningen.dk/upload/application/pdf/0092efe8/20060817.pdf

Eurojust Decision

www.eurojust.europa.eu/official_documents/Eurojust_Decision/l_06320020306en00010013.pdf
www.eurojust.europa.eu/official_documents/Eurojust_Amended_Decision/l_24520030929en00440045.pdf

SECI Center Agreement

www.secicenter.org/p160/Legal_framework_SECI_Agreement

REGIONAL CO-OPERATION FRAMEWORKS

Prüm Convention

www.register.consilium.europa.eu/pdf/en/06/st11/st11130.en06.pdf

South-East Europe Police Convention

www.eu2006.at/de/News/information/
SEE_Police_Convention_270406_Final_text.pdf

DATA PROTECTION RULES

Council of Europe Convention No 108 on Data Protection 1981

www.conventions.coe.int/Treaty/en/Treaties/Html/108.htm

Council of Europe Recommendation (87)15 on Police Processing of Personal Data

www.coe.int/t/e/legal_affairs/legal_co-operation/combating_economic_crime/
1_standard_settings/Rec_1987_15.pdf

Interpol Rules on Processing of Information

www.interpol.int/Public/ICPO/LegalMaterials/constitution/info/default.asp

Eurojust Rules on Data Protection

www.eurojust.europa.eu/official_documents/Data_Protection_Rules/
c_06820050319en00010010.pdf

Europol Rules on Analyst Files

www.europol.europa.eu/index.asp?page=AWfiles_regs_en

CAPACITY BUILDING

UN Convention against Transnational Organized Crime

www.unodc.org/pdf/crime/a_res_55/res5525e.pdf

UN Single Convention on Narcotic Drugs 1961

www.unodc.org/pdf/convention_1961_en.pdf

UN Convention on Psychotropic Substances 1971

www.unodc.org/pdf/convention_1971_en.pdf

UN Convention Against Illicit Traffic in Narcotic Drugs and Psychotropic Substances 1988

www.unodc.org/pdf/convention_1988_en.pdf

UN Convention Against Corruption

www.unodc.org/pdf/crime/convention_corruption/signing/Convention-e.pdf

Council of Europe Criminal Law No 173 on Corruption

www.conventions.coe.int/Treaty/EN/Treaties/Html/173.htm

Inter-American Convention Against Corruption

www.oas.org/juridico/english/Treaties/b-58.html

Council of Europe Convention No 185 on Cybercrime

www.conventions.coe.int/Treaty/EN/Treaties/HTML/185.htm

Council of Europe Convention No 198 on Money Laundering

www.conventions.coe.int/Treaty/EN/Treaties/Word/198.doc

Council of Europe Convention No 141 on Laundering, Search, Seizure and Confiscation of the Proceeds from Crime

www.conventions.coe.int/treaty/en/Treaties/Html/141.htm

Financial Action Task Force 40 Recommendations on Money-laundering

www.fatf-gafi.org/dataoecd/7/40/34849567.PDF

MUTUAL LEGAL ASSISTANCE

Council of Europe Convention on Extradition CETS No 024

www.conventions.coe.int/Treaty/Commun/QueVoulezVous.asp?NT=024&CM=8&DF=7/23/2007&CL=ENG

Council of Europe Convention on Mutual Assistance in Criminal Matters CETS No 030

www.conventions.coe.int/Treaty/Commun/QueVoulezVous.asp?NT=030&CM=8&DF=7/23/2007&CL=ENG

EU Council Act on Mutual Assistance in Criminal Matters 2001

www.europa.eu.int/eur-lex/en/archive/2001/c_32620011121en.html

EU Council Framework Decision on European Arrest Warrant 2002

www.europa.eu.int/eur-lex/en/archive/2002/l_19020020718en.html

EU Council Template for Requesting Mutual Legal Assistance

www.consilium.europa.eu/uedocs/cmsUpload/FormRequestEN.pdf

Appendix 7

Glossary of acronyms

ACCP	Association of Caribbean Commissioners of Police
ALAT	Assistant Legal Attaché
AIMC	Arab Interior Ministers' Council
ASEANAPOL	ASEAN Chiefs of National Police
BCOC	Bureau for the Co-ordination of Combating Organised Crime
CAPCCO	Central African Police Chiefs Co-operation Organisation
CARICC	Central Asian Regional Information and Coordination Center
CCLEC	Caribbean Customs Law Enforcement Council
CIS	Commonwealth of Independent States
CTITF	Counter-Terrorism Implementation Task Force
DEA	Drugs Enforcement Agency
EAPCCO	East African Police Chiefs Co-operation Organisation
EIS	Europol Information System
EJN	European Judicial Network
ENU	Europol National Unit
EPIC	El Paso Intelligence Center
E-POC	European Pool Against Organized Crime
Eurojust	European Judicial Co-operation Unit
Europol	The European Police Office
FATF	Financial Action Task Force
FIU	Financial Intelligence Unit
FPO	Focal Point Office (Frontex)
Frontex	European Agency for the Management of Operational Co-operation at External Borders
HENU	Heads of Europol National Units (a committee)
ICAID	Interpol's child abuse image database
ICC	International Criminal Court
ICSE	Interpol/G8 child sexual exploitation image database project.
ICTY	International Criminal Tribunal for the former Yugoslavia
Interpol	The International Criminal Police Organisation (ICPO)

I-24/7	Interpol's communications and information network
Legat	Legal Attaché
NCB	National Central Bureau (Interpol)
NCP	National Contact Point (WCO)
NFP	National Focal Point (SECI Center)
OLO	Overseas Liaison Officer
PCTF	Police Chiefs Task Force
PICP	Pacific Islands Chiefs of Police
PTCCC	Pacific Transnational Crime Coordination Centre
RETCOD	Inter-American Telecommunications Network for Drug Control
RILO	Regional Intelligence Liaison Officer (WCO)
RSS	Regional Security System (Caribbean)
SECI	Southeast European Cooperative Initiative
SEPCA	Southeast Europe Police Chiefs Association
SIS	Schengen Information System
SIRENE	Supplementary Information Request at the National Entry (Schengen)
SITCEN	Situation Centre (EU Brussels based group for Counter Terrorist information)
SAARC	South Asian Association for Regional Co-operation
SARPCCO	Southern African Regional Police Chiefs Co-operation Organisation
SEEPAG	South-Eastern European Prosecutors Advisory Group
SICA	System of Central American Integration
SLTD	Interpol's stolen or lost travel documents database
SMV	Interpol's stolen motor vehicle database
SRB	Sub-Regional Bureau (Interpol)
UNODC	United Nations Office on Drugs and Crime
WAPCCO	West African Police Chiefs Co-operation Organisation
WCO	World Customs Organization

Appendix 8

Further reading

BOOKS

M. Anderson and M. Den Boer (eds), *Policing across National Boundaries* (London: Pinter Publishers, 1994).

P. Andreas and E. Nadelmann, *Policing the Globe: Criminalization and Crime Control in International Relations* (Oxford: Oxford University Press, 2006).

K. Aromma, S. Leppä, S. Nevela and N. Ollus (eds), *Crime and Criminal Justice in Europe and North America 1995–1997: Report on the Sixth United Nations Survey on Crime Trends and Criminal Justice Systems* (Helsinki: HEUN, 2003).

C. Bradley (ed), *Criminal Procedure: A Worldwide Study* (Durham, NC: Carolina Academic Press, 1999).

M. Cherif Bassiouni, *International Extradition, United States Law and Practice* (3rd edn, New York: Oceana Publications, 1996).

N. Cope, N. M. Innes and N. Fielding, *Smart Policing – the Theory and Practice of Intelligence-led Policing* (London: UK Home Office, 2001).

P. Ekblom, *Getting the Best out of Crime Analysis*, Crime Prevention Unit Paper no 10 (London: UK Home Office, 1998).

J. Fraser, J. and R. Williams (eds), *Handbook of Forensic Science* (Cullompton: Willan Publishing, forthcoming).

Home Office, *Maximising the Opportunities for Sharing DNA Information across Europe* (London: UK Home Office, 2006).

Home Office, 'Memorandum of Evidence' in House of Commons Science and Technology Committee, Seventh Report of Session 2004–05, *Forensic Science on Trial*, Volume II, Oral and Written Evidence, HC 96-II (London: The Stationery Office Limited, 2004).

D. M. Hopkins, L. T. Kontnik and M. T. Turnage, *Counterfeiting Exposed: Protecting Your Brand and Customers* (Hoboken: John Wiley & Sons, 2003).

House of Lords EU Committee, 'Judicial Co-operation in the EU: the role of Eurojust', 23rd Report of Session 2003–04 (London: The Stationery Office Limited, 2004).

A. W. LaForest, *Extradition to and from Canada* (Aurora: Canada Law Books, 1991).

M. Leaf (ed), *Cross-Border Crime: Defence Rights in a New Era of International Judicial Co-operation* (London: Justice, 2006).

H. L. McQueen (ed), *Money Laundering*, Hume papers on Public Policy Vol. 1 No. 2 (Edinburgh: Edinburgh University Press, 1993).

M. Naím, *Illicit: How Smugglers, Traffickers and Copycats are Hijacking the Global Economy* (London: William Heinemann, 2005).
J. F. Nijboer and W. J. J. M. Sprangers (eds), *Harmonisation in Forensic Expertise: An Inquiry into the Desirability of and Opportunities for International Standards* (Amsterdam: Thelma Thesis, 2000).
P. Reichel (ed), *Handbook of Transnational Crime and Justice* (London: Sage Publications, 2005).
I. A. Shearer, *Extradition in International Law* (Manchester: Manchester University Press, 1971).
J. Sheptycki (ed), *Transnational Policing* (London: Routledge, 2000).
United Nations, *Report on the Sixth United Nations Survey on Crime Trends and Criminal Justice Systems* (Helsinki: HEUNI, 2003).
T. Vander Beken, *European Organised Crime Scenarios for 2015* (Antwerpen: Maklu, 2006).
G. Vermeulen, *Essential Texts on International and European Criminal Law* (4th edn, Antwerpen: Maklu, 2005).
A. Wright, *Organised Crime* (Cullompton: Willan, 2006).

JOURNALS

B. Bowling, 'Sovereignty vs. security: transnational policing in the contemporary caribbean' in Caribbean Journal of Criminology and Social Psychology, 10(1–2)(2005).
S. W. Brenner, 'Private-public sector co-operation in combating cybercrime: in search of a model' in Journal of International Commercial Law and Technology, 2(2)(2007).
S. Brown, 'The meaning of criminal intelligence' in International Journal of Police Science and Management, 9(4)(2007).
Lionel Frei and Stefan Freschal, 'Origins and application of the United States – Switzerland Treaty on Mutual Assistance in Criminal Matters' in Harvard International Law Journal, 31 (1990).
M. D. Goodman and S. W. Brenner, 'The emerging consensus on criminal conduct in cyberspace' in UCLA Journal of Law and Technology, 6(1)(2002).
Bart de Schutter, 'International criminal law in evolution: mutual assistance in criminal matters between the Benelux countries' in Netherlands Journal of International Law, 14 (1967).

INTERNET REFERENCES

BBC, 'Virtual theft' leads to arrest', www.news.bbc.co.uk/1/hi/technology/7094764.stm.
W. Bruggeman, (2000) 'Europol – A European FBI in the making?', www.cicerofoundation.org/lectures/p4bruggeman.
K. DiGregory, 'Fighting Cybercrime – What are the Challenges facing Europe', www.usdoj.gov/criminal/cybercrime/EUremarks.htm.
S. EL Zein, 'Reconciling Data Protection Regulations with the Requirement of Judicial and Police Co-operation', www.pcpd.org.hk/english/infocentre/files/elzein-paper.doc.

EMCDDA, 'The state of the drugs problem in Europe: Annual Report 2007', www.emcdda.europa.eu/html.cfm/index41535EN.html.

Eurojust Annual Report 2006, www.eurojust.europa.eu/press_annual.htm.

Eurojust, 'Findings of Eurojust in the Area of International Co-operation – Difficulties and Successes', (2007) Strasbourg: Council of Europe, www.coe.int/t/dg1/legalcooperation/ccpe/meetings/bureau/CCPE-Bu(2007)02%20Eurojust%20activities_en.asp.

Europol, 'EU Terrorism Situation and Trend Report' and 'EU Organised Crime Threat Assessment', www.europol.europa.eu/index.asp?page=publications&language=.

B. Etter, 'Critical Issues in Hi-tech Crime', paper at *Embracing the Future Together Conference 2002*, www.acpr.gov.au/pdf/Presentations/cpacongNov02.pdf.

Friends of the Presidency, 'Friends of the Presidency's report to the future of Europol', (2006) Council of the European Union 9184/1/06, www.statewatch.org/news/2006/may/eu-fop-future-of-europol-06.

Interpol, Various Reports, www.interpol.int/Public/Icpo/Publications/default.asp.

McAfee, 'McAfee Virtual Criminology Report', (July 2005), www.mcafee.com.

OLAF Seventh Activity Report 2006, www.ec.europa.eu/anti_fraud/reports/olaf/2006/report_en.pdf.

OLAF Manual, www.bookshop.europa.eu.

J. S. Park, 'Establishing a High-Tech Cyber Crime Response System', undated, www.innovation.go.kr/include/file_down.php?id=2190.

M. Roure, 'Policing Europe – Europol Liaison Officers', www.europarl.europa.eu/news/expert/briefing_page/6149-087-03-13-20060313BRI06148-28-03-2006-2006/default_p001c014_en.htm.

M. Shaw, 'Typologies of Transnational Organised Crime Groups', www.unodc.org/pdf/crime/training/typologies.pdf accessed.

M. Valsamis, 'Police Co-operation: What are the main Obstacles to Police Co-operation in the EU?', 2007, www.libertysecurity.org/article1379.

PRESS AND MEDIA

BBC, 'Man guilty of burning body murder', 11 October 2005, www.news.bbc.co.uk/1/hi/england/4382872.stm.

BBC, 'Two blame each other for murder', 19 October 2005, www.news.bbc.co.uk/1/hi/england/4332846.stm.

D. Campbell, 'Operation Ore Flawed By Fraud', www.guardian.co.uk/crime/article/0,,2059880,00.html.

P. Clarke, 'Man who helped Polly Peck boss escape felt he "deserved a break"', London: The Independent, 23 July 1998.

R. Cowan, 'Smuggling in suburbia: how two men ran cartel flooding UK with £1bn of cocaine', London: The Guardian, 7 December 2006.

Daily Telegraph, 'World's First Arrests for Virtual Theft', London: Daily Telegraph, 14 November 2007.

B. Deane, 'Body of evidence', Police, March 2006, www.polfed.org.

'FBI Agent Charged with Hacking', www.msnbc.com/news/563379.asp?0na=x22034Q2p.

'Fight against organised crime: the Commission recommends common methodologies', 2 June 2005, www.europa.eu/rapid/pressReleasesAction.do?reference=IP/05/659&format=HTML&aged=0&language=EN&guiLanguage=en.

S. Freeman, 'Colombian drug lords who ran UK cocaine trade are jailed', London: The Times, 6 January 2006.

'GMA presents Nigerian man arrested for cocaine trafficking', 31 July 2002, www.gov.ph/news/printerfriendly.asp?i=1728.

H. Goldstein, 'Who killed the virtual case file', www.spectrum.ieee.org/sep05/1455.

T. Green, 'Kaspersky seeks help from international police to fight cybercrime', www.networkworld.com/news/2007/013107-kaspersky-cybercrime.html.

The Guardian, 'Mystery Victim Buried with No Name,' London: The Guardian, 21 July 2003.

S. Gutterman, '10 Held in Russian Journalist's Killing', Guardian Unlimited, www.guardian.co.uk/worldlatest/story/0,,-6878634,00.html.

'Interpol DNA Database Online', in The Police Chief, April 2007.

'Interpol records 100th international DNA match. More countries urged to use unique global database', Interpol media release, 29 November 2006, Lyon: Interpol.

D. Leppard, 'Child porn suspects set to be cleared in evidence shambles', London: The Times, 3 July 2005, www.timesonline.co.uk/tol/news/uk/article539974.

J. Leyden, 'Cybercrime more lucrative than drugs', www.channelregister.co.uk/2005/11/29/cybercrime/.

New York Times, 'Pentagon to Close Disputed Database', New York Times, 22 August 2007; 'Pentagon ditches controversial security database', www.reuters.com/article/topNews/idUSN2135960020070821?src=082107_1359_DOUBLEFEATURE_envoy_slams_ progress.

J. Roach and K. Pease, 'DNA evidence and police investigations: a health warning', Police Professional, May 2006.

K. Sekyere, 'ID Theft left me in Slovenian Prison', www.news.bbc.co.uk/go/pr/fr/-/1/hi/magazine/6902922.stm.

M. Timmins, 'Ident 1 and Livescan Help Forensic Investigation', Norfolk Constabulary website article, www.norfolk.police.uk.

S. Todd, 'Yes, his name is Bond . . . but he is no fraudster', www.news.scotsman.com/topics.cfm?tid=779&id=241292003.

OTHER INTERESTING WEBSITES

European Network of Forensic Science Institutes
www.enfsi.org

Federal Bureau of Investigation
www.fbi.gov

The Netherlands Forensic Institute
www.forensischinstituut.nl/NFI/en

The Forensic Science Service
www.forensic.gov.uk
(a private company albeit, at the time of writing, 100 per cent government owned)

Nuffield Council on Bioethics
www.nuffieldbioethics.org

UN Office on Drugs and Crime
www.unodc.org

Drugs Enforcement Agency
www.usdoj.gov/dea/index.htm

Index